D1363408

SHIFTING
SHADOWS

An Anthology of Essays About the Christ

B. Neil Shaw

WESTBOW
PRESS®
A DIVISION OF THOMAS NELSON
& ZONDERVAN

WestBow Press books may be ordered through booksellers or by contacting:

WestBow Press
A Division of Thomas Nelson & Zondervan
1663 Liberty Drive
Bloomington, IN 47403
www.westbowpress.com
1 (866) 928-1240

ISBN: 978-1-9736-1691-7 (sc)
ISBN: 978-1-9736-1692-4 (hc)
ISBN: 978-1-9736-1690-0 (e)

Library of Congress Control Number: 2018901249

Print information available on the last page.

WestBow Press rev. date: 09/26/2018

CONTENTS

ACKNOWLEDGEMENTS

I owe a debt of gratitude to those men of the ministry who led me and my family, as new-born Christians, from the shallow waters of rebirth to the ever-deepening waters of the River of Life of Jesus Christ. Our first pastor in Christ was Dr. Charles Stanley to whom we turned as new Christians and whom we watched every Sunday on the television. His sage words of wisdom inspired by the Holy Spirit led us to a little Christian chapel in Medford, New Jersey named *Fellowship Alliance Chapel* where we were shepherded as lambs in the Lord by a man after God's own heart, Reverend Marty Berglund. His love for Christ was awe-inspiring. Then the Holy Spirit led us to *Applegate Christian Fellowship*, an "on-fire for the Lord" evangelical church in Ruch, Oregon led by Pastor Jon Courson. Under Pastor Jon's tutelage, we went through the Bible, page by page, book by book, and cover to cover wherein we learned so much about God's Word. Pastor Jon is a master of communicating the Gospel of Jesus Christ. Presently, we are being shepherded by a professor of the Gospel, Dr. Rick Booye of *Trail Christian Fellowship* in Eagle Point, Oregon. Pastor Rick is a teacher *par excellence*. He is a professor at *Pacific Bible College* wherein I have had the privilege of attending three of the courses taught by Pastor Rick at the College. To all of these shepherds of Christ we are indeed grateful.

In completing this work, I received valuable comments and suggestions from my wife, Cheryl Shaw whose insights were filled with much wisdom and added greater clarity to the many essays as they were written over the years for the magazine, *The Christian Journal*. I also wish to acknowledge my appreciation for the valuable insight and comments from time to time shared with me by Pastor Chad McComas, editor of *The Christian Journal* and Senior Pastor of *Set Free Christian Fellowship*, Medford, Oregon. *The Christian Journal* is a non-profit ministry of *Set Free Christian Fellowship*. Pastor Chad is an inspiration for many who are disciples of Jesus Christ, especially those whose God-given gift is writing about the Lord. Additional thanks are due my grandson, Zachary Schneider, whose technical assistance in formatting the book was invaluable. My appreciation is also due to my friend Lin Engelhorn whose stenographical skills enabled me to finalize the book in its present form. Finally, I very much appreciate the skills of Linda Kincaid who designed the meaningful cover of the book.

But most importantly, I ascribe all of this work to the guidance of the Lord, Jesus Christ, and the Holy Spirit Who planted thoughts in my mind and inspired me to do this work. Jesus said, "Whoever confesses Me before men, him I will also confess before My Father who is in heaven" (Matthew 10:32). It gives me a great sense of fulfillment to do just that—acknowledge Him before men and women of this world. If only one person comes to believe in Jesus Christ by reading this work, I shall be forever grateful.

> "Not unto us, O LORD, not unto us,
> But to Your name give glory,
> Because of Your mercy,
> Because of Your truth" (Psalm 115:1).

AN INSPIRATION

"God, think Thy thoughts in my mind.
What dost Thou desire written?
Here is my hand; use it.
Pour Thy wisdom through my hand."

By: Frank C. Laubach*

* From "The Game With Minutes" written by Frank C. Laubach (1884-1970) published by Dr. Robert S. Laubach, his son, in the book "Letters by a Modern Mystic" by Frank C. Laubach, copyright ©. "Excerpts of 'The Game With Minutes' were originally published by SeedSowers Publishing House, Jacksonville, FL, in the book "Practicing His Presence" by Brother Lawrence and Frank Laubach. "Letters by a Modern Mystic" was published by Dr. Laubach, copyright ©, with Purposeful Design Publications, Colorado Springs, CO 80962-5130. Used with permission. All rights reserved.

PREFACE

Writing has always been one of my pleasant pastimes. From the days in eighth grade English when one of my favorite teachers, Mr. Mathewson, inspired me to write, I have enjoyed writing about people and things. In the legal profession where I spent most of my working days, I did a lot of writing and often found it flowing easily out of me, albeit some of the works were on subjects that many would find non-inspirational.

As I have described in a few of the essays, in 1983 Jesus Christ reached out His hand and touched me. It was a "special revelation," a truly regenerative conversion, so awe inspiring to me that it was and is difficult to put into words. That wondrous event was the beginning of a lifetime journey seeking to know more about Jesus.

In 2001, the Lord opened a door for me to write about Him in a regional Christian magazine, *The Christian Quarterly* which is now known as *The Christian Journal*. The editor of *The Christian Journal*, Pastor Chad McComas, is the Senior Pastor of *Set Free Christian Fellowship* in Medford, Oregon. Pastor Chad continues to publish the monthly magazine as a ministry of *Set Free Christian Fellowship*. You can read *The Christian Journal* on its web site: www. thechristianjournal.org. For almost ten years, I submitted monthly essay-type articles to Pastor Chad and he graciously included them in the magazine.

In 2007, I embarked on a project that I'd had in the back of my mind for years: writing a book. In 2014, after seven years of research, drafting and editing and re-editing, I published an historical novel, *The Crossover People, an Incredible Journey from Darkness into the Light*. You can see a video highlighting the story at www.thecrossoverpeople.com.

After *The Crossover People* was published, the Holy Spirit placed upon my heart the desire to write another book, an anthology of the many essays I'd written for *The Christian Journal*. With the encouragement of my wife Cheryl and with the inspiration of the Lord, I reviewed, edited, embellished and in some cases wrote anew, ninety essays about Jesus Christ. My goal in writing *Shifting Shadows, an Anthology of Essays About the Christ*, was to do my part in the Great Commission of Jesus Christ (Matthew 28:19–20), "Go therefore and make disciples of all nations teaching them to obey everything I have commanded you." It is my desire and prayer that many will be inspired about our Lord Jesus Christ as I have been in writing about Him.

Since my goal for this book is to do my part in The Great Commission of the Lord Jesus Christ, it is my hope that a person reading the book will find it easier to understand the inspired words of God in the context of the essays as they are written on various life/spiritual subjects.

B. Neil Shaw
Winter, 2018

BELIEF

Jesus said, "If I do not do the works of My Father, do not believe Me; but if I do, though you do not believe Me, believe the works that you may know and believe that the Father is in Me, and I in Him" (John 10:37–38).

THERE'S POWER IN HIS WORKS

What do you say to a friend who doesn't believe in God? How do you convince your friend that the gospel is the truth? The Bible says that only through and with the power of God can anyone convince another that Christ is the only way to eternal salvation. Unless the Holy Spirit works in a person's heart, the wise words of the speaker won't be heard by the nonbeliever (1 Corinthians 2:4–5).

There is a science and art in Christianity that deals with responding to those who ask about, criticize or oppose the gospel. It is called *apologetics*, a term derived from the Greek legal term *apologia* which means defense, vindication, or answer. Apologetics has been utilized throughout Christian history in defending the faith. The apostle Peter wrote, "Always be ready to give a defense to everyone who asks you a reason for the hope that is in you, with meekness and fear; having a good conscience, that when they defame you as evildoers, those who revile your good conduct in Christ may be ashamed" (1 Peter 3:15–16).

The classical method of apologetics uses the power of reason in responding to persons who disbelieve the gospel. The apostle Paul used classical biblical apologetics in interfacing with the non-believing culture of his time. Acts 17:16–34 describes how Paul reasoned with the non-believing Epicurean and Stoic philosophers in Athens, a city known for its people of reason: "Now while Paul waited for them at Athens, his spirit was provoked within him when he saw that the city was given over to idols. Therefore he reasoned in the synagogue with the Jews and with the Gentile worshipers, and in the marketplace daily with those who happened to be there" (Acts 17:16–17). All apologetics ends at the resurrection of Jesus Christ. Thus, Paul "preached to them Jesus and the resurrection" (Acts 17–18). He proclaimed to the philosophers at Athens that God "commands all men everywhere to repent, because He has appointed a day on which He will judge the world in righteousness by the Man whom He has ordained. He has given assurance of this to all by raising Him from the dead"(Acts 17:30–31).

Christianity is a religion of people who reason. The Lord desires His disciples to "know and believe" (John 10:38). He wants us to view reality from the way He sees it. For example, Jesus Christ responded to the criticisms of the Jewish leaders when they challenged Him in the portico of Solomon. The Jewish leaders said to Jesus, "'If you are the Christ, tell us plainly.' Jesus answered them, 'I told you and you do not believe. The works that I do in my Father's name, they bear witness of Me. If I do not do the works of My Father, do not believe Me; but if I do, though you do not believe Me, believe the works, that you may know and believe that the Father is in Me, and I in Him'" (John 10:24–26, 37–38). Jesus said that if they didn't believe who He said He was, they should look around and see what He'd done and was doing as proof that He is the Messiah. In exhorting nonbelievers to believe His works, Jesus pointed them not only to the miracles they'd seen but also the power of God in His creation—His works.

The ancient prophet wrote about the works of God,

> "He has made the earth by His power, He has established the world by His wisdom, And He has stretched out the heavens at His discretion...He causes the vapors to ascend from the ends of the earth. He makes lightening for the rain, He brings the wind out of His treasuries" (Jeremiah 10:12-13).

The apostles witnessed the Lord's great power while in the midst of a storm on the Sea of Galilee, "Then He...rebuked the winds and the sea, and there was a great calm. So the men marveled, saying, 'Who can this be, that even the winds and the sea obey Him?'" (Matthew 8:26–27).

We experience the power of God's great works every moment of our lives. Did you ever wonder why the sun always stays ninety-three million miles from the earth? It's just right for life on earth. What about the atom with its electrons, protons and neutrons? There's a power that holds all of them together in a certain relationship so as to form all matter in the universe: "And He is before all things, and in Him all things consist" (Colossians 1:17). Just as the prophet Jeremiah observed, the characteristics of the universe, fine-tuned by God to make life possible and sustainable, are all from His outstretched hand—the power of God.

When a person asks, criticizes or opposes the gospel, speak as the apostle Paul spoke of the glorious splendor of God's kingdom and the power to make known His mighty works, "Because what may be known of God is manifest in them [unrighteous men], for God has shown it to them. For since the creation of the world His invisible attributes are clearly seen, being understood by the things that are made" (Romans 1:19–20). Similarly, the psalmist wrote, "All your works shall praise You, O LORD, And Your saints shall bless You. They shall speak of the glory of Your kingdom, and talk of Your power, To make known to the sons of men His mighty acts, and the glorious majesty of His kingdom" (Psalm 145:10–12).

By the grace of the Holy Spirit, the searching person will see and hear the power of God in His works. Belief in Him is the next rational step in the seeker's walk toward faith in the Lord. This person will then shout with glee, "For You, LORD, have made me through Your work; I will triumph in the works of Your hands" (Psalm 92:4).

COMMITMENT

Jesus said, "Be faithful until death, and I will give you the crown of life" (Revelation 2:10).

HE'S COMMITTED TO GIVE
US A CROWN OF LIFE

Jesus died for you and for me. Are we willing to die for Him? (John 13:38).

He proclaims that it was to Him that we are to commit our hearts. He said, "You believe in God, believe also in Me" (John 14:1).

But to what degree does the Lord, our God, expect us to commit our lives to Him? He tells us, "Be faithful until death" (Revelation 2:10). To the point of death? Yes, to the point of death!

But what if we are told by a government official, "You cannot pray in public" or, "You cannot display the Cross" or, "You cannot use the words *Under God* in the pledge of allegiance to your country" or on and on until we are told one day, "You cannot worship Jesus Christ" or, "You cannot have a Bible" or, "Religious practices except those determined by the government are not permitted."

Finally, what if we are told one day that the only way we can buy goods or do business is if we accept the government's identification computer chip under the skin of our forehead or our right hand? (Revelation 13:16–17). What would we do?

The book of The Revelation of Jesus Christ states that these foreboding events will occur: "All who dwell on the earth will worship him [Satan], whose names have not been written in the Book of Life of the Lamb slain from the foundation of the world" (Revelation 13:8). Faced with these edicts, many will refuse to comply with the dictates of the anti-Christ and will die in the name of Jesus Christ. Many have and are already dying for Him in this troubled world: "And they overcame him [the accuser, Satan] by the blood of the Lamb and by the word of their testimony, they did not love their lives to the death" (Revelation 12:11).

Are we willing to die for our faith? The answer must be yes! We must say, "Yes, Jesus, I am willing to be faithful to you even unto death." Why? Because Jesus said more than that in Revelation 2:10,

"Be faithful until death, and I will give you the crown of life." He will give us eternal life at His throne. He assures us that anyone whose name is written in the Book of Life will not be thrown into the lake of fire, the "second death" (Revelation 20:12–14). Being victorious is achieving the blissful state in which God and humans are restored to perfect fellowship as it existed before sin entered the world. By being faithful to our Lord Jesus Christ we are assured that we shall enjoy eternal life with Him and have nothing to fear from the death of our flesh.

In *Foxe's Book of Martyrs* (prepared by W. Grinton Berry), it is described how the apostle Andrew, Peter's brother, was totally committed in faith to our Lord. Andrew preached in an area now known as Ethiopia. He brought many to the faith of Christ. Aegeas, the Roman proconsul, commanded Andrew not to teach about Christ. He warned Andrew that if he did, he would be crucified "with all speed." Andrew responded that he would not have preached the honor and glory of the cross if he feared the death of the cross. Foxe described Andrew's strong faith (see page 9), "Andrew, going toward the place, and seeing afar off the cross prepared, did change neither countenance nor colour, neither did his blood shrink, neither did he fail in his speech, his body fainted not, neither was his mind molested, nor did his understanding fail him, as it is the manner of men to do, but out of the abundance of his heart his mouth did speak...he said, 'O cross, most welcome and long looked for! with a willing mind, joyfully and desirously, I come to thee, being the scholar of Him which did hang on thee: because I have always been thy lover, and have coveted to embrace thee.'"

Unbending faith—total commitment to Jesus Christ, earned Andrew a crown of eternal life. When it is our time, we too shall be with Him and when that time comes, He will be faithful unto us and will give us the crown of eternal life. May we be worthy in our commitment to Jesus—faithful to Him, even unto death.

LET YOUR YES BE YES,
AND YOUR NO, NO

A commitment is a pledge to do something. If to the Lord, it is a sacred vow. It is not something to be made and broken without consequences. "If a man makes a vow to the LORD, or swears an oath to bind himself by some agreement, he shall not break his word; he shall do according to all that proceeds out of his mouth" (Numbers 30:2). Jesus said, "But let your 'Yes' be 'Yes,' and your 'No,' 'No.' For whatever is more than these is from the evil one" (Matthew 5:37).

The Bible describes many ancients who made vows to the Lord. These Biblical accounts illustrate the importance of keeping a commitment. One whose commitment to the Lord is mentioned along with Abel, Enoch, Noah, Abraham and others is Jephthah the Gileadite (Hebrews 11:32).

Jephthah's childhood was troubled. His mother was a prostitute and his brothers drove him out of the family home condemning him (Judges 11:1–2). Perhaps it was during these troubled times that the LORD cultivated in Jephthah strong faith and courage—he became a great warrior. Although driven away from Gilead, the elders of Gilead later sought his help because the Ammonites made war on Israel. They asked him to be their leader against their enemy (Judges 11:6). After prayer (Judges 11:11), he agreed to serve as their commander and leader.

At first, Jephthah tried diplomacy with the Ammonites. He sent a message to the Ammonite king saying, "I have not sinned against you, but you wronged me by fighting against me. May the LORD, the Judge, render judgment this day between the children of Israel and the people of Ammon" (Judges 11:27). In essence, Jephthah was willing to leave the battle in the Lord's hands. His faith and commitment to the Lord were immovable. The Ammonite king ignored his message. The holy battle was joined.

As Jephthah advanced against the Ammonites the Holy Spirit

came upon him (Judges 11:29). It was then that Jephthah made a vow, an unbreakable commitment to the Lord. He said, "If You will indeed deliver the people of Ammon into my hands, then it will be that whatever comes out of the doors of my house to meet me, when I return in peace from the people of Ammon, shall surely be the LORD's, and I will offer it up as a burnt offering" (Judges 11:30–31).

The Lord acknowledged Jephthah's vow by granting Israel victory over the Ammonites. As Jephthah approached his home after the battle, who should come out to meet him but his daughter, his only child! (Judges 11:34). "When he saw her he tore his clothes, and said, 'Alas, my daughter! You have brought me very low! You are among those who trouble me! For I have given my word to the LORD, and I cannot go back on it'" (Judges 11:35).

Jephthah had taught his daughter well for she knew that once made, a vow is not to be broken. She replied to his outcry of anguish that since he had given his word to the Lord and the Lord had avenged his enemies, he must do to her as he had vowed to God, that is, offer her up as a burnt offering to the Lord (Judges 11:36). Her one request to Jephthah was to "Let me alone for two months, that I may go and wander on the mountains and bewail my virginity, my friends and I. And it was so at the end of two months that she returned to her father, and he carried out his vow with her which he had vowed. She knew no man" (Judges 11:37, 39).

There is disagreement as to the meaning of the words, *he carried out his vow*. Some expositors believe that Jephthah sacrificed his daughter as a burnt offering. Others interpret the reference to her virginity and that she would never marry to mean that Jephthah committed his daughter's life to the Lord just as Hannah did with Samuel. Whether Jephthah sacrificed his daughter as a burnt offering or committed her to a celibate life of devotion to the Lord isn't the issue here. The principle taught is that Jephthah kept his commitment, no matter what.

When we make a commitment, we are to keep it whether it causes difficulty, sacrifice or suffering. In marriage, in business, or in life in general, our word must be our bond. "What we have solemnly vowed to God, we must perform, if it be possible and lawful, though it be difficult and grievous to us." *Matthew Henry's Concise Commentary on the Whole Bible*, 251.

The wisest of kings, Solomon, spoke about vows, "When you make a vow to God, do not delay to pay it; For He has no pleasure in fools. Pay what you have vowed—Better not to vow than to vow and not pay" (Ecclesiastes 5:4–5).

Our "yes" must mean "yes," and our "no", "no."

COURAGE

Our courage comes not from men or women, but from God who is our "Wonderful Counselor, Mighty God, Everlasting Father, Prince of Peace" (Isaiah 9:6).

DEBORAH: A WOMAN OF COURAGE

The Bible is filled with accounts of men and women who have lived courageous lives. One of the heroines of the Bible is Deborah, a prophetess and a judge (Judges 4–5). She was a woman who had deep faith in the Lord, a faith which gave her wisdom, the gift of prophecy, and above all, resolution, confidence and bravery that brought her people "rest [for] forty years" (Judges 5:31).

The setting for her story appears in Judges 4:1–3: "The children of Israel again did evil in the sight of the LORD. So the LORD sold them into the hand of Jabin king of Canaan...And the children of Israel cried out to the LORD; for Jabin had harshly oppressed the children of Israel [for twenty years]."

This oppressive state of affairs for the children of Israel was assured when the angel of the LORD said to them, "You have not obeyed My voice...Therefore...I will not drive them [the Canaanites] out before you; but they will become thorns in your side" (Judges 2:2–3).

Deborah led Israel when Jabin reigned (Judges 4:4). "She would sit under the palm tree of Deborah between Ramah and Bethel in the mountains of Ephraim. And the children of Israel came up to her for judgment" (Judges 4:5). Bethel is north of Jerusalem and was in the lands of the tribe of Benjamin. The Israelites came to Deborah to resolve their disputes.

As a prophetess, the angel of the Lord spoke to her and provided the means by which the children of Israel could be freed from the terror of the Canaanites. Deborah sent for Barak who lived in Kedesh in the tribe of Naphtali in the extreme northern area of present day Israel near Mt. Hermon. She said to him, "Has not the LORD God of Israel commanded, 'Go, and deploy troops at Mount Tabor; take with you ten thousand men of the sons of Naphtali and Zebulun: and against you I will deploy Sisera [commander of Jabin's army]...and I will deliver them into your hand?'" (Judges 4:6–7).

Northern Israel is a mountainous area. Barak and his fellow

Napthalites and Zebulunites were men who lived in the mountains. They were rugged individuals who were used to the rigorous life of people who live and battle in rough terrain. Mount Tabor is to the east of the Plain of Megiddo, the main pass that runs northeast in Israel through the mountains surrounding the plain of Sharon and the fertile Valley of Jezreel. It was at that time a main travel route of commerce. Megiddo (in Hebrew, *Har Megiddo*) is the place described in Revelation 16:16 in which the final battle, the battle on the great day of God Almighty, will occur (Armageddon). It is interesting to note that one of Israel's key air bases is located underground in the Plain of Megiddo. From the nearby Mount Carmel you can see runways on the floor of the Plain that begin in the middle of nowhere and end just as they begin.

Jabin would have no trouble defeating the Israelites if the battle were to occur in the vast treeless Plain of Megiddo since he had nine hundred iron chariots and the Israelites had none. But God told Deborah to instruct Barak to lead the way to Mount Tabor wherein the Lord would cause Sisera with his chariots and his troops to go to the Kishon River and there give him into the hands of the children of Israel (Judges 4:6–7).

The area around Megiddo, especially the Valley of Jezreel, is one of Israel's most productive agricultural areas. Mount Carmel is the area where the prophet Elijah prophesied about drought to Ahab, king of Israel. After defeating the four hundred fifty false prophets of Ahab's wife Jezebel, Elijah prophesied that it would rain after three years (1 Kings 17:1, 18:1). In the Valley of Jezreel there is significant rainfall, often in such deluges as to cause the Kishon River to flood. The flooded Kishon River was used by Napoleon in achieving victory over the Turkish army in 1799. *NIV Study Bible*, *Judges*, note 4:7. The Lord's plan for victory over the dark forces of Jabin was firmly established since chariots don't do well in a flooded plain or in a battle fought at the base of a mountain against mountain men!

But Deborah was confronted by another problem unrelated to Jabin: Barak's lack of faith in the LORD. Barak told Deborah that he would fight for Israel only if she would accompany him (Judges 4:8).

Deborah told Barak that the Lord had assured her that Sisera would be given into Barak's hands. But Barak's faith, if any, was misplaced. He placed it on a person, Deborah, rather than on the Lord. Barak, which in Hebrew means *thunderbolt*, lacked courage to do battle because of misplaced faith. Thankfully, Deborah's faith was unshakable. She knew the Lord was with her. No matter what happened, she had great confidence that she would be safe in His hands.

She replied to Barak, "I will surely go with you; nevertheless there will be no glory for you in the journey you are taking, for the LORD will sell Sisera into the hand of a woman" (Judges 4:9). In spite of her admonition, Barak faltered in his faith and Deborah, keeping her word, accompanied him into battle.

Deborah risked her life and supported Barak in battle. She gave him the courage that he lacked. She encouraged him, "Up! For this is the day in which the LORD has delivered Sisera into your hand. Has not the LORD gone out before you?" (Judges 4:14). You can imagine her prayer to the Lord as she entered the battle (similar to what the Psalmist wrote): "Not unto us, O LORD, not unto us, but to Your name be the glory, because of Your mercy, because of Your truth" (Psalm115:1).

The Thunderbolt thundered down from Mount Tabor followed by his army of ten thousand mountain men. The sounds of the battle trumpets echoed in the hills surrounding the green Jezreel Valley. "And the LORD routed Sisera and all his chariots and all his army with the edge of the sword before Barak...and all the army of Sisera fell by the edge of the sword; not a man was left" (Judges 4:15–16). Being the coward he was, "Sisera alighted from his chariot and fled on foot" (Judges 4:15). After the battle was lost, the exhausted and beaten Sisera sought refuge in the house of Heber, an Israelite. He was encouraged by Jael, Heber's wife, to rest and while he slept, Jael drove a tent peg through his temple (Judges 4:21). In the end, Sisera was done in by two women.

It was the Lord who routed Sisera. Deborah never doubted that the Lord would be true to His Word. This gave her great courage for she knew that it was the Lord's battle, not hers. It always is!

B. NEIL SHAW

The lesson to be learned here is clear: in our own lives, of ourselves we can do nothing (John 5:30). Courage comes not from men or women, but from God, our "Wonderful Counselor, Mighty God, Everlasting Father, Prince of Peace" (Isaiah 9:6). Just as Moses encouraged his people, we too must "Be strong and of good courage, do not fear nor be afraid of them; for the LORD your God, He is the One who goes with you. He will not leave you nor forsake you" (Deuteronomy 31:6).

Jesus' last words to His disciples were also words of assurance, "Lo, I am with you always, even to the end of the age" (Matthew 28:20). Be like Deborah, a woman of courage who knew that the Lord was with her. After all, "If God is for us, who can be against us?" (Romans 8:31).

COVENANT

"God's covenant is a relationship of love and loyalty between the Lord and His chosen people." *

---

* *Vine's Complete Expository Dictionary of Old and New Testament Words*, 51.

THE MARRIAGE COVENANT

In His creation, God willed that when a man and woman fall in love, they are to leave their parents and cleave to each other as one flesh. In so doing they make an irrevocable covenant with God and to each other that they shall live their lives as husband and wife "until death do us part." This is the holy marriage covenant.

In Genesis, the Word of God provides, "God created man in His own image; in the image of God He created Him; male and female He created them" (1:27). But then God said, "It is not good that man should be alone; I will make him a helper comparable to him" (2:18). So God took one of the man's ribs and made a woman as a mate for life. "Adam said, 'This is now bone of my bones And flesh of my flesh; She shall be called Woman, Because she was taken out of Man.' Therefore a man shall leave his father and mother and be joined to his wife, and they shall become one flesh" (2:23–24).

"Then God blessed them, and God said to them, 'Be fruitful and multiply; fill the earth and subdue it'" (Genesis 1:28). Everything in life is planned for us by God. The psalmist wrote, "Your eyes saw my substance, being yet unformed, And in Your book they were all written, The days were fashioned for me, When as yet there were none of them" (Psalm 139:16).

God intended that procreation be the result of the holy covenant of marriage between a man and a woman. In marriage, a man cleaves to his wife and she cleaves to him. This is God's will. For over fifty-four years, this has been my personal experience as a husband. Before we were born God intended that my wife and I be husband and wife. To discard this relationship is not just a breach of a legal contract, but a broken covenant with God. Once joined together as one flesh, it was not God's plan that we part before death and cleave to another.

There was a time when God allowed our marriage covenant to be tested. After fourteen years, our marriage was in trouble. But because of our strong belief in God and the covenant we'd made with Him; because of the long history of our relationship including our children born to us; but most of all because of His grace and mercy, we weathered the storm. It was a time of deep pain for both of us, but with God's limitless love and guidance we worked through the issues we faced with each other. It was by no means easy. It was hard! In fact there were many occasions when we felt it would be *easier* to walk away. Now, looking back at those times over fifty-four years ago, we are aware of the lessons God intended for us in His marriage covenant. No matter how good or bad the times; no matter how rich or poor we are; no matter whether we are in good health or in sickness; no matter how hard it is or easy, God put us together to be husband and wife for His reasons and not ours. After all, the deeper He tests us, the greater the joy when He brings us through troubled times.

My wife and I have been best friends for many years now and we know that God's hand was in it all. After all, He is a party to our marriage covenant.

"Therefore what God has joined together, let not man separate" (Matthew 19:6).

DEATH

"To everything there is a season, A time for every purpose under heaven: A time to be born, And a time to die" (Ecclesiastes 3:1–2). As a saved soul, when I die I shall be with my Maker joining with my brethren singing His praise—forever.

IS THIS MY LAST DAY?

I'll never forget the day my uncle died—he was buried in the morning and yet, the afternoon news broadcast rush hour traffic the same as it did the day before. The earth continued to go around. Not a mention of my Uncle Harold! Life went on as if he'd never lived. Though I'd been to funerals before, this one for some reason impressed upon me how tenuous this life really is. "Where is Harold now?" I thought. Out of over seven billion in the world, there are only a few souls who are even aware of Harold's life before his last day on this earth. To the rest of the world, it's as if he never existed.

At the time I thought, "Is this what I want my life to stand for?" In a worldly context, my death and the thought of it was so final. But this was before I knew Jesus Christ. I thank God that I am one of the many souls who were blessed to find the Messiah, the Holy One of God. Since my rebirth in Christ, death has become a concept of fearless anticipation. I used to live my life as though there was no tomorrow, nothing beyond this, but now I pray that I live my life for Christ's sake, for He lives within me! As a saved soul, when I die I shall be with my Maker joining with my brethren singing His praise—forever. What a pleasant thought that is!

Thomas A' Kempis wrote an essay, *Thinking About Death,* in his book (edited by William C. Creasy) entitled *The Imitation of Christ*, 55. He wrote, "Very soon it will be over with you here...Today we are, and tomorrow we are gone. And when we are taken out of sight, we soon pass out of mind...This being the case, you ought to master yourself in every act and thought as if you were to die today."

In the biblical story of King Hezekiah, we learn of one who was told by God to keep the hour of death before his eyes (2 Kings 20:1–7). Hezekiah was deathly ill. Isaiah, the prophet, received word from the Lord that he should tell Hezekiah to get his house in order for he would soon die. Being a God-fearing man filled with the wisdom of God, Hezekiah did what he knew to do in the face of fear and darkness—he prayed to the Lord. He asked God to remember that he walked before Him in truth and with a loyal heart. He reminded God that he had done "what was good in Your sight" (2 Kings 20:1–3). While praying he wept bitterly.

Hearing the mournful prayer of the king, the Lord felt compassion for Hezekiah and told the prophet to tell Hezekiah that He'd heard his prayer and that He would add fifteen years to his life. He also assured Hezekiah that He would defend him and Jerusalem from the hand of the king of Assyria (2 Kings 20:4–6). God even told Isaiah how to heal Hezekiah's illness. He instructed the king's servants to lay a lump of figs on the king's boil "and he recovered" (2 Kings 20:7).

For the remainder of his days, Hezekiah continued to keep the hour of death before his eyes. This was so because other than the prophet Isaiah, he was the only human on earth who knew when he was going to die. It had to take a strong believer in the Lord, as Hezekiah was, to carry on his days knowing the day and the hour when he was going to die.

The story of King Hezekiah brings to mind a dear brother in the Lord. He'd written, "God performed an amazing miracle in my life...I have promised the Lord that as long as I live, I would tell anyone I could about His mercy and goodness in my life! I praise God daily now in, and for my life. May all love, honor, praise and gratitude be given to the Lord." (See article in *The Christian Quarterly*, Fall, 2001 by Mark Schiavone, *He Saved my Life, a Personal Testimony*). Mark was a man who, like Hezekiah, kept the hour of death before his eyes in his waning days.

Mark loved Jesus Christ with all of his heart and all of his soul. He had a strong desire to know all he could about the Lord and His Word. He was reborn when he read Josh McDowell's book, *Evidence That Demands a Verdict*. Mark's life reflected his deep love for Jesus. Then the bottom fell out. On August 8, 2000, while on a family vacation, he had a heart attack and collapsed in his hotel. He was rushed to the hospital where he "flat lined and went into a coma." If the definition of death is one's heart stopping, he died. The doctors worked frantically "to shock his heart back to life. After some time, they got a faint beat." He later wrote, "Things didn't look good for me and three separate doctors told my wife and son that I would die that night...I actually felt myself dying!...As I closed my eyes to die, all of a sudden I got this image of my wife on one side of my bed and my son on the other side, both praying for me. I remember saying to the Lord, 'Please Jesus, don't take me now. I don't want to leave my family yet'...I had no strength left! I just repeated over and over again to myself, 'Not in my strength but in Jesus.'"

The many prayers for Mark by his family and brethren were answered by the Lord. The man whose heart had given out "was sitting up and eating in eleven hours." As it turned out, the Lord gave Mark almost two more years "to set his house in order." The Lord "brought the shadow ten degrees backward, by which it had gone down on the sundial of Ahaz" (2 Kings 20:11). He gave Mark additional time. Like Hezekiah, Mark cried out to the Lord; he prayed for healing; and the Lord said, "I have heard your prayer, I have seen your tears; surely I will heal you" (2 Kings 20:5). During those extra years, Mark and his family lived each day as we all should, as if today is our last. The Lord dramatically showed Mark that he was on borrowed time. His attitude was as if the hour of death was before his eyes. He knew the Lord would take care of him and his family and each day was a reflection of this assuredness in the Lord. The only fear that my friend Mark knew during the brief time that the Lord had given him was fear of the Lord Himself. Now Mark is with Him. My friend is with my Friend.

Mark's story and that of King Hezekiah show us that when thinking of our own deaths, we should follow the sage advice of Thomas A' Kempis (*supra* at 56), "Who will remember you after your death, and who will pray for you? Do, do now...whatever you can do, because you do not know when you will die...Gather everlasting riches while you have time. Think of nothing except your eternal well-being. Care only for the things of God...Keep yourself as a pilgrim and stranger on earth, a person to whom the affairs of the world mean nothing apart from Christ. Keep your heart free and lifted up to God, for this world is not your permanent home; you are simply passing through. With heartfelt love, direct your prayers and sighs to your eternal home, so that after death your spirit may be worthy to pass happily to the Lord. Amen."

DISCERNMENT

Discernment is righteous judgment—a matter of judging wisely through prayer. By loving God, He enables us to love our neighbor. By loving our neighbor, we are able to discern with wisdom our neighbor's inward motives without condemnation.

DISCERNMENT: A MATTER OF PRAYER

In life, we judge, for out of necessity we must distinguish the good from the bad whether it is a person, matter or thing. The Bible exhorts us to "Test all things, hold fast what is good. Abstain from every form of evil" (1 Thessalonians 5:21–22).

But Jesus Christ commanded on the mountain overlooking the Sea of Galilee, "Judge not, that you be not judged. For with what judgment you judge, you will be judged" (Matthew 7:1–2). Is there a contradiction between our need to form an opinion about someone and God's commandment not to judge? In His Sermon on the Plain, Jesus clarified what He commanded in His Sermon on the Mount. He said, "Judge not, and you shall not be judged. Condemn not, and you shall not be condemned" (Luke 6:37).

In judging about someone, we are not to judge by condemnation, but for identification. *Jon Courson's New Testament Application Commentary*, 42. Judging for identification is another way of saying that we are to discern what is wise with respect to a person. *Discernment* is the act of "determining the excellence or defects of a person or thing." *Vine's Complete Expository Dictionary of Old and New Testament Words*, 171.

But in examining the character of another, how do we make a righteous judgment (discernment) without committing a sinful judgment (condemnation)? The process of righteous discernment versus sinful condemnation involves first examining our own motives in seeking to evaluate the character of another. As humans, we naturally desire that others accept our worldview. Often, in judging others our own character traits get in the way of wise determination. We do not like what we see because our own stuff gets in the way. If we find something that we don't like in another, it may be because we don't like that same trait in ourselves. If we don't like our own trait, there may be a bit of self-condemnation in the thought process. That negative view of our own conduct may be projected onto the character of the other person we are seeking to judge and becomes a sinful condemnation rather than an unbiased righteous discernment.

Pastor J. Vernon McGee identified the theme of Matthew 7 as "The relationship of the child of the King with other children of the King *maintained by prayer*" (my emphasis added). He wrote, "These verses [Matthew 7:1–2] do not mean that a child of God is forbidden to judge others, but it does mean that we are not to judge the inward motives of others in the sense of condemning them. We do not know or understand why a brother in Christ does a certain thing. We see only outward acts. God doesn't forbid our judging wrong and evil actions...It is important to make discernment [judging righteously] a matter of prayer." McGee, *Thru the Bible*, Vol. IV, 40–41.

If we ask the Father for guidance in forming an opinion about a person, He'll give us the wisdom to have a "good understanding" of that person's character (see Psalm 111:10). Jesus instructed us to "Ask, and it will be given to you; seek, and you will find; knock, and it will be opened to you. For everyone who asks receives, and he who seeks finds, and to him who knocks it will be opened" (Matthew 7:7–8). In essence, righteous discernment is a matter of prayer.

Jesus said that the two most important commandments are to "love the Lord your God with all your heart, with all your soul, with all your mind, and with all your strength [and to] love your neighbor as yourself" (Mark 12:29–31). By judging wisely through prayer, we are showing respect for God and loving Him. By loving God, He enables us to love our neighbor. By loving our neighbor, we are able to discern with wisdom our neighbor's inward motives without condemnation.

Discernment, make it a matter of prayer!

DISCIPLESHIP

"Jesus came and spoke to them, saying, 'All authority has been given to Me in heaven and on earth. Go therefore and make disciples of all nations, baptizing them in the name of the Father and of the Son and of the Holy Spirit, teaching them to observe all things that I have commanded you'" (Matthew 28:18–20).

WHAT IS WRONG WITH OUR COUNTRY?

What is wrong with our country? We have lost our way. Those are familiar words, perhaps said in a slightly different way by the prophet Habakkuk, "O LORD, how long shall I cry, And you will not hear?...For plundering and violence are before me; there is strife, and contention arises. Therefore the law is powerless, And justice never goes forth. For the wicked surround the righteous; Therefore perverse judgment proceeds" (Habakkuk 1:2–4).

Like the prophet, I look around and I see my decaying nation. Morality is in a downward spiral. It's on a slippery slope. Right and wrong are no longer determined by reference to Reality (God), but are determined by "Me'ism," that is, "If it's good for me, it's OK." Like the time of the judges in Israel where the people had lost their way with God, many in our culture do what's "right in his own eyes" (Judges 21:25). We're told there is no truth, but that truth is just relative (moral relativism, "I can do as I like so long as no one else is harmed"). Corruption, dishonesty and greed are the rule rather than the exception. Babies are being killed by the millions, not burned alive in the arms of Molech, the Canaanite god recorded in the Bible, but on the abortionist's table. Crime and drug use are rampant. The media idolizes sex, profanity and violence. Even dishonesty in reporting news ("fake news") has become the standard. Commitment means nothing. Cheating is not an unusual occurrence in our educational system. Many of our politicians are unwilling to take a stand for righteousness, but in obedience just go along with the establishment agenda so as to retain their position of power.

What is wrong with the United States of America? *Bottom line: it is no longer a nation of disciples but a nation that is unwilling to follow God.*

The Lord, our Designer, our Creator, sets the standards by which we are to live our lives. Those standards are written in His inerrant

Word, the Bible. The Lord "teaches sinners in the way. The humble He guides in justice, And the humble He teaches His way" (Psalm 25:8–9). Without God, there is no standard for what is right and what is wrong. The Bible is the moral reference by which mankind has lived for over five thousand years. And yet, so many of our citizenry have never read the Bible, They have rejected it or have just not bothered to read it. By so doing, they have rejected God. Without a moral reference, our culture meanders along a directionless path to a point of destruction, mostly in a downward spiral, away from God, from the light into darkness.

God wants us to be His disciples. A disciple is a learner, "one who follows one's teaching." *Vine's Complete Expository Dictionary of Old and New Testament Words*, 171. The apostle Paul wrote in Romans 1:5 that through Christ "we have received grace and apostleship for obedience to the faith among all nations for His name." The *obedience* that Paul spoke of is not just a trust in Jesus Christ, but it is a willingness to obey Him. That obedience enables the disciple to be lifted out of his sinful nature and emulate the Teacher. The result is justification, that is, as if I'd never sinned. The fruit of being a disciple of Jesus Christ is integrity, righteousness, purity, and correctness of thinking, feeling and acting. People who ascribe to Christ's teachings live fulfilling lives that are guided by high moral standards, truth, honor, righteousness, justice and a sensitive respect for others.

Contrary to what the secularists assert, most of our country's forefathers were disciples of Christ. They had the courage, individualism and fortitude to live their lives as disciples. They risked all for the honor of living the teachings of the Lord. Our Constitution and the Declaration of Independence are living documents which reflect the Godly concepts practiced by our forefathers under which our nation was founded.

The Preamble to the Constitution evidences the intent of the founders for our nation in 1789. It reads, "WE THE PEOPLE of the United States, in Order to form a more *perfect Union*, establish *Justice*, insure domestic *Tranquility, provide for the common defence, promote the general Welfare,* and secure the *Blessings of Liberty* to ourselves and our Posterity, do ordain and establish this Constitution for the United States of America" (my emphasis added). The forefathers intended to form a nation of disciples of Christ who live by God's standards.

The Holy Spirit spoke through Azaria the prophet to King Asa, "The LORD is with you while you are with Him. If you seek Him, He will be found by you, but if you forsake Him, He will forsake you" (2 Chronicles 15:2). To Zechariah the priest He said, "Why do you transgress the commandments of the LORD so that you cannot prosper? Because you have forsaken the LORD, He also has forsaken you" (2 Chronicles 24:20).

Fellow Americans, we have lost our way as a nation of people who live a righteousness that comes from God. But why have we lost our way? It's because many in our nation seek to eliminate God in the guise of political correctness. "Take God out of everything," argue the secularists. But who is really behind "secularism?" The apostle Paul wrote, "For we do not wrestle against flesh and blood, but against principalities, against powers, against the rulers of the darkness of this age, against spiritual hosts of wickedness in the heavenly places" (Ephesians 6:12). Who is behind the movement to eliminate God from our nation? It's God's adversary, Satan. We are in a great spiritual battle for our nation's very existence.

What is wrong with our country? *Many have turned away from the Lord.*

The Lord is saying, "Yes, I have cursed them already, Because you do not take it to heart" (Malachi 2:2). But there is still hope. Jonah exhorted the Ninevites to repent from their wicked ways. They repented and believed God (Jonah 3:4–5). When God saw that the Ninevites had repented from their sin, He held back His right hand and did not destroy them (Jonah 3:10).

Fellow Americans, pray for repentance and revival by our citizenry that we may all stand in God's kingdom as a nation of His disciples. Pray for Christ's light to overcome the forces of evil permeating our land. Pray that Americans turn to Jesus Christ for He alone can set hearts to honor His Name. "Let the peoples praise you, O God...Then the earth shall yield her increase; God, our own God, shall bless us" (Psalm 67:5–6).

SERVING OTHERS IS SERVING THE LORD

Jesus said, "All authority has been given to Me in heaven and on earth. Go therefore and make disciples of all nations, baptizing them in the name of the Father and of the Son and of the Holy Spirit, teaching them to observe all things I have commanded you" (Matthew 28:18–20).

This exhortative teaching of Jesus Christ is known as His *Great Commission*. Using "plain meaning" as a means of interpreting His intention in giving this command to His disciples, it would appear that the Lord's intention was that His disciples tell the world about all the things He taught them and in so doing, make all the people in the world His disciples.

But how does the Lord want us, His disciples, to carry out His Great Commission to "make disciples of all nations?" The answer to this question lies in the "greatest commandments" upon which He said, "hang all the Law and the Prophets" (Matthew 22:40). He told us, (1) to "love the LORD your God with all your heart, with all your soul, and with all your mind" and (2) to "love your neighbor as yourself" (Matthew 22:37, 39). Jesus taught us to live our lives honoring God in every respect and to love our neighbors in the same manner that we care for ourselves.

But how should we love our neighbors as we love ourselves? Jesus answered this question. He said, "For even the Son of Man did not come to be served, but to serve" (Mark 10:45). Jesus Christ is the Servant, the Messiah, about whom the prophet wrote in Isaiah 52:13 – 53:12. He wants us to emulate Him and be servants to others. By serving our neighbors, we show that we care (love) about them as we do ourselves. By serving our neighbors, we are serving the Lord. By doing this, our neighbor may see what it means to be a disciple of Jesus Christ, follow our example, and become a disciple of the Lord thus fulfilling the Lord's Great Commission.

Not only does the Lord tell us to serve Him by fulfilling His Great Commission, but He also provides the means by which His disciples are able to carry it out. By His grace He gave us gifts which, through the guidance of His Holy Spirit within us, enables us to serve Him (1 Corinthians 7:7). The apostle Paul gave examples of the God-given gifts the Lord provides to His disciples: faithful prophesying, ministry (service), exhortation, teaching, encouraging, giving, diligent leadership, cheerful mercy, sincere brotherly love, fervent spirit, hospitality, and most important, the gift of "serving the Lord" (Romans 12:6–13). The last gift is fulfilled by serving others, that is, by loving our neighbors.

Christian ministers are those who serve the cause of Jesus Christ. The Lord, by His grace, has given them gifts that are used in teaching others about Him. We all have an innate sense of what our God-given gifts are and which instill in us a desire to serve the cause of _____. You fill in the blank space. For example, one of my ministries is writing about Jesus Christ. That is my way of serving others as commanded by Jesus Christ in Matthew 28. If one person sees and hears the Lord because of these writings, I shall have followed His exhortation to "make disciples of all nations."

Serving the cause of Jesus Christ can take many forms. The apostle Paul wrote about the many forms of ministry in his epistles to the early Christians. In Romans 15:15–16 he speaks of himself as an evangelist, a minister to the Gentiles.

Another example of a ministry spoken of by Paul is that of Epaphras (Colossians 1:7–8). Epaphras' ministry was the establishment of the Church at Colossi. Tychicus, an associate of Paul who traveled as his representative, was a minister of encouragement whose job was to let Paul's brothers in the Lord know how he was, how his ministry was progressing "and that he may comfort your hearts" (Ephesians 6:21–22). Timothy was a minister of truth of the faith, whose ministry as appointed by Paul was to reveal the deceiving spirits and things taught by false teachers (1 Timothy 1:3–4).

Paul, Epaphras, Tychicus and Timothy obeyed the Lord's command to go and make disciples of all nations. They served others and in so doing served the Lord.

The apostle John writes in his gospel about an invalid man who'd been lying next to the pool at Bethesda for thirty-eight years. The paralyzed man along with many others who were ill and infirm were lying at the pool's edge believing that an angel would come and stir up the water. They were of the belief that the first one in the water after the angel stirred it would be healed. The man was so transfixed with the water that he was startled when the Lord asked him if he wanted to be healed (John 5:6). The man didn't respond to the Lord with a resounding, "Yes!" No, he replied that he had no one to assist him into the water when it was stirred up. He said that every time he tried to get into the water, someone stepped in front of him (John 5:7). Just as described in the essay *Shifting Shadows* later in this book, his eyes were focused on the things of the flesh, the material, the *self*, rather than on the spiritual gift of life being offered to him by the Lord.

J. Vernon McGee in his commentary, *Thru the Bible*, on John 5:6, Vol IV, 395, says in his usual direct and honest way,

> "The condition of so many people today is just like the man who was watching that pool, waiting for something to happen. I'm bold enough to say that it is the condition of all of us in these days. We are waiting. Just think of the people in our churches, waiting for some great, sweeping emotion to engulf them. Then there are those who are postponing making a decision for Christ. They are not willing to turn to Him because they are looking for an emotion; they are looking for something to happen...Because they were entranced by the material, they lost sight of Jesus Christ."

In essence, Pastor McGee is saying that many people are focused on *self* rather than on the Lord.

This brings me back to the definition of *minister*. So many Christians do not obey the Great Commission of our Lord to go and make disciples of others. As a result, they aren't able to fill in the blank space. But that doesn't mean that they cannot be one of His ministers.

God has made all of us competent to be His ministers. He has made us "ambassadors for Christ, as though God was pleading through us" (2 Corinthians 5:20).

But you might say, "I don't know the Bible well enough to be a minister." God never gives us more than we can handle (1 Corinthians 10:13; Matthew 11:28–30). He's given each one of us a special gift. The apostle Paul had his own special gift of words and Godly wisdom as he wrote about the gifts God has given each of us. He wrote, "There are diversities of gifts, but the same Spirit. There are differences of ministries, but the same Lord. There are diversities of activities, but it is the same God who works all in all" (1 Corinthians 12:4–6).

Each of us has been given "the manifestation of the Spirit...for the profit of all" (1 Corinthians 12:7). Some have been given words of wisdom from the Holy Spirit; others have been given knowledge from the Holy Spirit; others faith; some, the gifts of healing; others, the ability to work miracles; a few, the gift of prophecy; others, discernment of spirits; some can speak in tongues; and some can interpret the language of tongues spoken. "But one and the same Spirit works all these things, distributing to each one individually as He wills" (1 Corinthians 12:7–11).

Let's not wait and watch like the man did at the Pool of Bethesda. He waited for thirty-eight years! If you've already filled in the blank space above, may the Lord continue to bless you. If not, please pray that you can do as He commanded, that is, to "go and make disciples of all nations" (Matthew 28:19). He wants us all to be His ministers, to serve Him by loving (serving) others.

ETERNITY

Eternity is forever: "For God so loved the world that He gave His only begotten Son, that whoever believes in Him should not perish but have everlasting life" (John 3:16).

THE SEA CHANGER A SHORT STORY

My name is John A. Gnostic and as I tell you this, I am speaking words given to me by the Holy Spirit. I am writing to you Bill, my friend, because you say that you do not believe in Jesus Christ. It is the Lord's desire that you repent of your sinful ways and change your mind about Him. By His grace, I changed my mind, and I must recount to you my experience with God before it is too late for you.

On earth it is Tuesday, October 17, 2021. About four years ago, on October 3, 2017 at 4:30 P.M. millions of people disappeared from the face of the earth. Coincidentally, all the people who disappeared were believed to be Christians. Up to that time, I regarded myself as a Christian since my parents were Christians. But I was a Christian in name only. Except for Christmas and Easter, I didn't attend church and rarely read the Bible.

Coincidentally, in 2017, the governments of the world formed a one-world government headquartered in Rome and called themselves, the "United Nations of the World" (UNW). The Chairman of UNW, Sergius S. Sexton, a Middle Easterner by birth, was appointed by acclamation by the former leaders of the world governments. Mr. Sexton convinced the Arab nations to sign a peace treaty with Israel. As a result, Israel built a new temple on the Temple Mount in Jerusalem side by side with the existing mosques. For the first time known to modern man, peace had come to the Middle East and to the world.

In that same year, 2017, all of the religions of the world joined together to form The World Church (TWC). TWC is led in Rome by its Supreme Bishop, the spiritual advisor to Sexton. The theology of TWC is based on false and anti-Biblical premises: that the gods of all religions are the same; that the Judeo-Christian Bible is based on ancient myths and is not relevant in an enlightened society; that everyone in the world is good so long as in their actions, they don't harm anyone else; that negotiation and compromise are the only methods for resolving world differences; that political correctness is mandatory; that the ideas and thoughts of an individual are inappropriate in any given situation (only the collective consensus of one's peer group will determine the correctness of any given action or idea of an individual in that group); and that diversity, compassion and tolerance are required guidelines for societal behavior.

The official explanation offered by the UNW and the Supreme Bishop for the mass disappearance of millions all over the world was that the multitude who'd taken flight were opposed to the UNW and TWC and that UNW forces would soon locate them. My wife and I didn't believe the official explanation since our parents disappeared at that time. We needed a better answer to this burning question: was the sudden disappearance of so many people the *Rapture* as described in 1 Thessalonians 4:13–17 and 1 Corinthians 15:51–53 of the Holy Bible?

In our quest for an answer, we joined the Rogue Temple, an affiliate of the TWC. Its pastor, Tom Lukewarm, was formerly a pastor in a Christian denominational church that had been forced to close in 2018 due to theological differences with the TWC. My parents attended Pastor Lukewarm's church before it closed. They often spoke of Lukewarm's opposition to the denominational church's doctrine concerning issues such as abortion and same sex marriage— he favored both.

According to UNW Rule 16:36A, ownership and/or study of the Bible is a capital crime. Notwithstanding this rule, we attended a secret Bible study to examine the Rapture. We needed better answers concerning the disappearance of our family members and friends. We were aware of the great risk if we were caught studying the Bible.

On October 1, 2020, the UNW Chairman issued an executive order that required all people of the world to have a computer chip implanted in their right hand. The chip is known as the "MARC," which stands for "Multi-technology Automated Reader Chip." The MARC had been developed and first used by the United States Army in 1997 to track its personnel. Without the MARC, a person is unable to work or buy anything, not even food. The MARC contains the complete personal and medical history of a person and enables the

UNW to track the whereabouts of that person at any time. Refusal to accept the MARC is a capital crime.

Revelation 14:10 provides that anyone who receives the mark of the beast will be subject to the wrath of God. Acceptance of the MARC symbolizes worship of the beast, the anti-Christ. One evening, while studying the verses in Revelation which deal with the mark of the beast (Revelation 13:16–17 and 14:9–11), a miracle occurred: Jesus Christ appeared to all of us in a vision and spoke to us. He said, "Because you have kept My command to persevere, I also will keep you from the hour of trial which shall come upon the whole world, to test those who dwell on the earth." These are the same words He spoke to the believers in the ancient church at Philadelphia (Revelation 3:10).

We were overwhelmed. I trembled with both fear and excitement. All were speechless and without energy and everyone fell to their knees. There was utter silence. No one could speak a word. After what seemed like a long while, Pastor Lukewarm broke the silence. In tears, he repeated the words spoken by Jesus in Revelation 3:10 (see above). He also spoke the words of Jesus in John 14:6 that He is the only way to the Father.

For the first time in my life, I truly believed in Jesus Christ and accepted Him as my Lord and Savior. No longer was there any doubt in my mind that He was God. I felt joy and peace as I had never felt before. I'd been transformed—a sea change had occurred in my life. It is called being "born-again."

The faces of the people in the room were bright with smiles of joy. I didn't know it until someone told me that my face shined with great happiness. The pastor's face beamed from ear to ear with a broad smile—it may be that he for the first time truly believed in Jesus as his Lord and Savior. The pastor led us through the sinners' prayer: we confessed that we were all sinners; that we believed in our hearts that Jesus died for us and sacrificed Himself for our sins; and that He was buried in a grave and rose from death to save us from our sins. The room was filled with indescribable love!

Unbeknownst to us, someone had reported the pastor and his

Bible study group to the regional bishop of TWC who asked the UNW police to investigate. When the police arrived, we were all arrested. We were taken to an old building without windows and kept in solitary confinement for days. They tortured us, deprived us of food and water, and subjected us to relentless questioning. They tried to get me to deny my faith in Jesus and to sign a paper to that effect. I refused and they tortured me even more. Then they tied me down and implanted the MARC in my right hand. They returned me to my solitary cell and again deprived me of food or water. The torture continued for days and I grew weaker and weaker. I kept repeating to myself the words of Proverbs 3:5–6, "Trust in the LORD with all your heart, And lean not on your own understanding; In all your ways acknowledge Him, And He shall direct your paths."

The Lord got me through. He directed my path to Him. This morning at 7:00 A.M., I was put to death. As I approached the windowless room where I was given a lethal injection, I felt the hand of the Lord guiding me through the death process. Words are inadequate to describe how I felt. All I know is that when I passed, I saw brilliant white light—its brilliance was like that of a precious jewel, like jasper, clear as crystal. Colors of the spectrum abounded—red, white, blue, green, all melded into a peace that I'd never experienced before. All of the burdens that I'd carried in the world were gone.

Now, as I recount this to you, I am on my knees with a great multitude of Christian believers in the majestic Temple in heaven and I see the Lord who is sitting on His throne. Just as John had described in Revelation, His head and hair are white like wool, as white as snow, and His eyes are like blazing fire. His feet are like bronze glowing in a furnace. His voice is like the sound of rushing waters. His face is like the sun shining in all its brilliance (Revelation 3:21).

The millions who disappeared mysteriously on that fateful October afternoon were the people on earth who believed in Jesus Christ—born-again Christians. Just as written in the Bible, they ascended in the Rapture to the Lord's kingdom in heaven.

Without believers in Christ, wickedness and discord are pervasive throughout the earth. Without anyone to set a Godly example to inhibit evil in the world, there is no moral reference to guide the people of the world. All who remain on the earth are living their lives in accordance with what is right in their own eyes just as they did at the time of the Judges of the Bible (Judges 21:25).

I'm not sure what the Lord has in mind for those still down there, but Revelation states that even in the midst of the Tribulation, our Lord calls out to those who want to overcome evil and seek truth, righteousness and justice. The Bible says that all will have eternal life. Those who believe in Jesus Christ will be resurrected to life and spend eternity in heaven with Him. But those who scorn the Lord will be resurrected to condemnation (judgment) and thrown into the lake of fire, forever (John 5:28–29; Acts 24:15).

Please believe me, Bill, you too can overcome evil. In spite of the tribulation now being waged on the earth, it may not be too late. All you need to do is confess with your mouth, "Jesus is Lord" and believe in your heart that God raised Him from the dead, and you will be saved. For Jesus said in John 16:33, "These things I have spoken to you, that in Me you may have peace." In so doing, He overcame the world and so can you! Become a sea changer and join us in eternity with Him!

FAITH

"Real faith means that you have really received the Lord Jesus Christ as your personal Savior." *

---

* J. Vernon McGee, *Thru the Bible* at Hebrews 10:22, Vol V, 575.

FAITH IN CHRIST: HE MAKES IT EASY

Watchman Nee wrote in *The Spiritual Man* that "We should inquire once again as to what the life of faith is. It is one lived by believing God under any circumstance." Brother Nee gives an example of the man of God, Job, who experienced those circumstances. Brother Nee quotes Job 13:15, "If he slay me," says Job, "yet would I trust in Him." Brother Nee also wrote: "He who is able to accept everything gladly from the Lord...and completely disregard self is he who lives for Him." *The Spiritual Man*, Volume II, 244–245.

Hebrews 11, sometimes called the "Hall of Faith," lists many Godly men and women whose faith in the Lord was unshakable. Abel's faith required that he offer to God a better sacrifice than Cain—Abel offered the Lord the first fruits of his flock of sheep whereas Cain gave the Lord just "An offering of the fruit of the ground" (Genesis 4:3–4; Hebrews 11:4). Enoch's faith pleased the Lord so much that He spared Enoch the process of dying (Genesis 4:24; Hebrews 11:5). By his faith Noah became an heir of the righteousness of God, by His grace, for Noah was the only man on earth who, with his family, was chosen to survive the flood of God's wrath on the corrupt (Genesis 6:8–8:22; Hebrews 11:7). Abram obeyed God's command to go to a place even though he did not know where it would lead him (Genesis 12:1–4; Hebrews 11:8). Moses gave up his right as an Egyptian royal to bear the suffering and castigation of his own people, the people of God (Exodus 2:11–12; Hebrews 11:24–26). By her faith Rahab, a Gentile harlot of Jericho, helped the children of Israel by shielding two of their spies from the king of Jericho's men (Joshua 2:1–22; Hebrews 11:31). The Lord credited the faith of these Godly men and women as righteousness. "For Christ is the end of the law for righteousness to everyone who believes" (Romans 10:4).

In spite of all the examples in His Word of faithful servants, we sometimes hear it said, "It's so hard to believe when I can't see or hear God." Jesus even heard this from His disciples. (See for example Thomas in John 20:25 and Philip in John 14:8–9). After all the miracles they'd seen Him perform, they still expressed confusion and doubt as to Jesus' deity.

But the Lord is visible and can be heard if we just take the time to look and listen. He makes it easy for us to believe in Him. Jesus Christ said, "Believe Me that I am in the Father and the Father is in Me, or else believe Me for the sake of the works themselves" (John 14:11). In essence Jesus said that if you can't believe in Him without seeing or hearing Him, then look around and see the miracles He did and continues to do. Jesus told the two disciples of John the Baptist that He'd cured the blind and lame, cleansed the lepers, gave hearing to the deaf, resurrected the dead, and preached the gospel to the poor (Matthew 11:5).

But you say, "That was then; this is now!" Be assured. Have faith that He is indeed the Creator of all the visible and the invisible (Hebrews 11:3). Look and see His wondrous works. For example, see and be aware of the limitless sky, the countless stars, the light of the sun by day, the light of the moon at night, the air we breathe (just the right amount of oxygen), the abundance of water available for us to drink, the food He provides, the health He gives, the temperature range on earth that is perfect for life, and the mind He gives us that enables us to know Him. The list of His "works" is endless. The psalmist with heavenly words describes the wondrous works of the Lord in Psalm 104. It's not just the miracles of old that were seen and heard. It is ongoing.

"In the beginning God created the heavens and the earth" (Genesis 1:1). He created light, the evening and the morning, the first day and every day thereafter, the waters of the earth, the sky above, the plants and trees, the sun and the moon, every living and moving thing, and He created us! Jesus says to look at His works if you have any doubt that He is who He says He is. "All things were made through Him, and without Him nothing was made that was made" (John 1:3).

Remember the faith of the ancients and "Remember those who rule over you, who have spoken the word of God to you, whose faith follow, considering the outcome of their conduct. Jesus Christ is the same yesterday, today, and forever" (Hebrews 13:7–8). Be like the centurion of whom Jesus said, "Assuredly, I say to you, I have not found such great faith, not even in Israel!" (Matthew 8:10). The centurion didn't even need to see Jesus' works, for his faith alone confirmed that Jesus would heal his servant just by the Lord's spoken Word.

It's easy to have faith in Jesus Christ as our Lord and Savior. Just "Ask, and it will be given to you; seek, and you will find; knock, and it will be opened to you. For everyone who asks receives, and he who seeks finds, and to him who knocks, it will be opened" (Matthew 7:7–8).

O Lord, may we live our lives by believing in Him as Brother Nee urged: "under any circumstance."

THE LEGACY

A legacy is something handed down from a prior generation. There were many things handed down to me from my father which I recall with great fondness.

It was Christmas, 1943, a crisp, snowy December morning. My sister and I got up very early, before dawn, and snuck downstairs. It was still dark outside. We could smell the sweet aroma of the Christmas tree. We put on the light and there, set up around the base of the beautiful Christmas tree, was a Lionel electric train! There was a black steam engine which pulled a coal tender and three blue and white passenger cars. All were sitting on steel tracks. There was even a homemade passenger station with a white picket fence (my father was very handy with wood). I was so excited since the train was exactly like the trains that our family had taken to visit New York City!

A few minutes later, my parents came down the stairs and joined us in our excitement. My father immediately took over the controls of the train. After all, I was only three and might break the train. He told me that he'd run it until I got a little bit older, that is, "until I understood how to operate it." I suspect that I was probably an excuse for him to get a model train since I wasn't allowed to touch it for quite a while. My father and I enjoyed many hours together watching those steel cars going round and round. To this day, that train is a legacy from my father that I shall never forget. I still have it. It will be passed down to my granddaughter who loves trains.

But of all the things handed down to me from my father, one surpasses all. My father, a Jewish man, loved God with all his heart and all his soul. Every chance he got, he taught me about God. He spoke about Him all the time. He showed me that God was his guiding light in the world. His faith was unshakable. Despite the economically tough post-war years for our family, my father never lost his great love for God. I can therefore say with confidence that ever since I was a small child, I too have believed in God.

Like my father before me, I married and started a family. Now that I was the family's father, it was my time to hand something down. One day, while on a retreat, God spoke to me and introduced me to His Son, Jesus Christ. I re-devoted my life to the Lord. From that time on, my life and that of my family hasn't been the same. Over the course of many years, we have all come to know and love Jesus Christ. That's His legacy for my family—His grace. Our hunger and thirst for the Lord's guidance is unquenchable. By His mercy He has given us great peace and comfort in knowing and loving Him.

Yes, my earthly father left me a great gift, one that's been passed on to my children and grandchildren. It's a love for the Lord that burns within my family's heart. What a legacy!

BE FAITHFUL, FOR IF YOU ARE FAITHFUL TO HIM, YOU WILL HAVE ETERNAL LIFE

Do you live your life in accordance with the teachings of the Bible? Or do you look upon the Word of God as merely history recorded or perhaps, even myths? Do you live a life of empiricism, that is, by what you see, hear, taste, touch or smell? Do you believe that this is it in life and that there's nothing beyond the grave?

If you fall into the first group, that is, living your life as the Bible tells us to live, you are a person of faith in the Lord. The Bible describes God's faithful. They are the righteous ones who live their lives "By His faith" (Habakkuk 2:4). "For I am not ashamed of the gospel of Christ, for it is the power of God to salvation for everyone who believes...For in it the righteousness of God is revealed from faith to faith; as it is written, 'The just shall live by faith'" (Romans 1:16–17). The righteous are those who commit their way to the Lord, who are still before Him, and as the Bible teaches, "wait patiently for Him...[who are] meek...[whose ways are upright]...[who possess little]...[who] show mercy and gives...[who are] ever merciful, and lends...[who] speaks wisdom and...talks of justice...[who are]...blameless..." and are men of peace (Psalm 37:7, 9, 11, 21, 26, 30, 37).

However, if you are one who trusts the five human senses but doesn't believe in the Eternal God, the only thing you can be sure of is physical death. The psalmist says that those who do not believe in Him "shall soon be cut down like grass...they shall be no more" (Psalm 37:2, 10). If you read any part of the Bible, you will quickly learn that the Lord will not forsake His faithful ones, for "The righteous shall inherit the land, And dwell in it forever" (Psalm 37:29). But for those who do not believe in the Lord, the prophet Isaiah exclaimed, "Woe to the wicked! *It shall be ill with him*" (Isaiah 3:11).

The apostle John summed up the outcome of both the faithful and the faithless. He wrote, "He who believes in the Son has everlasting life; and he who does not believe the Son shall not see life, but the wrath of God abides on him" (John 3:36).

The Word of the Lord teaches that if I seek to be righteous and believe in Him, I will inherit the land and dwell peacefully in it forever (Isaiah 3:10). "The work of righteousness will be peace, And the effect of righteousness, quietness and assurance forever" (Isaiah 32:17). If I strive to be a righteous and faithful person, the Lord will give me the desires of my heart. "He shall bring forth [my] righteousness as the light, And [my] justice as the noonday." He will "uphold" me; my "inheritance shall be forever...in the days of famine"...I "shall be satisfied." My steps will be firm. Though I may stumble on my path, I shall not fall and my feet will not slip—He will uphold me "with His hand." My children will not beg for bread. He will protect me from the wicked and will not permit them to condemn me when I am "judged." He will deliver me "from the wicked." He will save me because I "trust in Him" (Psalm 37:4, 6, 17–19, 23–25, 33, 40).

On the other hand, if I do not strive to be righteous, if I do not place my faith in Him, His Word tells me with certainty that I shall not enter the peace of His kingdom (Psalm 95:11).

Jesus Christ said, "I am the resurrection and the life. He who believes in Me, though he may die, he shall live. And whoever lives and believes in Me shall never die" (John 11:25–26). "When we know Him by faith, we need not fear the shadow of death...When you face your last enemy, death, you want the Savior [to be with you]...In Jesus Christ, every doctrine is made personal (1 Corinthians 1:30). When you belong to Him, you have all that you ever will need in life, death, time, or eternity!" Warren W. Wiersbe, *Be Alive,*137.

It's never too late to seek righteousness, to be faithful to God (Matthew 19:30). Believe what our Lord tells us that He is the only way to everlasting life (John 14:6). "...one who believes in Christ has eternal life that transcends physical death. If he is living and believing, he will never die but will make an instant transition from the old life to the new life." Frank Gaebelein and Merrill C. Tenney, *The Expositors Bible Commentary*, Vol. 9, 118.

Be faithful to the Lord, for if you believe in Him, you will have eternal life.

HAVE FAITH IN JESUS CHRIST: THERE'S MORE WHO ARE WITH US THAN THOSE WHO ARE WITH THEM

The writer of the Book of Hebrews wrote, "Now faith is the substance of things hoped for, the evidence of things not seen" (Hebrews 11:1). But what did he mean by this teaching? The Old Testament is a picture of the teachings of the New Testament. In Second Kings the Lord paints a beautiful word canvas which illustrates this teaching. The Word describes the life of a man of vision, the Prophet Elisha, a man of God whose spirit was aligned with the Holy Spirit. He could see evidence of things not seen—not with his eyes, but with his spirit. He saw things from God's perspective (See 2 Kings 6:15–17).

Aram (Syria) was at war with Israel. The Aramean king set up camp east of the Jordan River perhaps at Ramoth Gilead (2 Kings 6:8; 8:28). Each time the king moved his camp, Elisha knew the new location since the Holy Spirit was speaking to him. Each time the Aramean camp moved, Elisha told Ahaziah, the king of Israel, the location of the new camp of Hazael, king of Syria (2 Kings 6:9). Each time the king of Israel found the Arameans precisely where Elisha had said they would be (2 Kings 6:10).

Because his camp was discovered each time, the Aramean king became enraged. He suspected that one of his own men was a spy. When he confronted his officers, one said that it was Elisha who not only told Ahaziah the location of the Syrian camp, but even the words spoken by Hazael in his own bedroom (2 Kings 6:12). The king then ordered his horses and chariots and a strong force to Dothan where Elisha was staying. They went by night to surround the city (2 Kings 6:14).

The next morning, Elisha's servant went outside and saw that the Aramean army had surrounded the city. He ran in to Elisha and asked with great fear what they should do (2 Kings 6:15). Elisha answered him saying, "Do not fear, for those who are with us are more than those who are with them" (2 Kings 6:16). And he prayed that the Lord would open his servant's eyes so that he could see what Elisha saw. The Lord answered Elisha's prayer instantly, "Then the LORD opened the eyes of the young man, and he saw. And behold, the mountain was full of horses and chariots of fire all around Elisha" (2 Kings 6:17). In response to Elisha's prayer, God enabled his servant to see the evidence of things not seen in our temporal world—the unseen reality of the Heavenly Hosts.

"Faith is the whole man rightly related to God by the power of the Spirit of Jesus Christ." Oswald Chambers, *My Utmost for His Highest*, October 30. Elisha was a person in the right relationship with God through the Spirit of Jesus Christ.

Faith is seeing the things that are unseen—seeing things as God sees them—the spiritual rather than the temporal view. Pastor Ray Stedman described God's perspective from heaven, "In the Bible, heaven is the realm of the invisible—another dimension...wherein God reigns hidden from our eyes but present among us. It is a spiritual kingdom that surrounds us on every side, but one we cannot taste, touch or see—yet it is utterly real, more real than this plane of existence that we call 'real life!'" Ray Stedman, *Adventuring Through the Bible*, 788.

As believers in Christ "we do not look at the things which are seen, but at the things which are not seen. For the things which are seen are temporary, but the things which are not seen are eternal" (2 Corinthians 4:18). The apostle Paul continued in his letter to the Colossians: "So we are always confident, knowing that while we are at home in the body we are absent from the Lord. For we walk by faith, not by sight. We are confident, yes, well pleased rather to be absent from the body and to be present with the Lord" (2 Corinthians 5:6–8).

Examining the Old Testament picture, what did Elisha do that enabled him to see the unseen? Elisha was a man who lived his life guided by his spirit aligned with God's Holy Spirit. To him, his body was but a temple in which the Holy Spirit was welcome. His spirit ruled his temple. We who are in the flesh often have difficulty with faith since our spirits are dominated by our flesh rather than the opposite. Remember, as earthly beings, we are spirit, mind (will/soul), and body (flesh). Our mind is the referee between spirit and flesh. But while on earth, our mind is distracted by worldly things. It often favors the flesh over the spirit. When that occurs, our spirit is stifled and our faith, our ability to see the substance of things hoped for, is likewise stifled— sometimes even snuffed out.

How can we redirect our minds to favor our spirit so as to align ourselves with the Lord's Spirit as Elisha did? The apostle Paul wrote, "So then faith comes by hearing, and hearing by the word of God" (Romans 10:17). We must pray without ceasing, daily, if not more often. We must study His Word. We must be part of His body, the Church so as to give and receive the benefits of fellowship and offer our God-given gifts to others. By doing these things, our mind will be filled with the things of God, our spirit will be in Him, and we shall be people who are in the right relationship with God through the power of the Spirit of Jesus Christ.

The apostle James wrote, "He who looks into the perfect law of liberty and continues in it, and is not a forgetful hearer but a doer of the work, this one will be blessed in what he does" (James 1:25). The "perfect law" mentioned by James is "[T]he moral and ethical teaching of Christianity, which is based on the Old Testament moral law, as embodied in the Ten Commandments (see Ps 19:7), but brought to completion (perfection) by Jesus Christ." Note to James 1:25, *The NIV Study Bible*, 2376.

See life through the Lord's eyes as the Prophet Elisha saw it. By faith know that He is with us forever and ever. "Finally, my brethren, be strong in the Lord and in the power of His might. Put on the full armor of God [by prayer and supplication], that you may be able to stand against the wiles of the devil" (Ephesians 6:10–11). By doing these things we shall all be able to see that "those who are with us are more than those who are with them" (2 Kings 6:16).

HIS MERCY ENDURES FOREVER

"Oh, give thanks to the LORD, for He is good! For His mercy endures forever" (Psalm136:1).

How long is "forever"? Forever is a measure of time, but the concept of time is beyond comprehension by the human mind. It is a mystery of God.

The universe of space is also a concept beyond our human understanding. Take for example, the end of space. Where does it end if it ends at all? Even the idea of space itself is beyond our understanding. It is indeed another great mystery of God.

I can't see the wind but I know it's there. You can hear it and feel it. But where does it come from and where does it go? Jesus Christ said, "The wind blows where it wishes, and you hear the sound of it, but cannot tell where it comes from or where it goes" (John. 3:8). Incomprehensibility also applies to the wind—another mystery of God.

Life—why does it exist, if it exists? How long will I live? When I was younger, I didn't concern myself about how long I'd live. Now, I ask, "Where did all the years go?" Jesus assures us that life lasts forever—all we need to do is believe in Him and we shall have eternal life. There's that word again, forever! And the list of imponderables is endless.

God's Word indicates that it was not His intent that we know the answers to these imperceptible questions, at least not in this life in the flesh. "For now we see in a mirror, dimly, but then face to face. Now I know in part; but then I shall know just as I also am known" (1 Corinthians 13:12). Someday when we are with God at the foot of His throne in heaven, He'll reveal the answers if it is His will to do so. In the meantime, be at peace and enjoy the ride of life.

Adam, the first man, was faced with these same imponderables. Unfortunately for Adam and for us, his descendants, curiosity rather than faith in God got the best of him. What we know from the Scriptures and must learn from Adam's mistake is that God is in charge. Our job is to *have faith in Him* and He'll take care of the "forever" in our wondering.

The story of Adam's lack of understanding of the works of God is told in Genesis, the first book of the Bible. The Lord had a garden in Eden. He placed the first created man, Adam, in His garden (Genesis 2:8). God then commanded Adam, "Of every tree of the garden you may freely eat; but of the tree of the knowledge of good and evil you shall not eat, for in the day that you eat of it you shall surely die" (Genesis 2:16–17). In essence, the Lord tells us that so long as we stay away from the "knowledge" tree and look only to Him, He promises He'll give us all we shall *ever* need.

God is omniscient. As the Creator, He has the answers to all the questions that we may have about life, especially the imponderables. But He also states in unequivocal terms that those answers are for Him alone, for if we knew as much as Him, we'd be our own god and wouldn't need Him. The serpent in the Garden acknowledged this truth when he told Eve, Adam's wife, "You will not surely die... For God knows that in the day you eat of it your eyes will be opened, and you will be like God, knowing good and evil" (Genesis 3:4–5).

Adam and Eve, our first ancestors, disobeyed God's command and listened to the serpent by eating the fruit of the forbidden tree. The temptation offered by the serpent to Adam and Eve to know as much as God was too great for them. God knew they'd disobey Him for although He'd created them, He'd also given them free will, the right to obey or disobey Him. When Adam and Eve disobeyed Him, God knew that in their quest to be their own gods, they'd eaten from the forbidden tree (Genesis 3:22). He then forced Adam [and Eve] out of the garden so that they would not live forever. For the first time there was death and dying of humans on the earth. [A sidebar thought: if rejection from God's garden results in death and dying, perhaps God intended Adam and Eve to live forever in the garden so long as they obeyed Him].

Sure, Adam may have had some answers to his imponderable questions about life by eating the fruit of the forbidden tree of the knowledge of good and evil, but by his disobedience of God, that is, by his sin, he also lost the right to live forever with Him. Through this story God's Word tells us how to deal with our imponderables: by obedience to Him and by faith in Him, not in the serpent. Our duty in life is to trust Him. He'll provide all the answers. He'll provide all that we need (see Hebrews 11:3 and 12:1–2).

There is no need to be frustrated by our inability to know the answers to the imponderables of life. Someday, if He so chooses, the Lord will share the answers with us when we are with Him in heaven. For now, all we need to do is to have faith in our living and loving God, Jesus Christ our Lord, who forgives us for the sins of Adam and Eve (Mark 2:10) and who gives us everlasting life, forever. He says, "And lo, I am with you always, even to the end of the age" (Matthew 28:20).

The Lord's mercy endures forever.

THE BOY WHO WOULD BE KING

In ancient days when Saul was king, Israel was threatened with annihilation by its arch-enemy the Philistines. The two armies were about to battle each other in the Valley of Elah, on the Philistine-Israeli border. A menacing giant named Goliath taunted the Israelites to choose one man to fight him, claiming that the victorious fighter's nation would rule over the losing nation. "When Saul and all Israel heard these words of the Philistine, they were dismayed and greatly afraid" (1 Samuel 17:11).

Three of Saul's warriors were the eldest sons of Jesse the Ephrathite. Jesse's youngest son, David, a boy, ruddy and handsome, was a shepherd who tended sheep under the stars where he came to know the splendor of God. Jesse summoned David to take food to his sons. Just as David arrived at the Israeli camp, the Philistine giant shouted his daily insults challenging the Israelites.

The men standing near David spoke about the great reward being offered by King Saul to any man who would take up the sword and kill Goliath. The reward was a great temptation to many of the Israeli warriors, but none volunteered to fight the Philistine as they were "dreadfully afraid" (1 Samuel 17:24–25).

David, who later became known as a man after God's own heart, was incensed that the Gentile Philistine was defying the armies of God (1 Samuel 17:26). Not seeking the earthly rewards offered by Saul, but zealous to defend the honor of God, David volunteered to fight the giant. The older warriors including David's older brother Eliab scoffed at him for his youthful insolence. When Saul heard that David volunteered to fight, he summoned him to his tent. David said to Saul, "Let no man's heart fail because of him; your servant will go and fight with this Philistine" (1 Samuel 17:32). David knew in his heart that victory over Goliath would rest not on his own strength, but on the power of God whose honor had been attacked by the enemy and whose covenant promises were being ignored by His own people.

David armed himself with a sling and five smooth stones. The giant bellowed, "'Am I a dog, that you come to me with sticks?' And the Philistine cursed David by his gods. And the Philistine said to David, 'Come to me, and I will give your flesh to the birds of the air and the beasts of the field!'" (1 Samuel 17:43). David replied,

> "You come to me with a sword, with a spear and with a javelin. But I come to you in the name of the LORD of hosts, the God of the armies of Israel, whom you have defied. This day the LORD will deliver you into my hand, and I will strike you and take your head from you. And this day I will give the carcasses of the camp of the Philistines to the birds of the air and the wild beasts of the earth, that all the earth may know that there is a God in Israel. Then all this assembly shall know that the LORD does not save with a sword and spear; for the battle is the LORD's, and He will give you into our hands" (1 Samuel 17:45–47).

The Lord delivered Goliath into David's hands.

David sought not earthly rewards, but with deep faith and by the grace of God, he sought to honor the Lord. In everything he did, David had great success because the Spirit of the Lord was upon him. Ultimately, the young boy David, the Lord's servant, became king over the Lord's cherished land, Israel. He became the Lord's representative on earth. Could there be a greater reward?

BE TEMPERATE IN ALL THINGS, BUT ONE

The apostle Paul wrote, "Now to Him who is able to establish you according to my gospel and the preaching of Jesus Christ" (Romans 16:25). *Vine's Complete Expository Dictionary of Old and New Testament Words*, 206, defines *establish* as used by the apostle in his letter to the Roman Christians to mean "confirmation of the saints as the work of God." "Confirmation" means 'to make firm, establish, make secure'" *Vine's, supra* at 121.

It is through the Lord's gospel that we get to know and understand His plan for salvation for us and are thus established as Christians. Through His gospel we get to know the truth and are thus enabled to share it with others who are lost, that is, those who have eyes to see, but do not see, and ears to hear, but do not hear. Being established, we become more God-centered in our life's outlook, more secure in our faith, and more stable in life.

God intended His creations to exist in perfect balance. The apostle Paul counseled his companion and friend Titus to,

> "Exhort the young men to be sober-minded, in all things showing yourself to be a pattern of good works; in doctrine showing integrity, reverence, incorruptibility, sound speech that cannot be condemned, that one who is an opponent may be ashamed, having nothing evil to say of you" (Titus 2:6–7). "For the grace of God that brings salvation has appeared to all men, teaching us that...we should live soberly, righteously, and godly in the present age, looking for the blessed hope and glorious appearing of our great God and Savior Jesus Christ...zealous for good works" (Titus 2:11–14).

We are to be temperate or balanced in all things, but one: our faith in the Lord. Quoting the Scriptures, Jesus said, "You shall love the LORD your God with all your heart, with all your soul, and with all your mind" (Matthew 22:37; Deuteronomy 6:5). The Lord wants **all** of us, not just some of us. We are to love Him as He loves us, with boundless passion, zeal, fervor, and with fire in our hearts. To a church that was not balanced, that is, lukewarm in its faith (Laodicea), Jesus said, "I know your works, that you are neither cold nor hot...So then, because you are lukewarm and neither cold nor hot, I will vomit you out of My mouth" (Revelation 3:15–16).

Job was a stalwart man who trusted God no matter what the circumstances. He lived his life as a blameless and upright man who feared God and shunned evil (Job 1:1, 8). God blessed him with ten children and great wealth. Satan challenged God claiming that he could shake Job from his Godly faith. Knowing His child's limitless faith, God allowed Satan to proceed. In the arduous tests that ensued, Job's children were killed, he lost his health, and his wealth was taken away. In his deep sorrow, Job refused to waiver in his faith. He cried out, "Though He slay me, yet will I trust Him" (Job 13:15). In the face of the worst adversity, Job maintained his deep trust in the Lord. Job was zealous for God. His faith was boundless and God blessed him for it (Job 42:12–17).

Daniel's friends Shadrach, Meshach and Abed-nego also were men of limitless faith in God. All people of Babylon were ordered to bow down and worship the golden idol made by King Nebuchadnezzar. Anyone who was unwilling to do so was to be thrown into a fiery furnace (Daniel 3:5–6). Shadrach, Meshach and Abed-nego were unwilling to disobey God's commandment against the worship of other gods and were willing to die for their faith in Him. The king ordered them to be thrown into the blazing furnace. The fire was so hot that the soldiers who threw them into the furnace were burned up. Moments later King Nebuchadnezzar was shocked when he saw four men (not three) walking around in the fire and not burning up. Their hair wasn't even singed. He remarked in amazement that the fourth man's form was " like the Son of God" (Daniel 3:24–25). The king called to them to come out of the furnace and the three men came out unharmed by the raging fire! Nebuchadnezzar was so shaken by this incident that he blessed the God of Israel and proclaimed, "There is no other God who can deliver like this" (Daniel 3:28–29). The three friends of Daniel were restored by Nebuchadnezzar to a place of honor.

Note that Nebuchadnezzar said that he saw **four** men walking in the fire. Jesus said, "and lo, I am with you always, even to the end of the age" (Matthew 28:20). Surely it must have been Jesus who walked in the fire with the three Godly men!

The deeper our faith and the greater our trust in our Lord Jesus Christ, the more balance we experience in life. For the Lord's Word tells us that "the fruit of the Spirit is love, joy, peace, longsuffering, kindness, goodness, faithfulness, gentleness, self-control" (Galatians 5:22–23). The more we seek Jesus, the more temperate we become in all other things in life.

"Inward peace comes with absolute surrender to the will of God." Francois Fenelon, *The Seeking Heart*, 175. "Therefore gird up the loins of your mind, be sober, and rest your hope fully upon the grace that is to be brought to you at the revelation of Jesus Christ" (1 Peter 1:13).

Boundless faith and trust in the Lord will render us temperate in all things, but One.

VICTORY THROUGH FAITH

"For whatever is born of God overcomes the world. And this is the victory that has overcome the world—our faith" (1 John 5:4). Pastor J. Vernon McGee wrote, "Today we are saved by faith, and if we are going to overcome this world, we'll not overcome it by fighting it. We are going to overcome it by faith. That is the only way you and I can deal with this world in which we live, and that is the great message which is here for us." *Thru the Bible*, 1 John 5:4, Vol V, 815.

In these troubled days (the Great Recession*) many are struggling just to put food on the table. Some have lost the roof over their head. Multitudes are out of work and can't find a job. Small businesses are closing their doors. Many are living paycheck to paycheck.

What is the breadwinner of a family to do if he or she can't bring home the bread? Negative thoughts permeate our minds. Nighttime is especially hard. It's those sleepless 3 A.M.'s seeking answers out of desperation that are the worst. Our minds won't rest as we ponder, "Is there no end to these bad times? When will things get better? What are we to do?"

At times such as these, we are at war. We battle between things of the light and the pull of darkness. But do not listen to the darkness. Do not entertain its despairing suggestions. There are always options and opportunities in life, for everyone.

David faced many of the same issues and yet, he wrote with great wisdom, "I have been young, and now am old, Yet I have not seen the righteous forsaken, Nor his descendants begging bread. He is ever merciful, and lends; And his descendants are blessed...For the Lord loves justice, And does not forsake His saints" (Psalm 37:25–26, 28). David knew what it took to be victorious over the dark pull of the world. He wrote, "Trust in the LORD, and do good; Dwell in the land, and feed on His faithfulness. Delight yourself also in the LORD, And He shall give you the desires of your heart" (Psalm 37:3–4).

---

* Originally written in 2008

Overcoming the world occurs through *faith in Jesus Christ.* Believe in Him crucified and risen from the dead. He has overcome the world and through Him, so shall we. The present darkness will pass. How can I be so sure? I'm sure because Jesus Christ said so. He said, "Come to Me, all you who labor and are heavy laden, and I will give you rest. Take My yoke upon you and learn from Me, for I am gentle and lowly in heart, and you will find rest for your souls. For my yoke is easy and My burden is light" (Matthew 11:28–30).

Next time you can't sleep at 3:00 A.M., pick up your Bible and read the words of our Lord. I assure you that within minutes you will overcome the darkness and be at peace—and fall into a sound sleep!

FEAR OF MAN

Jesus said, "I do not receive honor from men" (John 5:41). "Be aware of men. Do not fear those who kill the body but cannot kill the soul. But rather fear Him who is able to destroy both soul and body in hell" (Matthew 10:17, 28).

ON BEING ACCEPTABLE TO GOD

A child experiences great pain when he believes that a parent doesn't approve of him. For many years before I accepted Jesus Christ, I struggled with the belief that no matter what I did or achieved, my father didn't approve of me. At least he never told me so. I don't say this to defame my father. On the contrary, as I ponder my relationship with him many years later, I have nothing but love and respect for him for I know now that he did the best he knew how.

Looking back at my youthful struggle to obtain the acceptance of others, I have come to the realization that seeking the approval of men is "grasping for the wind" (Ecclesiastes 1:14). No matter what a man does, he will not be totally acceptable or approved by men. This truth is due to the fact that humanity is naturally sinful, self-centered (Romans 1:18–32), and is unable to give love or acceptance as our heavenly Father does.

The Lord is the only Person from whom we should seek acceptance (Psalm 118:8). The apostle Paul wrote to the Roman believers, "I beseech you therefore, brethren, by the mercies of God, that you present your bodies a living sacrifice, holy, acceptable to God which is your reasonable service" (Romans 12:1). Paul sought to please God, not men. He concluded that if he aspired to please men, he "would not be a bond servant of Christ" (Galatians 1:10).

Jesus Christ is my Savior. Once I confessed with my mouth that He is Lord, believed in my heart that He died for my sins, and that God raised Him from the dead, I knew in my heart that He accepted me totally, without condition (just as I was and am) (Romans 10:9–10), and my soul was saved for eternity. He knows all of my sins, my indiscretions, my faults and imperfections. He sees the true condition of my soul. He knows my mind. Yet, He accepts me as His child. Above all, He loves me! Knowing that I have the love of Jesus and that I am saved for eternity gives me a broad perspective and with God's grace, the courage to speak the truth before men even though doing so risks their wrath. Now I can love others whether they accept me or not. Knowing this gives me great peace.

In his book, *The Imitation of Christ* (translated by William C. Creasy), Thomas A' Kempis wrote at page 119 as if Jesus were speaking, "Your peace does not depend on what other people say; whether they think well or ill of you, you remain the same person. Where is true peace and true glory? Is it not in Me [Jesus]? The person who has no wish to please others nor is afraid to displease them will enjoy great peace."

"Let the words of my mouth and the meditation of my heart Be acceptable in Your sight, O LORD, my strength and my Redeemer" (Psalm 19:14).

FEAR OF MAN IS A SNARE

One of the subjects of this essay is *affirmation*. *Roget's International Thesaurus* lists some synonyms for affirmation including *confirmation, acknowledgment, corroboration and ratification*. While praying for insight into affirmation, the Holy Spirit placed on my heart the words, *Fear of Man*. Why fear of man? Because so many times in our lives we look to man for affirmation rather than God and the effect of such misdirection is fear, worry and emptiness.

The consequences of seeking affirmation or approval of man rather than God were described by the prophet Jeremiah,

> "Thus says the LORD: 'Cursed is the man who trusts in man And makes flesh his strength, Whose heart departs from the LORD. For he shall be like a shrub in the desert, And shall not see when good comes... Blessed is the man who trusts in the LORD, And whose hope is the LORD. For he shall be like a tree planted by the waters, Which spreads out its roots by the river, And will not fear when heat comes; But its leaf will be green. And will not be anxious in the year of drought, Nor will cease from yielding fruit'" (Jeremiah 17:5–8).

Affirmation can be a process whereby human beings seek acknowledgment and confirmation that they are worthy. Measured by what standards? Acknowledged by whom? The answers to both of these questions should be God, not another man or woman (see Colossians 1:9–10).

We humans tend to look to other people for affirmation that we are acceptable as human beings. If we look to people for affirmation of our self-worth, earthly standards are applied not only by others but also by ourselves in concluding that we are beautiful or ugly, rich or poor, wise or unwise, powerful or weak, prominent or obscure, etc.

But looking to earthly standards as applied by other people leads to a dead end, for when we die, all of the things of the flesh that we regard as important in measuring our worth will be meaningless. Where then will be our beauty, our bucks, or our brains?

Solomon exclaimed in viewing his life, "'Vanities of vanities,' says the Preacher. 'All is vanity'" (Ecclesiastes 12:8). He added, "Let us hear the conclusion of the whole matter: Fear God and keep His commandments, For this is man's all. For God will bring every work into judgment, Including every secret thing, Whether good or evil" (Ecclesiastes 12:13–14).

Our Lord Jesus Christ taught that we should look to the Father, not man, for affirmation. He said, "I do not receive honor from men" (John 5:41). "Do not fear those who kill the body but cannot kill the soul. But rather fear Him who is able to destroy both soul and body in hell" (Matthew 10:28).

Pastor Jon Courson in his *Application Commentary, New Testament*, 476, wrote, "Is your validation coming from your own accomplishments, or from others patting you on your back? It'll never be enough. You'll always be one pat shy of satisfaction. Validation for your life will not come from someone pointing out how good you are. Nor will it come from your own achievements. True validation comes when you hear the voice of the Father in your heart, saying, 'Well done, good and faithful servant.'"

King David had it right. He knew that the only affirmation we need is from the Lord. He wrote, "The LORD shall judge the peoples; Judge me, O LORD, according to my righteousness, And according to my integrity within me" (Psalm 7:8). David's wise son Solomon concluded, "The fear of man brings a snare, But whoever trusts in the LORD shall be safe" (Proverbs 29:25).

If we find ourselves needing affirmation of what we are, do, or have on earth, we should look not to the things on earth, but to the things which are not seen, in heaven. The apostle Paul wrote,

> "Therefore we do not lose heart. Even though our
> outward man is perishing, yet the inward man is

being renewed day by day. For our light affliction, which is but for a moment, is working for us a far more exceeding and eternal weight of glory, while we do not look at the things which are seen, but at the things which are not seen. For the things which are seen are temporary, but the things which are not seen are eternal" (2 Corinthians 4:16–18).

BE STRONG AND OF GOOD COURAGE

Moses said to the Israelites as they were about to enter the land promised to them by God, "Be strong and of good courage, do not fear nor be afraid of them; for the LORD your God, He is the One who goes with you. He will not leave you nor forsake you" (Deuteronomy 31:6).

There have been many who have lived their lives by this Biblical truth. John Hus, an ordained priest and a Bohemian scholar at the University of Prague was a "man for all seasons." Hus feared not men and knew the Lord would not forsake him. Courageously, he expressed his moral indignation against the corruption of the church at the time. In Hus' time, 1409, the church was split from top to bottom. There were three popes, a French Pope Gregory at Avignon, an Italian Pope John at Rome and a Spanish Pope Benedict in Aragon. The rival Popes fought over ecclesiastical offices, and the clergy, including Hus, were demoralized. Power and money were more important than spiritual guidance. The Avignonese Popes systemized the established methods of taxation and invented new ones. The *annates* (first year's income earned by the most important clergy) and the *procurations* (visitation fees earned by visiting bishops from the diocesan churches) were claimed by competing popes. *Simony* (the sale of church offices) was the norm.

In England and elsewhere, the cries for church reform were deafening. John Wyclif, a scholar at Oxford, wrote powerful articles protesting the papal supremacy and the wealth of the clergy. He denied the power of the clergy to grant absolution from sins. His ideas were read throughout Europe. John Hus was greatly influenced by the truths uttered by Wyclif concerning the church. He accepted the writings of Wyclif and used them as a basis for his own defiant preaching and writings. Because he opposed the leadership of the church, he was regarded as undisciplined by the hierarchy and accused of heresy.

In 1414, a General Council was convened at Constance to resolve the papal leadership schism in the church. At that time, Pope John XXIII was waging war against one of his rivals and was giving full remission of sins to all who would assist him in his war. Hus was outraged by the Pope's acts of absolution in exchange for the purchase of *indulgences*, financial support to fight a war. He openly referred to the Pope as the "antichrist." The citizens of Prague were divided between those who supported Hus and those who did not. Fearing insurrection, King Wenceslaus removed Hus from his church and banned him from Prague.

Hus courageously challenged the king's decree banning him from Prague. Openly and defiantly he stated that the Pope and his cardinals were not the true successors of Peter and the apostles; Christ, not the Pope, was the Head of His church; Christ's faithful people, not the cardinals, were the body of the Catholic Church; the Pope and his cardinals were not the final word, but the Holy Scripture was the inspired Word of God; and the high clergy were falsifiers of the Holy Scriptures. See *Foxe's Book of Martyrs* prepared by W. Grinton Berry at 94–95.

Hus was excommunicated and imprisoned for his stand against ecclesiastical corruption. He was charged with heresy for speaking against the church. A General Council at Constance was again convened to try Hus as a heretic. The questions posed to Hus at the "trial" bring to mind the trial of Sir Thomas More. He was falsely accused of heresy when they sought to remove him as Lord Chancellor of England. As Lord Chancellor, Sir Thomas had defied king Henry VIII in his effort to break with Rome and start his own church wherein he could divorce queen Catherine (who hadn't given him a male heir) and marry Anne Boleyn. Sir Thomas More stood his ground for the Lord. His deep faith in Christ was unshakeable, even unto death.

At the trial of Hus by the General Council at Constance, he was required to do three things in order to establish his innocence: (1) confess that he erred in writing the articles attacking the church and the Pope; (2) agree not to continue preaching the subject matter of the articles; and (3) recant the articles he'd written criticizing the church. Hus refused, for he believed he'd spoken truth placed before him by the Lord. He knelt before the Council and prayed, "Lord Jesus Christ! Forgive mine enemies, by whom Thou knowest that I am falsely accused, and that they have used false witness and slanders against me; forgive them, I say, for Thy great mercy's sake." *Foxe's Book of Martyrs*, 128.

Hus was condemned to death by the Council and was thereafter taken to the place of execution where he, while praying and reciting Psalms 31 and 51, was burned at the stake on July 6, 1415. In his last breaths, Hus was heard uttering the words, "Jesus Christ! the Son of the living God! have mercy on me." *Foxe's Book of Martyrs*, 133.

John Hus was a man of great faith in Jesus Christ. He did not fear his transgressors for he knew that the Lord was with him. The Lord did not forsake him. The Lord did not fail him. "For in that He Himself has suffered, being tempted, He is able to aid those who are tempted" (Hebrews 2:18). The Lord led Hus to speak the truth no matter what the earthly consequences.

SUBMIT YOUR LIFE TO JESUS CHRIST, NOT TO CAESAR *

In these troubled economic times, people hope that something or someone will save them from a world that is collapsing around them. Many delude themselves into believing that it isn't possible for things to get worse and that the government ("Caesar") will save them from total disaster. In so doing, they forget completely about God.

One could really work him or herself into a frenzy thinking about the desperation of our current economic situation. Many thought this way in "The Great Depression." Yet, notwithstanding volumes of government programs initiated in that era, people throughout the world suffered for a long time, many without the basic necessities of life: food, water, a roof over their head, clothing on their back, and a job in order to earn a living.

I have found myself thinking on occasion, "I've worked all my life and whatever I have to show for it could disappear into thin air. In such a case, where will my family live, what will we eat, what will I do for a livelihood? How will we survive?" It's very easy to get caught up in all the negative news and look at things from a worldly point of view.

How quickly we lose sight that God is in charge. He's allowed all of these economic troubles to occur. He has His reasons, reasons which are beyond our understanding. But then again, there's a familiar ring to all of this. Just read the prophets such as Isaiah or Jeremiah and their writings become very contemporary (see for example Isaiah 1–3 or Jeremiah 6:9–15). At a time when God's people were defiant of Him, Jeremiah wrote the spoken words of wrath of the Lord, "Hear, O earth! Behold, I will certainly bring calamity on this people—The fruit of their thoughts, Because they have not heeded My words Nor My law, but rejected it...I will lay stumbling blocks before this

---

* Originally written May 15, 2009 in the "Great Recession"

people, And the fathers and the sons together shall fall on them. The neighbor and his friend shall perish" (Jeremiah 6:19, 21).

I sometimes find myself getting caught up in the bad financial tidings of Bloomberg News, CNBC, or CNN Money. But then I hear "a still small voice" (1 Kings 19:12) that says, "I am in charge. Trust in me and I shall give you peace." It is then that I recall words spoken by the apostle Peter, "Therefore humble yourselves under the mighty hand of God, that He may exalt you in due time, casting all your care upon Him, for He cares for you" (1 Peter 5:6–7). Suddenly, all my pre-baby-boomer worries are cast aside and I no longer have a concern that my family and I will be OK in all ways.

Our Lord loves us and wants us to submit to Him in times of trouble. That's why He allows troubles to occur from time to time. He will see to it that we are fed, clothed and sheltered for He assured us,

> "Therefore I say to you, do not worry about your life, what you will eat or what you will drink; nor about your body, what you will put on. Is not life more than food and the body more than clothing?... Therefore do not worry, saying, 'What shall we eat?' or 'What shall we drink?' or 'What shall we wear?'... For your heavenly Father knows that you need all these things. But seek first the kingdom of God and His righteousness, and all these things shall be added to you" (Matthew 6:25, 31–33).

When trouble occurs such as we are experiencing this day, remember the words of the psalmist, "The LORD is my rock and my fortress and my deliverer; My God, my strength, in whom I will trust; My shield and the horn of my salvation, my stronghold" (Psalm 18:2).

"Be anxious for nothing, but in everything by prayer and supplication, with thanksgiving, let your requests be made known to God; and the peace of God, which surpasses all understanding, will guard your hearts and minds through Christ Jesus" (Philippians 4:6–7). "The humble person in the midst of trouble is filled with peace, for he depends on God alone." Thomas A' Kempis, *The Imitation of Christ*, 67.

Submit your life to Jesus Christ, not Caesar, and you will have peace in these troubled times.

FEAR OF MAN OR FEAR OF THE LORD: IT'S YOUR CHOICE

God commanded Adam, "Of every tree of the garden you may freely eat; but of the tree of the knowledge of good and evil you shall not eat, for in the day that you eat of it you shall surely die" (Genesis 2:16–17). At the urging of the serpent, Satan, who was also in the Garden of Eden, Adam and his wife Eve disobeyed God's command and ate the fruit of the tree of the knowledge of good and evil. The result of Adam and Eve's disobedience of God's command: fear! For it says in Genesis 3:10 that Adam "was afraid." Why was he afraid? He was afraid because he'd made the wrong choice by disobeying God and feared the consequence—death.

God uses fear in two ways in the Bible: (1) in the context of love or light, that is, reverence for Him, and (2) in the context of darkness, that is, worry, anxiety, terror, lack of peace and torment. The apostle John wrote, "God is love, and he who abides in love abides in God, and God in Him...There is no fear in love; but perfect love casts out fear, because fear involves torment. But he who fears has not been made perfect in love" (1 John 4:16, 18). In a Biblical sense, fear boils down to a choice in life of (1) a path of good where worldly fear doesn't exist, or (2) a path of evil in defiance of God's will. One is a choice of life, eternal life in the light with God; the other, a choice of death, eternal life in the darkness of condemnation.

The Bible describes two types of fear: (1) fear of man (darkness; evil) and (2) fear of the Lord (light; goodness; love; respect). *Fear of man* means worldly concern of injury to *self* (even death) caused by intimidation from or judgment by others due to one's actions or inactions.

When we fear man, we are choosing death because fearing man is rejection of God, a sin, and "the wages of sin is death" (Romans 6:23). If I am concerned about what others think about me, in essence I am concerned about the survival of *self*, my fleshly well-being, my life. Some of the fears we experience in our lives are fear of failure, fear of humiliation, fear of rejection, fear of loss, and fear of judgment by others. When in fear of man, our minds race with thoughts of imminent disaster. Questions go through our minds such as: "Will I be OK?" "Will I lose everything I own?" "Will I be hurt and suffer pain?" "Will I die?" All of these dark thoughts are not from the Lord, but from the accuser, Satan. The devil would like nothing better than to see me squirm and suffer, live a life of despair and anguish, and worrying myself, first to illness and then death! Therefore, when I am choosing to fear man rather than revering the Lord, I am choosing death. "Thus says the LORD: 'Cursed is the man who trusts in man And makes flesh his strength, Whose heart departs from the LORD'" (Jeremiah 17:5).

On the other hand, when I turn to the Lord in the midst of my worries, death is not a concern for He is with me. God's Word tells us not to fear man, but to fear or have reverence (love; obedience; and respect) for the Lord. The psalmist wrote,"Behold, the eye of the LORD is on those who fear Him, On those who hope in His mercy, To deliver their soul from death" (Psalm 33:18–19).

God said to Abram in a vision, "Do not be afraid, Abram. I am your shield, your exceedingly great reward" (Genesis 15:1). To the children of Israel, He exhorted through his servant Moses, "Be strong and of good courage, do not fear nor be afraid of them; for the LORD your God, He is the One who goes with you. He will not leave you nor forsake you" (Deuteronomy 31:6). Through the inspired word of God, David declared, "The LORD is my light and my salvation; Whom shall I fear? The LORD is the strength of my life; Of whom shall I be afraid?" (Psalm 27:1).

In life, as we walk deeper with the Lord, our fleshly tendency to fear man diminishes and our decision to love the Lord strengthens. By confessing that we are sinners and that we need a Savior; that Jesus Christ is our Lord and Savior; that He died for our sins; that He rose again, and that He is with us—we are saved for eternity and our salvation is forever assured. Our body may die, but our spirit will live for eternity with the Holy One. With confidence, we can boldly tread through life, free of fear (of man; of death), and with a deepening sense of peace and well-being.

As we study the Lord's Word, participate in His body (the Church), practice fellowship, and live as children of God by carrying out His most important commandments to love Him with all of our heart, soul, mind, and strength, and love one another (Mark. 12:29-31), we experience a perfecting love and a growing confidence towards God. As our walk with God deepens, our fear of worldly matters will diminish and the light of God will brighten in our lives. The apostle Paul wrote to Timothy, "For God has not given us a spirit of fear, but of power and of love and of sound mind" (2 Timothy 1:7). I believe that the fear that John speaks of in 1 John 4:18 (above) is fear of man, for if I fear what others think about me and fear not God, I shall not have in my life the power, love, and sound mind Paul speaks of in Second Timothy.

Paul summed it up in Romans 8:31, "What then shall we say to these things? If God is for us, who can be against us?" If we fear the Lord, He will care for us. "Therefore humble yourselves under the mighty hand of God, that He may exalt you in due time, casting all your care upon Him, for He cares for you." 1 Peter 5:6-7). "Because he has set his love upon Me, therefore I will deliver him; I will set him on high, because he has known My name. He shall call upon Me, and I will answer him; I will be with him in trouble; I will deliver him and honor him. With long life will I satisfy him, And show him My salvation" (Psalm 91:14–16).

The poet wrote, "I shall be telling this with a sigh, Somewhere ages and ages hence: Two roads diverged in a wood, and I—I took the one less traveled by, And that has made all the difference." *The Road Not Taken*, Robert Frost. Make a difference in your life: choose the small gate and the narrow road, the "one less traveled by." Fear not man, but fear the Lord. Choose Jesus Christ! He will make all the difference in your life.

FELLOWSHIP

"BEHOLD, how good and how pleasant it is For brethren to dwell together in unity!" (Psalm 133:1).

WHY I'M IN A BIBLE STUDY

The question was once posed to me, "Why are you in a Bible study?" While pondering this question during my daily morning devotions, the words of Psalm 133:1 came to mind, "BEHOLD, how good and how pleasant it is For brethren to dwell together in unity!" The Hebrew of these words has been eternalized in an ancient Hebrew song (transliterated as follows), "He nay mah tovu manayim, shevat achim gam yachad!"

What a privilege it is to arise early in the morning and pray, worship and study the Word of God with people who are like-minded. Our Lord set the example of praying early in the morning, which to me is the best time of the day to study His Word. The apostle Mark wrote, "Now in the morning, having risen a long while before daylight, He went out and departed to a solitary place; and there He prayed" (Mark 1:35).

Every Monday morning for a number of years, I got up very early, drove twenty-five miles, and joined many other Christian men in a Bible study. Why did we do that?

Because:

1. We wanted to show the Lord that we love Him with all of our hearts, all of our souls, and all of our minds.
2. We wanted to know Him and His Word in a deeper way.
3. We wanted to do what He set as an example for each of us.
4. We wanted to live our lives as men of God.
5. We wanted to arm ourselves with His plate of armor for the comings day(s) (Ephesians 6:11).
6. We wanted to please Him.
7. We wanted to share the unity of Christ with our brethren.
8. We wanted to share the blessings His Word offers to each of us every minute of every day of our lives.

9. We wanted to have accountability with others who live by His Word.
10. We wanted a safe place where we could share life issues with brethren who truly cared about our concerns, who could give each other insights and support for those issues, and where we could practice Jesus' exhortation to love "your neighbor as yourself" (Luke 10:27).

How did we do all of those things? By studying His Word, by praying with and for others, by sharing our innermost thoughts, by living as He taught us, and by being together with our brethren in unity in Christ.

FREE WILL

"And the LORD God commanded the man, saying, 'Of every tree of the garden you may freely eat; but of the tree of the knowledge of good and evil you shall not eat, for in the day that you eat of it you shall surely die'" (Genesis 2:16–17).

ALL AUTHORITY IN HEAVEN AND ON EARTH

No one likes to be told what to do or how to live their life. Since the Garden of Eden, man has been in rebellion against authority and particularly against God. Rebellion against God is sin.

Man's rebellion against God intensified in the late eighteenth century when modernist philosophers such as Friedrich Nietzsche wrote that the "autonomy [*self*-will] of the individual is the dominant philosophical ideal before which all other concepts including the existence of God, must be eliminated...[T]he ideal figure is the 'superman'...who creates his own values and who is answerable to no one but himself." Reverend James Boice, *Foundations of the Christian Faith*,120. Nietzsche declared that "God is dead." In his view, there is no authority over our individual lives other than our own. What a hopeless worldview! What chaos!

The apostle Paul wrote about the depraved condition of man in Romans 1:18–32. If left to his own will, man rejects goodness and chooses evil. Look, for example, at the actions of a two year old if left unsupervised! "Let all divine restraints be removed and man be left absolutely free [of God], and all ethical distinctions would immediately disappear, the spirit of barbarism would prevail universally, and pandemonium would reign supreme." Boice, *ibid* at 177–178 citing Arthur W. Pink, *The Sovereignty of God*. That statement succinctly describes the direction of our culture today as it eliminates God from all aspects of society. Everyone is doing as he or she sees fit in their own eyes (Judges 21:25)!

Self-will has never worked. Adam defied God and declared himself to be the authority over his own life. The result: eternal separation from God which led to depravity and death. Even worse, Adam's defiant act, original sin, has been imputed to us all. Paul wrote, "Therefore, just as through one man sin entered the world, and death through sin, and thus death spread to all men, because all sinned" (Romans 5:12).

Contrary to modernist worldview, there is and can be only one Authority that is truly in control of the universe. The prophet Daniel stated that "The Most High God rules in the kingdom of men, and appoints over it whomever He chooses" (Daniel 5:21). As the Creator of all moral order in the universe, it was God's intent that we be subject to *His* will, not our own. God reserved for His Son Jesus Christ "All authority...in heaven and on earth" (Matthew 28:18; Luke 5:24). We may think we have free will or authority over our own lives, but in reality it is *God's will* that determines the course of our lives. I had no say over when I was born nor do I have any say when I am going to die. It was and is God's will! "By the grace of God I am what I am" (1 Corinthians 15:10).

But, do I have any say in my own life?

Yes, God gave us a choice. He gave us free will to choose Him or to reject Him, that is, to choose the Tree of Life, or to choose to violate His command to not eat of the Tree of the Knowledge of Good and Evil. God desires that we, His children, love Him as He loves us. Forced love is not true love. Therefore to create the ability within man to truly love another, He created the mechanism of choice within man. He housed within man a principle which enabled man to determine his own actions. "For man to obey God, it requires a willingness on his part, because God never compels him... until he gives his consent God will not make His way into the man." Watchman Nee, *The Spiritual Man*, Vol. III, 77.

On the other hand, if man chooses as Adam did (he rejected God), his wrong choice condemns him to an eternal life of death and darkness, separated forever from God. In God's eyes the wrong choice regarding Him is sin. "For to be carnally minded is death, but to be spiritually minded is life and peace" (Romans 8:6). As rebellious offspring of Adam, we have the God-given ability to acknowledge that we are sinners. Without God, our lives will be like Adam's—hopeless. But in faith and with our God-given free will, we can wisely choose to repent (change our mind), to invite Jesus Christ into our lives, to pray for His forgiveness of our sins, and ask that by His grace He save us from eternal separation from the love that is the glory of God.

> "Blessed be the name of God forever and ever, For wisdom and might are His...He gives wisdom to the wise And knowledge to those who have understanding. He reveals deep and secret things...I thank You and praise You, O God of my fathers; You have given me wisdom and might [to choose wisely]" (Daniel 2:20–23)

Praise the One with all authority in heaven and on earth..

GIVING

"But as you abound in everything—in faith, in speech, in knowledge, in all diligence, and in your love for us—see that you abound in this grace also" (2 Corinthians 8:7).

GENEROSITY, THE GRACE OF GIVING

Jesus said, "It is more blessed to give than to receive" (Acts 20:35). By His grace, the Lord blesses each of us by providing that which enables us to give to others. Willingness to share from one's heart is the true motivation of generosity. The apostle Paul called this Godly principle of generosity the *grace* of giving (2 Corinthians 8:7).

The widow's offering described in The Gospel According to Mark illustrates this principle: "Now Jesus sat opposite the treasury and saw how the people put money into the treasury. And many who were rich put in much. Then one poor widow came and threw in two mites [small copper coins worth a fraction of a penny]" (Mark 12:41–42). She'd put in everything that she had to live on. Jesus remarked to His disciples, "Assuredly, I say to you that this poor widow has put in more than all those who have given to the treasury" (Mark 12:43).

Generosity is an act of righteousness (Psalm 37:21). At God's calling, Abram left ancient Babylon and went to the land of Canaan. There he acquired great wealth for he was blessed by the Lord. His nephew Lot who accompanied Abram, also had acquired "flocks and herds and tents" (Genesis 13:5). But Lot's herdsmen quarreled with Abram's herdsmen because the dry land could not support them both. Being a generous man, Abram said to Lot that there was plenty of good pasture available for both of them and that they shouldn't argue over it. He urged Lot to seek the best land for himself and if Lot went in one direction from where they stood, he would go in the opposite direction (Genesis 13:8–9). Abram was confident by his faith in God that the Lord's grace would cover them both. He gave his nephew the opportunity to choose the best land for himself. Abram's great faith in God blessed him with many things including the grace of giving and the Lord "accounted it to him for righteousness" (Genesis 15:6).

In his second letter to the Corinthians, Paul provides the most complete biblical discussion of the "grace of giving" (see 2 Corinthians 8 and 9). The Christians in Jerusalem were being persecuted and were impoverished. Paul took up a collection for the physical relief of the Jerusalem brethren. Whereas the Christians of Macedonia gave generously out of poverty, the wealthy Corinthians were not fulfilling the pledges they'd previously made. Paul exhorted the Corinthians to excel in this grace of giving. He reminded them, "He who sows sparingly will also reap sparingly, and he who sows bountifully will also reap bountifully. So let each one give as he purposes in his heart, not grudgingly or of necessity; for God loves a cheerful giver" (2 Corinthians 9:6–7). In essence, Paul was telling the Christians at Corinth and us that through His grace, God will make sure we have all we need in life and that we shouldn't worry about how much to give. By His grace, we'll have such abundance that we'll have a deep desire to give.

"The real test of any person lies in what he gives...Giving is part of our worship to God. If we do not have the grace of giving, we should pray to God and ask Him to give us a generous, sharing spirit." *Thru the Bible*, J. Vernon McGee, 2 Corinthians 8:6, Vol V, 127.

GOD'S LOVE

"Greater love has no one than this, than to lay down one's life for his friends" (John 15:13).

AGAPE, THE SACRIFICIAL LOVE OF GOD

In his book *The Glorious Journey*, 377, Pastor Charles Stanley defines *agape*, a Greek word, as a "sacrificial commitment; dedicated to the well-being of another." *Agape* is the Lord's love for us. Pastor Oswald Chambers concluded that "The love of God means Calvary, and nothing less! The love of God is spelt out on the Cross and nowhere else." *My Utmost for His Highest,* November 19. Thomas A' Kempis wrote, "In the cross is salvation...life...protection...heavenly sweetness...strength of mind...spiritual joy...supreme virtue; in the cross is perfect holiness. There is no salvation for the soul nor hope for eternal life, except in the cross." *The Imitation of Christ*, 78.

Jesus said, "Greater love has no one than this, than to lay down one's life for his friends" (John 15:13). Jesus gave up His human life for us on the cross. But for what purpose would Jesus do this? What was the plan of God in sending His only Son to the cross? The answer lies in John 3:16, "For God so loved the world that He gave his only begotten Son, that whoever believes in Him should not perish but have eternal life." Jesus went to the cross to save us, mortal sinners, from eternal damnation! He laid down His life because of His great love for us.

When I turned 40, my many roles in life consisted of husband, father, son, brother, friend and co-worker. Yet at mid-life I was lost, without direction, without hope, and without God. In quiet desperation I cried out to God from the darkness which surrounded me: "Where does this end?" "Will I ever be happy in life?" "How can I relieve the pit in my stomach?" My mind raced with dark thoughts because my marriage was failing and my family was about to fall apart. The pressures of work fueled my need to please others, not God. I had no time for anything, especially my family. I had anger at my father for the hurts I'd stored from early childhood. I felt incomplete and unfulfilled in my spiritual life. I believed that I didn't have time for God. I was in deep despair and saw no way out of the darkness.

In searching for answers, I drifted into *New Age*, a spiritual movement that had its origins in the late 60's. Perhaps, I thought, Buddha would provide solace to me in my path to enlightenment. In a quest for answers to my pain, I attended a "human potential" seminar, the purported subject-matter of which was "introspection into one's self—finding truth." In the midst of that search into my very being, the Lord Jesus Christ appeared to me in a vision.

In an evening session of the seminar while contemplating questions such as, "Who am I?" "What is this all about?" "Is there more to this than what I see, hear, touch, etc.?", I suddenly saw in my mind's eye (with my eyes closed) Jesus Christ on the cross. I felt His presence in the deepest part of my soul. I experienced all the emotions as if I were there at Calvary observing the Lord dying on the cross. Great sadness came over me and I sobbed uncontrollably. Yet, at the same time, I felt indescribable joy for He was beckoning me through His sacrificial death to believe in Him, to repent from my sinful ways, and to follow Him. It is woefully inadequate to put into words the *agape* love I felt from Him on that cross.

Since that September evening in 1983, my life has not been the same. The Lord took my despairing soul, my darkened spirit, and breathed new life into me. I felt like a baby in His arms. I felt immeasurable peace for the first time in my life.

Now, back in the valley of life, I recall with joyful tears, the wondrous experience I had on that mountaintop in Vermont. The love our Lord showed me on that distant evening lives on in me like a burning torch. It is and was His *agape* love. He plucked me, a woeful sinner, out of the abyss and set me on His straight path.

Jesus said to His disciples, "You did not choose Me, but I chose you and appointed you that you should go and bear fruit, and that your fruit should remain, that whatever you ask the Father in My name He may give you" (John 15:16). I say this not as a boast, but humbly as a fact: He chose me out of the abyss as He has done for multitudes of others who believe and have faith in Him. What a privilege it was (and is) to become one of His disciples that special evening in Vermont! What *agape* love from Him!

Now, older and hopefully wiser, I know that visions and wonders are not what He is all about. It is His daily Word and His grace that sustains me in this valley of the shadow of death. It is not the aspiration to live on a mountaintop, but it is faith in Him and His Spirit dwelling within me that plucked me out of a crowd and now gets me through life. I shall be forever grateful and blessed by His glorious act of *agape* love on the cross.

> "In you, O LORD, I put my trust;
> Let me never be put to shame.
> Deliver me in Your righteousness,
> and cause me to escape;
> Incline Your ear to me, and save me.
> Be my strong refuge,
> To which I may resort continually;
> You have given the commandment to save me,
> For You are my rock and my fortress" (Psalm 71:1–3).

HARMONY

"But Jesus knew their thoughts and said to them: 'Every kingdom divided against itself is brought to desolation, and every city or house divided against itself will not stand'" (Matthew 12:25).

PRAY FOR HARMONY IN OUR LAND

The ancient Israelites fought each other for seven and one-half years until God brought the House of Saul and the House of David together (see 2 Samuel 2:8–3:1). After years of bloody strife, all of the tribes of Israel united under David. They exclaimed, "Indeed we are your bone and your flesh. Also, in time past, when Saul was king over us, you were the one who led Israel out and brought them in; and the LORD said to you, 'You shall shepherd My people Israel, and be ruler over Israel.'" (2 Samuel 5:1–2). David rejoiced to see the Lord bringing all his brethren together in harmony, peace and unity. He wrote of his joy, "BEHOLD, how good and how pleasant it is For brethren to dwell together in unity!" (Psalm 133:1).

The bitter strife of the Israelites brings to mind what is occurring in our own land today. The adversity that exists between our citizens has divided our land. That adversity is encouraged by partisan politicians. It's as if many of our representatives in government no longer desire to continue this Godly plan called the *United States of America.*

Many elected officials in government do not seek to do right for right's sake, but merely to perpetuate their position in power. It troubles me to recall the difference between today and my earlier days, days when parents and teachers taught their children to be polite. I remember how my mother often told us to live by the *Golden Rule.* She taught us to do unto others as you would have them do unto you. It was Jesus Christ who first spoke this Godly principle on that hillside on the northern shore of the Sea of Galilee: "Therefore, whatever you want men to do to you, do also to them, for this is the Law and the Prophets" (Matthew 7:12).

The dysfunction in our land is cutting our national fiber to the bone. Why can't we Americans live together in peace, harmony and unity? Why do friends oppose friends and families oppose families? We have become immersed in worldly darkness, an abyss that is fast becoming an irreversible slippery slope, a culture without moral reference. *What is going on in America that has brought about such bitter disharmony?*

The answer: our nation, a Christian nation, has turned away from Jesus Christ. God is allowing this to occur. I'm not sure why, but perhaps He is pouring out His wrath on this nation for excluding Him from our lives, our schools, our culture! Jesus said to the Pharisees, "Every kingdom divided against itself is brought to desolation, and every city or house divided against itself will not stand" (Matthew 12:25). "He who is not with Me is against Me, and he who does not gather with Me scatters abroad" (Matthew 12:30). The people of the United States have become a house divided that will be scattered by God if as a nation we don't *change* (repent) and turn back to Christ.

At times, I get upset over the opposing points of view in our land, feeling anger, frustration, and even despair about the direction of our country. But then, thanks be to God, I catch myself and remember that God is in charge! I remember that no matter how bad things appear, the Lord is guiding and directing all that occurs. The psalmist wrote about his realization that God has it all planned, "Your eyes saw my substance, being yet unformed. And in Your book they all were written. The days fashioned for me, When as yet there were none of them" (Psalm 139:16).

Fellow Christians, pray for the peaceful harmony in our land that David wrote about in his Psalm (133:1). May Jesus' prayer for unity be our prayer, "Holy Father, keep through Your name those whom You have given Me, that they may be one as We are" (John 17:11). Pray for our fellow Americans so that their eyes will be opened and their ears unblocked. Pray for them so that our nation will once again look to Jesus Christ as its Lord and Savior. How marvelous it will be when we can all exclaim, "BEHOLD, how good and how pleasant it is For brethren to live together in unity!"

HEALING

Jesus Christ, the Messiah, is the Great Healer. "By His stripes, we are healed" (Isaiah 53:5).

THE BLESSINGS OF BEING HEALED BY OUR LORD

My father-in-law received an email from a Jewish woman to whom he'd been witnessing about Jesus Christ on the East Coast. The woman, a widow whom I shall call Rachel, is very ill and is suffering deeply. In her suffering, she openly acknowledged that she was "searching and hoping for unshakeable faith." She acknowledged that the message about Jesus Christ is a powerful one, but in her view "it doesn't address the questions: Why does God allow such unspeakable pain and suffering on those He made and loves? Could you in your most evil moments visit any of these things on your daughter? Then why did a loving God include these things in His plan? These questions rock my soul and my searching toward complete belief and no one has given me the answer yet that can satisfy."

Rachel asks age-old questions. While she is not a believer in Jesus Christ, she is seeking answers. She is seeking the truth. In essence she is asking, "Why the suffering; Why the pain?" She cannot understand how God, Whom she acknowledges loves us, can at the same time "allow such unspeakable pain and suffering."

Many Biblical scholars have addressed these issues: F.W. Bosworth in the book *Christ The Healer,* Jon Courson in his book *A Future and a Hope*, and Watchman Nee in his book *The Spiritual Man.* These Christian writers suggest that suffering, whether due to illness or otherwise, can possibly be attributed: (1) to the consequences of our sin (our disobedience of God's will); (2) to preparation for a future ministry; or (3) for the glory of God. But I could read every book on the subject and still not understand God's purpose in a given situation. So I turn to the true source for answers to life's issues, the Bible. The Holy Bible tells us that whatever God's purpose for allowing sickness and suffering, He, as our heavenly Father, has our well-being in mind. The apostle Paul summed it up when he wrote, "And we know that all things work together for good to those who love God, to those who are the called according to His purpose" (Romans 8:28).

No matter how bright we are, no matter how educated we are, we are simply incapable of knowing all the answers to life's challenges. Paul concluded, "There is none who understands" (Romans 3:11). Similarly, the prophet Isaiah concluded that the intellectualism of "wise men" does not assist them in finding God, "For the wisdom of their wise men shall perish, And the understanding of their prudent men shall be hidden" (Isaiah 29:14). In this post-modern age, it is fashionable to try to gauge the existence of something by its empirical evidence. But the fact that we cannot see, hear, touch, smell or taste something doesn't mean that it doesn't exist. Therefore, in life when we reach the limit of human understanding, we must make a quantum leap to the Great Beyond! That leap is called *faith*. "Now faith is the substance of things hoped for, the evidence of things not seen" (Hebrews 11:1).

If we are faced with a serious illness, the first thing we must see is that it has been allowed by God in our lives for a good reason. That reason will become apparent as our faith becomes stronger. How does our faith in God become stronger? "Faith comes by hearing, and hearing by the word of God" (Romans 10:17). Life's challenges can only be understood through our faith in the Lord and our faith can only be strengthened by knowledge of His will through His Word. Thus, when we don't know the answers to life's challenges, we should turn to God's Word, the Bible.

Watchman Nee wrote in *The Spiritual Man*, Vol. III, 158, that "Sickness...is the sequel to sin and the prologue to death...Had Adam not sinned, sickness would not have come upon the earth." The source of sin is not God, but Satan, for the definition of sin is disobedience of the will of God. Satan led the way to evil by rejecting God and fell from heaven (Luke 10:18). "He who sins is of the devil, for the devil has sinned from the beginning" (1 John 3:8). "There is none righteous, no not one" (Romans 3:10). Because we are all sinners derived from Adam's fall, we must all consider sin as a source of our suffering.

Sinners suffer from illness that may result in death. Aside from the physical manifestations of illness, there are underlying spiritual reasons for illness. Paul wrote, "Many are weak and sick among you, and many sleep. For if we would judge ourselves, we would not be judged. But when we are judged, we are chastened by the Lord, that we may not be condemned with the world" (1 Corinthians 11:30–32). Watchman Nee explains the apostle's statement, "Sickness is one type of the Lord's chastening. Owing to their having erred before the Lord, believers are chastened with illness to prompt them to judge themselves and eliminate their mistakes. In chastening His children, God deals graciously towards them that they may not be condemned with the world...Illness is frequently the chastisement of God employed to draw our attention to some sin we may have overlooked so that we may forsake it. God *permits* these sicknesses to fall upon us that He may discipline us and purge us from our faults. God's hand bears down on us to direct our eyes to some unrighteousness or some debt, some pride or love of this world, some self-reliance or greediness in work, or some disobedience to God. Sickness is consequently God's open judgment of sin." Nee, *ibid*, Vol. III, 161–162.

God doesn't inflict sickness upon us, but He allows it. Why? The apostle Paul suffered from an affliction and delighted in it since it <u>turned him to Christ</u>. He wrote,

> "A thorn in the flesh was given to me, a messenger of Satan to buffet me, lest I be exalted above measure. Concerning this thing I pleaded with the Lord three times that it might depart from me. And He said to me, 'My grace is sufficient for you, for My strength is made perfect in weakness.' Therefore most gladly I will rather boast in my infirmities, that the power of Christ may rest upon me. Therefore I take pleasure in infirmities, in reproaches, in needs, in persecutions, in distresses, for Christ's sake. For when I am weak, then I am strong" (2 Corinthians 12:7–10; Nee, *ibid*, Vol. III, 161–162).

A person who is ill (such as Rachel) must "place [herself] completely in God's light for examination, having an honest desire to learn if [she] is being chastened because of some lack. [She] should judge [herself]. Thus the Holy Spirit shall point out to [her] where [she] has failed. And whatever [she] is shown, it must be immediately confessed and forsaken... [She] should offer herself afresh to God and be disposed to obey His will fully." Nee, *ibid,* Vol. III, 162. Only through Jesus Christ, the Great Mediator, is this possible. If she hasn't confessed that she is a sinner, she should do so, recognizing that Christ died for her sins and arose again from His grave that she might be saved for eternal life. He is a loving God. If Rachel has faith in Him, she will be pardoned by the Lord for her sins and will be cleansed from any unrighteousness (1 John 1:9).

There are other reasons why God *allows* us to suffer. An example of this is the blind man who was blind from birth. "Now as Jesus passed by, He saw a man who was blind from birth. And His disciples asked him, saying, 'Rabbi, who sinned, this man or his parents, that he was born blind?' Jesus answered, 'Neither this man nor his parents sinned, but that the works of God might be revealed in him'" (John 9:1–3). "So far as mankind is concerned, sickness does come from sin; but in relation to the individual it may or may not be the case...aside from natural causes there is additionally the *control of Providence.*" Nee, *ibid,* Vol. III, 180, 182 (my emphasis added). If the blind man was born blind so that the work of God might be displayed in his life, his blindness was permitted so that his life should be a witness for the glory and honor of the Lord. Joni Erickson-Tada is a contemporary example of this.

We don't know who may be affected by Rachel's illness and suffering. It may be that her "searching and hoping for unshakeable faith" may be an inspiration or a seed for another's re-birth. "But the ones [the seeds] that fell on the good ground are those who, having heard the word with a noble and good heart, keep it and bear fruit with patience" (Luke 8:15).

Rachel's searching reflects her desire to know God. Rachel refers to Him in her letter as a "loving God." Whatever the reason for her suffering, even in her uncertain belief, she still sees that God's purpose is a loving one.

But what advice does one give to Rachel regarding her present suffering? The Word of God provides the answer: "Therefore humble yourselves under the mighty hand of God, that He may exalt you in due time, casting all your care upon him, for He cares for you" (1 Peter 5:6–7). Rachel must have faith in the Lord Jesus Christ; she must come to know Him by His Word; and she must see that His Word tells her who He is in relation to Father God and her. He is the Great Healer. He cares for Rachel. He loves her. Moreover, she must see that it is the enemy Satan who wants to see her fall to death through sickness. By admitting that she can't handle her problems without God, He will stand in the gap for her. "God resists the proud, but gives grace to the humble. Therefore humble yourselves under the mighty hand of God, that he may exalt you in due time" (1 Peter 5:5–6).

Referring to the Messiah, the prophet Isaiah had the prescription for illness, "Surely He has borne our griefs And carried our sorrows; Yet we esteemed Him stricken, Smitten by God, and afflicted. But He was wounded for our transgressions, He was bruised for our iniquities; The chastisement for our peace was upon Him And by His stripes we are healed" (Isaiah 53:4–5). Jesus Christ, the Messiah, is the Great Healer.

HEAVEN

Heaven is God's abode. It is the place where He is everlasting in His love, all powerful, all knowing, ever-present, unchangeable, and infinite beyond understanding. By His Son, Jesus Christ, He has blessed us with His grace to experience in part, now, every spiritual benediction in His heavenly places (Ephesians 1:3–6; 1 Corinthians 13:12). By accepting Jesus Christ as our Lord and Savior, we can live our lives in the kingdom of heaven, now.

THE KINGDOM OF HEAVEN IS NOW

Before I knew Jesus Christ, I believed that if I led a clean life and did good deeds, I would go to heaven when I died. Now that I believe in Jesus Christ, I know by His grace and not on the basis of anything that I've done, that I'll be with Him in heaven (Ephesians 1:13–14). Moreover, as I have walked with Him deeper in His River of Life, I have come to know that heaven is not a place that I shall know only when I die. It is the place that I have known ever since the Lord chose me as one of His elect (I say that humbly). Jesus said, "You did not choose Me, but I chose you and appointed you that you should go and bear fruit, and that your fruit should remain, that whatever you ask the Father in My name He may give you" (John 15:16).

Heaven is a spiritual dimension that is just beyond our human time/space continuum. The Bible is filled with examples of the presence of God's realm just beyond the sight of humans. The prophet Elisha prayed for his servant's eyes to be opened so that he could see the surrounding hills "full of horses and chariots of fire," filled with unseen angels ready to defend the prophet (2 Kings 6:15–17). The writer of Hebrews wrote that though unseen in our flesh "we are surrounded by so great a cloud of witnesses" (Hebrews 12:1). Angels surround us though we cannot see them with our eyes (1Corinthians 11:10; 1Timothy 5:21; Hebrews 13:2).

Jesus Christ came to earth as God in the person of a man to preach His kingdom and to teach that the kingdom of heaven is now (Luke 4:43). He proclaimed, "The time is fulfilled and the kingdom of God is at hand. Repent and believe in the gospel" (Mark 1:15). He came to change our destiny by believing in Him. His intention is to draw each of us nearer to Him so that we will be conformed to His heavenly image (Romans 8:29). By His Holy Spirit we are empowered to experience now, the fruits of the kingdom life: "love, joy, peace, longsuffering, kindness, goodness, faithfulness, gentleness and self-control" (Galatians 5:22–23). This is the heavenly life.

The apostle Paul wrote to the Corinthians, "For now we see in a mirror, dimly, but then face to face." We can experience heaven now, but in Paul's view, our flesh keeps us from seeing heaven clearly. He continued, "Now I know in part, but then I shall know just as I am also known" (1 Corinthians 13:12). The point Paul makes is that in our flesh we experience heaven now, but only in part. We don't have to die first in order to experience at least part of the kingdom of heaven. The part we can experience now is lovely—knowing and believing in the Lord.

Although as earthly beings we can only see through a glass dimly, the part of heaven that we can and do experience in this life, as apprentices of Jesus Christ, is glorious and wonderful. The realization that we are now in the Lord's kingdom of heaven enables us to have a totally different attitude toward others. We live uplifted lives with God's perspective. The Lord changes us and puts on our hearts the desire to be more considerate, more polite, more respectful and more loving of others.

In a recent teaching, Senior Pastor Rick Booye of Trail (Oregon) Christian Fellowship (paraphrasing in part, Dr. Dallas Willard) described the Lord's intention for His saints now into eternity, "God's intention for you as His child is that you will have a never-ending life of unutterable joy, peace, beauty and creativity. You will live in an entirely safe and secure, ever-expanding and constantly more powerful universe where you will contribute to and cooperate with unimaginably marvelous leadership and teamwork in the achievement of infinitely good and meaningful ends. Your relationships will all be profoundly deep and fulfilling and you will have infinite time and resources to develop them." Pastor Rick added, "The quality of this life begins now."

When we die, we shall sit at the foot of His throne and worship Him with multitudes of believers. We look forward to that glorious life. But now, although as fleshly beings we are only able to look in that heavenly mirror dimly, we are assured of more than just a taste of the fruits of the Spirit. By Christians' "union with the exalted Christ, [we] have already been made beneficiaries of every spiritual blessing that belongs to and comes from the heavenly realm." *NIV Study Bible*, 2270, note at Ephesians 1:3.

Rejoice in the Lord for the kingdom of heaven is now!

HOLINESS

"For I am the LORD your God. You shall therefore consecrate yourselves, and you shall be holy; for I am holy" (Leviticus 11:44).

HOLINESS IS WHAT WE YEARN FOR

To be holy is to be set apart, sanctified from sin and moral impurity.

> "Therefore gird up the loins of your mind, be sober, and rest your hope fully upon the grace that is to be brought to you at the revelation of Jesus Christ; as obedient children, not conforming yourselves to the former lusts, as in your ignorance; but as He who called you is holy, you also be holy in all your conduct, because it is written, 'Be holy, for I am holy'" (1 Peter 1:13–16).

The evil desires ("lusts") the apostle Peter referred to are summarized by the apostle John, "For all that is in the world—the lust of the flesh, the lust of the eyes, and the pride of life—is not of the Father but is of the world" (1 John 2:16).

There are at least two Biblical passages that illustrate John's sin-summary: the Fall of Man in Genesis 3 and the Temptation of Christ in Matthew 4. In both cases we are presented with pictures of temptations to sin, to reject God and to be unholy. In contrast to our Lord Jesus Christ who the apostle Paul called the "last Adam" (1 Corinthians 15:45) and who resisted the temptations offered by Satan, the first Adam fell into Satan's traps and took mankind with him. The Lord Jesus, being Holy, resisted Satan's offers of the lust of the flesh, the lust of the eyes, and the pride of life and by so doing, provided the human race with a means to avoid Satan's abyss and be saved from a life of those worldly lusts.

In Genesis 2:16-17, God commanded Adam that he could eat the fruit of every tree in the Garden of Eden except the fruit of the tree of the knowledge of good and evil. If he ate the fruit of that tree, he would know death. When tempted by the serpent, Adam and Eve chose to be disobedient of God and ate of the forbidden tree resulting in the Fall of Man (Genesis 3:6). The first Adam succumbed to three temptations offered to him by Satan: lust of the flesh (the fruit was food), lust of the eyes (it was pleasing to the eye), and if eaten, gave man the knowledge of good and evil (man, not God, would determine right from wrong—pride of life). J. Vernon McGee, *Thru the Bible Genesis 3, Vol I, 25.*

Satan offered the same three temptations to Jesus Christ.

The Holy Spirit led Jesus into the wilderness where He faced temptations of the devil. There He stayed and fasted for forty days and forty nights. Knowing that Jesus was hungry, Satan challenged Jesus to prove that He was the Son of God by commanding stones to become bread (Matthew 4:1–3). This was an appeal to the lust of the flesh. But being in the Father, Jesus said, "It is written, 'Man shall not live by bread alone, but by every word that proceeds from the mouth of God.'" (Matthew 4:4).

Tempting Jesus with the lust of the eyes, the devil then showed Jesus the world from a very high mountain. Satan offered Jesus the world if He would bow down before him and worship him (Matthew 4:8–9). Jesus responded, "Away with you, Satan! For it is written, 'You shall Worship the Lord your God, and Him only you shall serve'" (Matthew 4:10).

The devil then offered Jesus a third temptation by taking Him up to the highest point of the temple in Jerusalem. There he suggested to Jesus that if He was indeed the Son of God, He should throw Himself off the roof and the angels would save Him (Matthew 4:5–6). Jesus again resisted Satan's temptation that He could miraculously survive such a fall and in so doing, be prideful about Who He is. Jesus responded, "It is written again, 'You shall not tempt the Lord your God'" (Matthew 4:7).

Our Lord was as a rock in resisting the same temptations posed by Satan to Adam. As the rock of our faith, Jesus was not subject to shifting shadows as was Adam. Adam yielded to temptation; Jesus stood His ground. In each case, the Lord responded with "It is written" after which He proceeded to cite the Holy Scriptures of His Father in heaven as the basis to resist the temptations of life. Jesus offers us the same opportunity to resist the evil desires of the lust of the flesh, the lust of the eyes and the pride of life by knowing and following the Word of God.

Like our Father, the Lord wants us to be holy as He is. God said to Moses and Aaron, "I am the LORD your God. You shall therefore consecrate yourselves, and you shall be holy, for I am holy" (Leviticus 11:44). If knowing the Word of God is the key to being set apart to God—of being holy—we, as His children must do as He taught—to live our lives "by every word that proceeds from the mouth of God" (Matthew 4:4). Filling our minds daily with the Word of God and speaking the words to ourselves and others gives us the strength to resist the temptations of the evil one, renders us as good disciples of the Lord, and pleases Him.

It is written,

> "For in this we groan, earnestly desiring to be clothed with our habitation which is from heaven, if indeed, having been clothed, we shall not be found naked. For we who are in this tent groan, being burdened, not because we want to be unclothed, but further clothed that mortality may be swallowed up by life" (2 Corinthians 5:2–4).

Paul exhorted us that our mortal existence should be a life emulating Jesus Christ and not a life of darkness and uncertainty without Jesus, which is unto death.

Be holy—for holiness is what we yearn (groan) for. It is the Lord's will that we, His children, be consecrated (made holy) in His image as we progress in our earthly life toward the perfection of the glorious spiritual garment with which we shall be adorned in our heavenly dwelling.

HOLY SPIRIT

Jesus said, "But the Helper, the Holy Spirit, whom the Father will send in My name, He will teach you all things, and bring to your remembrance all things that I said to you" (John 14:26).

HONOR THE HOLY SPIRIT

If you are like me, your prayers have been primarily directed to the Father and His Son, Jesus Christ. However, it is important that we also acknowledge by prayer the role that the Holy Spirit plays in our lives, for the Holy Spirit has been accomplishing God's purposes in the creation from the beginning. "In the beginning God created the heavens and the earth...And the Spirit of God was hovering over the face of the waters" (Genesis 1:1–2). See also Numbers 11:17, 25 for other examples of the Holy Spirit at work in ancient times.

The Holy Spirit is the Person who Jesus Christ left in charge of our lives when He ascended to the right hand of the Father in heaven. When referring to the "Helper," the Holy Spirit, Jesus used the personal pronouns "He" and "Him" (John 14:16–17). As a Person, the Holy Spirit guides us, reproves us, rebukes us, convicts us, teaches us, intercedes for us in response to our prayers, leads us, communicates with us, comforts us, gives us words of Godly wisdom, inspires our faith, and is sometimes grieved by what He sees us do. His righteousness and justice produce good fruit within us, namely, "Love, joy, peace, longsuffering, kindness, goodness, faithfulness, gentleness, self-control" (Galatians 5:22). Where does the Holy Spirit do these things in us? He dwells within us (Romans 8:11).

The Holy Spirit is God. In Acts 5:3–4, Peter equates the Holy Spirit with God. The Holy Spirit is the Third Person of the Trinity. He shares one essence with the Father and the Son, yet He is distinct from the Father and the Son (Matthew 3:16–17).

Jesus Christ did everything by the power of the Holy Spirit (Acts 10:38; Luke 4:17–21). It is the Holy Spirit who anointed Jesus "To preach the gospel to the poor...to heal the brokenhearted...To proclaim liberty to the captives And recovery of sight to the blind, To set at liberty those who are oppressed" (Luke 4:18). It is He who brings glory to the Son "for He will take of what is Mine [Jesus] and declare it to you" (John 16:14). It is He who draws us to the Father and the Son. It is He who gives us new birth (regeneration): "That which is born of the flesh is flesh, and that which is born of the Spirit is spirit" (John 3:6). It is He who transforms our inner lives into the likeness of the Lord (sanctification): "But we all, with unveiled face, beholding as in a mirror the glory of the Lord, are being transformed into the same image from glory to glory, just as by the Spirit of the Lord" (2 Corinthians 3:18). It is He who convicts us of our sinful ways, corrects us with His righteousness, and reminds us of our accountability to God. He is the life in the body of Christ. Peter said to the crowd of his fellow Jews after which three thousand of them were baptized, "Repent and let every one of you be baptized in the name of Jesus Christ for the remission of sins; and you shall receive the gift of the Holy Spirit" (Acts 2:38).

But notwithstanding His station in the Godhead, the Holy Spirit is placed in a position of lesser importance in the minds of some. Many theologians have commented about the debate within the church of the importance of the Person and the work of the Holy Spirit. They point out that many Christians are not aware of the work the Holy Spirit does. At conversion (rebirth) we receive "the Spirit who is from God, that we might know the things that have been freely given to us by God" (1 Corinthians 2:12). Once we accept Christ, the Holy Spirit re-focuses our mind to heaven above (Romans 8:5–6). Once led by the mind of the Holy Spirit, we become the "sons of God" (Romans 8:14). "For you did not receive the spirit of bondage again to fear, but you received the Spirit of adoption by whom we cry out, 'Abba, Father.' The Spirit Himself bears witness with our spirit that we are children of God" (Romans 8:15–16).

By His Spirit, we are empowered, baptized, and filled with rivers of living water. We are given new life, everlasting life. It is so wondrous that God has revealed His secret wisdom of the Christ to us through His Holy Spirit and for that the Holy Spirit is to be honored!

HONESTY

Honesty is being truthful. Suppression of truth is dishonesty. Dishonesty is anathema to God. "Lying lips are an abomination to the LORD. But those who deal truthfully are His delight" (Proverbs12:22).

TRUTH AND HONESTY—THE MOST POWERFUL THINGS ON EARTH

Jesus Christ said to Thomas, His disciple, "I am the way, the truth, and the life. No one comes to the Father except through Me" (John 14:6). Pontius Pilate asked Jesus, "What is truth?" (John 18:38). Pilate posed this question cynically after Jesus had said, "For this cause I have come into the world, that I should bear witness to the truth. Everyone who is of the truth hears My voice" (John 18:37).

God is truth (Psalm 31:5). Jesus is truth (John 14:6). The Holy Spirit is truth (John 15:26). God's Word is truth and in His Word, the Lord testified to the truth. Truth is all that God is creating, has created and will continue to create for God's creation is perfect. Moses wrote, "Ascribe greatness to our God. He is the Rock, His work is perfect; For all His ways are justice, A God of truth and without injustice; Righteous and upright is He" (Deuteronomy 32:3–4).

If truth is God, if truth is God's Word, if truth is God's creation, if truth never changes, if truth is the most powerful thing on earth, it follows that it is essential that we honor God's Word and be honest and true in everything we do and in how we live our lives. Why? To do otherwise is to defy our Creator. Suppression of truth or dishonesty is anathema to God. "These six things the LORD hates, Yes, seven are an abomination to Him" (Proverbs 6:16). Of those seven things listed in the Bible, two are foremost, "A lying tongue [and] A false witness who speaks lies" (Proverbs 6:17, 19).

"Lying lips are an abomination to the LORD" (Proverbs 12:22). By lying, a liar rejects God and chooses the evil one. The devil is the father of lies "because there is no truth in him. When he speaks a lie, he speaks from his own resources, for he is a liar and the father of it" (John 8:44). "He who speaks truth declares righteousness, But a false witness, deceit" (Proverbs 12:17).

The ninth commandment of God is, "You shall not bear false witness against your neighbor" (Exodus 20:16). Indeed, false witness is lying, plain and simple. Our Lord wants us to obey His Word, to be honest, and not bear false witness. "He who says, 'I know Him,' and does not keep His commandments, is a liar, and the truth is not in him. But whoever keeps His word, truly the love of God is perfected in him" (1 John 2:4–5).

"The Law was given through Moses, but grace and truth came through Jesus Christ" (John 1:17). Our Lord wants us, His children, to speak and live the truth. But how do we know what the truth is when we speak and live the truth? By the Holy Spirit who Jesus Christ left with us and within our hearts when He first ascended to heaven to be with the Father (Acts 2:2–4). "And it is the Spirit who bears witness, because the Spirit is truth" (1 John 5:6). The Spirit is the Spirit of truth who testifies about Jesus Who is the truth (John 15:26).

My conscience, enlightened by the Holy Spirit within me, bears me witness (Romans 9:1). If we lie, we cannot remember what we said. But when we speak the truth, the truth is always the same for the truth is consistent, never changing, just as the creations of the Lord are consistent and never changing. "When He, the Spirit of truth, has come, He will guide you into all truth; for He will not speak on his own authority, but whatever He hears He will speak; and He will tell you things to come" (John 16:13). We can count on the sun rising every day just as we can count on the Holy Spirit showing us truth in everything we say or do. He is never changing. His shadows do not shift like ours. "Jesus Christ is the same yesterday, today, and forever" (Hebrews 13:8).

Be truthful in everything for that is what the Word of God tells us to do: "These are the things you shall do: Speak each man the truth to his neighbor; Give judgment in your gates for truth, justice, and peace...And do not love a false oath" (Zechariah 8:16-17). In doing these things, we can pray as King Hezekiah prayed, "Remember now, O LORD, I pray, how I have walked before You in truth and with a loyal heart, and have done what was good in Your sight" (2 Kings 20:3). If we are able to pray as King Hezekiah prayed, the love of the God of truth, Jesus Christ "shall cover you with His feathers, And under His wings you shall take refuge; His truth shall be your shield and buckler" (Psalm 91:4).

B. NEIL SHAW

HONOR

"Who can find a virtuous wife? For her worth is far above rubies...Strength and honor are her clothing...a woman who fears the LORD, she shall be praised" (Proverbs 31:10, 25, 30).

THE BOOK OF ESTHER: A STORY OF A WOMAN OF HONOR

King Xerxes of Persia was a man of great pride. He was a man to be defied only under penalty of death and yet, the two women who served as his queens both stood up to him and lived. The first, Queen Vashti, refused to be paraded before the king's court as a beautiful trophy of the prideful king. The consequence of her defiance was banishment.

After King Xerxes had banished Queen Vashti and his anger had subsided, pride prevented him from rescinding his decree of banishment. His attendants proposed that a search be made for a successor to Vashti (Esther 2:2). Many girls were brought to the king's palace including Esther. The king loved Esther more than any other women for she was very beautiful, filled with grace and favor in the sight of the king. "So he set the royal crown upon her head and made her queen instead of Vashti" (Esther 2:17).

Esther's cousin, Mordecai, a Jewish man who'd raised Esther since she was orphaned at a young age, stayed nearby in the city gate to find out what was happening to her in the king's palace. One day, Haman, one of the king's officials was being honored and the royal officials were commanded by the king to kneel down and pay homage to Haman as he passed through the city gate. But Mordecai, honoring the third commandment of the Lord, refused to kneel down or pay homage to Haman (Esther 3:1, 2). "When Haman saw that Mordecai did not bow or pay him homage, Haman was filled with wrath" (Esther 3:5). Haman, an evil man, began looking for a way to destroy Mordecai and all of the Jews throughout the kingdom. He falsely reported to King Xerxes that "certain people" in the kingdom did not obey the king's laws and that they should be destroyed (Esther 3:8). He purposely didn't tell the king that it was the Jewish people of Persia that he sought to kill. Unaware that he was issuing a death decree for all of the Jewish people in his kingdom (including his new queen Esther), the king authorized Haman to annihilate the alleged rebellious people—young and old, women and children—on a single day in the month of Adar and to plunder their goods. Esther 3:8, 13. Hearing of the decree, Mordecai and all the Jews went into great mourning "with fasting, weeping, and wailing; and many lay in sackcloth and ashes" (Esther 4:3).

Esther learned about Mordecai's distress, but didn't know why he was distressed. She sent her servant Hathach to find out the reason for his distress. Mordecai told Hathach about Haman's edict and asked Hathach to urge Esther to beg the king for mercy and "plead before him for her people" (Esther 4:8).

King Xerxes had established a law that if any man or woman approached the king in the inner court without being summoned, he or she was to be put to death (Esther 4:11). Esther told Mordecai about this law, but he exhorted Esther to speak to the king about Haman's evil edict for if she didn't, all of the Jews, including Esther, would perish. Esther requested Mordecai to gather all of the Jews in Susa, the capital city, and to fast and pray to God in intercessory prayer for her. After much fasting and prayer, Esther placed her fate completely in the hands of the Lord. She told Mordecai, "I will go to the king, which is against the law; and if I perish, I perish!" (Esther 4:16).

Thereafter, Esther held a banquet for the king. During the banquet and without being summoned, she approached the king risking a decree of death. She pleaded with him to spare her and the lives of her people. She told the king that the alleged "rebellious people" unjustly condemned by Haman were the Jewish people (of which she was one). The king was outraged by the deceit of his "trusted minister" Haman and ordered that Haman be hanged on the very gallows Haman had built to punish Mordecai. Esther's courage saved the day!

The story of Esther teaches among other things that the Lord gives us all we need in life. In Esther's case, He gave her the strength and honor to do that which needed to be done for her people. The Book of Proverbs sums up Esther's brave and honorable deed, "Who can find a virtuous wife? For her worth is far above rubies...Strength and honor are her clothing...a woman who fears the LORD, she shall be praised. Give her of the fruit of her hands, And let her own works praise her in the gates" (Proverbs 31:10, 25, 30–31).

HOPE

"Let Your mercy, O LORD, be upon us, just as we hope in You" (Psalm 33:22).

THE HOPE CHEST

I have fond memories of a cherished family heirloom: my mother's hope chest. I haven't heard much about hope chests these days, but back in the 1940's and 50's, hope chests were common. I recall how important that cedar chest was to my mother since it was handed down to her by her mother when she married my father. It had been in the family for many years.

Why was it called a "hope chest?" The things placed in it by a prospective bride were in many cases heirlooms from prior generations symbolic of a tradition of a life of happiness thus giving to the person having such family heirlooms a feeling of confidence, optimism and hope.

The contents of my mother's hope chest consisted of special things once owned by her mother and her mother's mother and perhaps beyond: fine linen, her wedding dress, crocheted table cloths, a feather quilt, lace doilies, embroidered handkerchiefs, an old doll, a family Bible, and many other items that today would be antiques. I'm not sure what became of that treasured hope chest. It has long since been gone. But one of the things in my mother's hope chest that has endured is the family Bible which sits on my bookshelf. It's no coincidence that the family Bible has endured while all the other possessions, including her hope chest, have since disappeared from view. The family Bible was, by tradition, given to me as the male child.

The hope chest is a place in which valued life possessions are stored in anticipation of earthly marriage. On the other hand, the Bible is a heavenly place in which great hope is recorded for eternity in anticipation of another wedding. Just as women in days of old stored their valued possessions in a hope chest in anticipation of a life of love and security with the man of their dreams, we, the Lord's bride, store up the treasured promise of God, not in hope chests, but in our hearts. His promise gives us great hope. What is that promise of God? Jesus said, "Behold, I am coming quickly! Blessed is he who keeps the words of the prophecy of this book" (Revelation 22:7). "Surely, I am coming quickly" (Revelation 22:20).

In the Book of the Revelation of Jesus Christ, the apostle John recounts the roar of the great multitude in heaven shouting for joy at the fulfillment of the Lord's promise,

> "And I heard, as it were, the voice of a great multitude, as the sound of many waters and as the sound of mighty thunderings, saying, 'Alleluia! For the Lord God Omnipotent reigns! Let us be glad and rejoice and give Him glory, for the marriage of the Lamb has come, and His wife has made herself ready.' And to her it was granted to be arrayed in fine linen, clean and bright, for the fine linen is the righteous acts of the saints" (Revelation 19:6–8).

Who is the bride that John speaks of? It is we who believe in Jesus Christ as our Lord and Savior, the body of Christ—the Church.

John saw what eternal hope fulfilled looks like,

> "Then I, John, saw the holy city, New Jerusalem, coming down out of heaven from God, prepared as a bride adorned for her husband. And I heard a loud voice from heaven saying, 'Behold, the tabernacle of God is with men, and He will dwell with them, and they shall be His people. God Himself will be with them and be their God. And God will wipe away every tear from their eyes; there shall be no more death, nor sorrow, nor crying. There shall be no more pain, for the former things have passed away.'" (Revelation 21:2–4).

Jesus Christ is our hope of heaven. His Word given to us as our Bridegroom assures us of the hope of salvation: "Let us who are of the day be sober, putting on the breastplate of faith and love, and as a helmet the hope of salvation" (1 Thessalonians 5:8). Like brides of old, we look forward with excited anticipation, not of earthly things which pass through our hands like hope chests, but of the things eternal that He provides to us: the hope of His mercy (Psalm 33:18), the hope of His truth (Isaiah 38:18), the hope of His righteousness (Galatians 5:5), the hope of His love that is stored up for us in heaven (Colossians 1:5), and the hope of His promise of eternal life (Titus 1:2), for He is called "the hope of glory" (Colossians 1:27).

My mother's hope chest has disappeared from view just as all things of earth will one day pass away (Revelation 21:1), but the Word of God endures as a heavenly hope chest providing eternal assurance of love and security—forever.

OUR HOPE IS IN HIS UNFAILING LOVE

The Bible is a Book of Hope. Psalm 33 is a prayer of hope in the Book of Hope to the God of Hope, Jesus Christ. "Behold the eye of the LORD is on those who fear Him, On those who hope in His mercy" (Psalm 33:18).

These words recently became very meaningful to me. My doctor used the word "serious" twice while examining the degenerating disks in my cervical (upper) spine. Many years ago, I was involved in an automobile accident—I was rear-ended. At that time, I dealt with my neck injuries as uneventful and routine—some therapy, a temporary neck brace and healing—or so I thought. It seems, however, that the Lord had something else in mind for me. As I have aged, arthritis set in and the disks in my neck have deteriorated. Now, they've ruptured which means they bulge between the vertebrae in my neck and out into the spinal cord which the vertebrae surround and protect. Two of the disks have actually bruised the cord. My doctor says that if left untreated, a significant jarring could leave me paralyzed! What? "Yes," he replied, "paralyzed." "Well, doctor," I said, "what kind of treatment are you talking about?" He replied, "Surgery." What? I said, "Well what about exercises or medication?" "No," he said, "exercise won't eliminate the problem. You have four disks that are herniated involving five vertebrae. This means that all four disks have to be removed and the five vertebrae fused with metal clamps." I asked, "How do you do this?" He replied, "We go in through the front of the neck since going through the back requires more cutting of tissue and bone. It is somewhat risky." Risky? What an understatement!

I free-associated as my mind raced: Surgery? Back surgery! He's talking about going through the front of my neck to get to my back! That's my neck and back he's talking about! What if the knife slips such as occurred to a friend of mine many years ago. He's spent his life in a wheelchair! What if the operation doesn't work? What if? What if? What if!!

In my morning devotions the next day, I was reading Psalms and I read, "Why are you cast down, O my soul? And why are you disquieted within me? Hope in God, for I shall yet praise Him For the help of His countenance" (Psalm 42:5). I can always count on the Bible to tell me where I am in life. Then as I continued to read my Bible "a still small voice" (1 Kings 19:12) brought the words of the God of Hope from the Book of Hope in focus and quieted me down, "Come to Me, all you who labor and are heavy laden, and I will give you rest. Take My yoke upon you and learn from Me, for I am gentle and lowly in heart, and you will find rest for your souls. For My yoke is easy and My burden is light" (Matthew 11:28–30). "Hey," I thought, "That's Jesus talking to me!"

Then reading on, the still small voice continued, "Trust in the LORD with all your heart, And lean not on your own understanding; in all your ways acknowledge Him, and he shall direct your paths" (Proverbs 3:5–6). "WO!" I thought. "That's it! Not my understanding, Lord, but yours!" And He continued with more, "Rejoice always, pray without ceasing, in everything give thanks; for this is the will of God in Christ Jesus for you" (1Thessalonians 5:16–18). I thought, "That's it, Lord! Prayer and more prayer! Grace! Mercy! They're all Yours to give—they're Your magic words of hope, of hope for me Jesus, a helpless sinner. In my heart, I know Lord that You are talking to me!"

The Lord's apostle Paul faced much greater trials than a mere back ache. Paul's problems also give me great perspective on my health issues. In his second letter to the believers at Corinth, he wrote about his sufferings,

> "I speak as a fool—I am more: in labors more abundant, in stripes above measure, in prisons more frequently, in deaths often. From the Jews five times I received forty stripes minus one. Three times I was beaten with rods; once I was stoned; three times I was shipwrecked; a night and a day I have been in the deep" (2 Corinthians 11:23–25).

Paul's sufferings were beyond reason (2 Corinthians 11:26–27).

Yet, through all of Paul's sufferings, the Lord's right hand was upon his shoulder. The Lord saw him through. The Lord assured him that he wouldn't give him more than he could handle. He comforted Paul with these holy words, "My grace is sufficient for you, for My strength is made perfect in weakness" (2 Corinthians 12:9). Paul looked solely to Jesus Christ to get him through. He explained to his brethren, "Therefore I take pleasure in infirmities, in reproaches, in needs, in persecutions, in distresses, for Christ's sake. For when I am weak, then I am strong" (2 Corinthians 12:10).

It may have been Paul who wrote at that time to the Hebrews, "Now faith is the substance of things hoped for, the evidence of things not seen" (Hebrews 11:1). Paul had great faith and hope in our Lord and Savior Jesus Christ to get him through!

After reading these things, my mind continued to stir: "So what am I to do Lord? Am I to do this surgery thing my doctor is recommending? Is this the right doctor for me whose hand will do the cutting? Please God," I prayed, "give me wisdom about this. Give me clarity as to what to do. Give me peace, please. Take my fears and concerns away." And that still small voice answered, "If any of you lacks wisdom, let him ask of God, who gives to all liberally and without reproach, and it will be given to him" (James 1:5). In other words, He will answer all my prayers. All I need to do is pray without ceasing. All I need to do is, "In all your ways acknowledge Him, and He shall direct your paths" (Proverbs 3:6). All I need to do is to cast "all your care upon Him, for He cares for you" (1 Peter 5:7). For Jesus is my God of Hope. With faith and hope in our Lord Jesus Christ, I need not have any fear, anxiety, or worry about a mere back problem. His unfailing love will rest on me and see me through.

I have since experienced a peace about this that passes my ability to understand. I know in my heart that everything will be fine.* He's given me great peace and confidence, for He is with me and will see me through.

"Let your mercy, O LORD, be upon us, Just as we hope in You" (Psalm 33:22).

---

* Author's note: As the surgeons wheeled me into the operating room, I shouted, "Hallelujah, praise the Lord." As I came out of the anesthesia after a skillful (and successful) 4 1/2 hour operation by the surgeons, my wife told me that in my post-op stupor I kept exclaiming "Hallelujah!" Praise the Lord for He is with us indeed!

INTEGRITY

A person with integrity has a clear conscience, clean hands, is upright in all things, is blameless, righteous, unwavering in obeying God, patient, blesses his or her children, speaks truth and lives honorably in every way.

THE IMPORTANCE OF BEING HONEST: HOW THE BIBLE DEFINES INTEGRITY

The Bible is a wonderful resource for the issues of how we should live our lives! Some even refer to the Bible as the manual of life provided to us by God—a how to do life book. The Bible tells us what we need to do in life in order to receive God's blessings and be His worthy children.

One of the life subjects defined by the Bible is *integrity*. What is integrity? How can we achieve it? Why does God want us to be people of integrity? The Bible says that a person with integrity has a clear conscience, clean hands, is upright, blameless, righteous, unwavering in obeying God, patient, blesses his or her children, speaks truth, and lives honorably in every way. God wants us to be persons of integrity so that others who do not believe "may, by your good works which they observe, glorify God in the day of visitation" (1 Peter 2:12).

In Genesis 20:1–6, the Bible describes Abraham's lack of integrity earlier in his life. In their journey from the Ur of Chaldes, Abraham and Sarah, his wife, traveled to Gerar in what is now called the *Sinai*. Abimilech was the king of Gerar. Sarah was an attractive woman. Fearing that Abimilech would kill him and take Sarah for his harem, Abraham lied and said that Sarah was his sister. Abimilech ordered that Sarah be taken into his courts. In a dream, the Lord spoke to Abimilech and told him that he was a dead man because he'd taken another man's wife. Abimilech pleaded with God not to destroy his righteous nation because he'd received Sarah into his courts relying on the untruthful words of Abraham that Sarah was his sister. In response, God acknowledged that Abimilech "did this in the integrity of [his] heart" (Genesis 20:6).

This passage doesn't speak kindly of Abraham's integrity, but it gives us encouragement. If Abraham stumbled earlier in his life and later became the father of our faith, we can have great hope that if we stumble, we can seek the Lord's help like Abraham and God will change our ways. It's never too late to change from our disingenuous ways. Look at Abraham,

> "The LORD appeared to Abram and said to him, 'I am Almighty God; walk before Me and be blameless... As for Me, behold, My covenant is with you, and you shall be a father of many nations...I will make you exceedingly fruitful; and I will make nations of you, and kings shall come from you...I will establish My covenant between Me and you and your descendants after you in their generations, for an everlasting covenant, to be God to you and your descendants after you'" (Genesis 17:1, 4, 6–7).

Notwithstanding his dishonesty with King Abimilech, Abraham (as he was then renamed by God) became the father of many nations.

Solomon was a man who like his father David, walked before God "in integrity of heart and in uprightness" (1 Kings 9:4). A person is upright if he or she keeps commitments made to others. God made a covenant with the Jewish people that if they followed His decrees and were careful to obey His commands, He would walk among them and be their God, and they would be His people (Leviticus 26:12). The Lord re-emphasizes to Solomon the importance of obedience to His covenant in order to experience blessings rather than curses, "Now if you walk before Me as your father David walked, in integrity of heart and in uprightness, to do according to all that I have commanded you, and if you keep My statutes and My judgments, then I will establish the throne of your kingdom over Israel forever" (1 Kings 9:4–5). In God's eyes, Solomon was a man of integrity; he walked in uprightness. God fulfilled His promise to Solomon by sending His Son, Jesus Christ, to rule and reign forever.

Job was another man of integrity. The Lord described him as "a blameless and upright man, one who fears God and shuns evil" (Job 1:8). Job maintained his integrity even though God allowed Satan to test Job's faith in God by killing his ten children and taking from him all that he owned. Notwithstanding the disaster inflicted upon him and his family, Job was unwavering in his belief that he had not sinned against the Lord. His wife, grieving the loss of their children, cursed him for his steadfastness. She cried to him in her deep grief, "Do you still hold fast to your integrity? Curse God and die!" (Job 2:9). Later, he cried out to his "friend" Bildad the Shuhite, "Till I die I will not put away my integrity from me. My righteousness I hold fast, and will not let it go" (Job 27:5–6). In the end, God acknowledged Job's honesty and steadfast faith by blessing the latter days of his life "more than his beginning" (Job 42:12).

David was a man of integrity. He wasn't afraid of man, but he feared God. He wrote, "Judge me, O LORD, according to my righteousness, And according to my integrity within me" (Psalm 7:8). David was a man who placed his hope in the Lord. He prayed that God would enable him to live a life of unmarred moral rectitude (Psalm 25:8). He wrote, "Vindicate me, O LORD, for I have walked in my integrity. I have also trusted in the LORD; I shall not slip" (Psalm 26:1). He relished God's presence in his life, "As for me, You uphold me in my integrity" (Psalm 41:12). But even David stumbled when he saw Bathsheba (2 Samuel 11:2–3). He later regretted that transgression and repented when he wrote in his psalm of contrition, "Have mercy upon me, O God, According to your lovingkindness... Blot out my transgressions. Wash me thoroughly from my iniquity, And cleanse me from my sin" (Psalm 51:1–2). Through His grace, the Lord turned David's weakness to strength and restored him as a man of integrity (Hebrews 11:32–34). God's forgiveness and grace are unending.

A person of integrity is patient. He or she waits for God's will to become manifest in his or her life. Daniel, prominent and of authority in Nebuchadnezzar's kingdom, was removed from power when Nebuchadnezzar died in B.C. 562. Twenty-three years later in B.C. 539, Daniel was called upon by King Belshazzar to interpret the writing on the wall by the fingers of a human hand (Daniel 5:13–16). He did so with Godly guidance. Thereafter, Daniel was restored by God to a position of prominence. Being a man of integrity, he did what we too must do: he remained patient but ready to serve when called upon to do so in God's time.

A person of integrity blesses his or her children by leading a life of unwavering righteousness. "The righteous man walks in his integrity; His children are blessed after him" (Proverbs 20:7). What could be more fulfilling than for a parent to see his or her child live a life of integrity in the pattern established by the Lord?

Finally, the Word of the Lord teaches us that a person of integrity is honest and speaks the truth. "The entirety of Your word is truth," said the psalmist regarding the Lord in Psalm 119:160. We are to "draw near with a true heart in full assurance of faith, having our hearts sprinkled from an evil conscience...for He who promised is faithful" (Hebrews 10:22–23). We are "to live honorably" in every way (Hebrews 13:18).

The Lord is eager to forgive us of our sinful ways. For His own sake, the Lord blots out our transgressions and remembers our sins no more (Isaiah 43:25). He went to the Cross for that purpose. He wants us to lean not on our own understanding, but to trust in Him that what He teaches us is true. He wants us to walk uprightly, be righteous, and speak the truth so that He is glorified through our lives (Psalm 15:2–5).

The Lord wants all of us to be people of integrity.

ISRAEL

Israel is God's special place. It is where His only Begotten Son, Jesus Christ, will ultimately return and rule and reign: "A Star shall come out of Jacob; a Scepter shall rise out of Israel" (Numbers 24:17).

EZEKIEL'S PROPHESY ABOUT THE MOUNTAINS OF ISRAEL

The nations of the world have great difficulty sharing this planet, particularly in the Middle East. Iran, a part of the ancient Assyrian Empire, is flexing its muscles. Iran's president continually rants that he intends to "wipe Israel off the map!" "They have said, 'Come, and let us cut them off from being a nation, That the name of Israel may be remembered no more.'" (Psalm 83:4).

Why is Iran so obsessed with hatred against Israel, a country that is approximately one percent of the size of Iran? Could it be because Israel is the place to which Jesus Christ will return and Satan is doing all he can to prevent that from occurring?

Israel's vitriolic enemy Iran is gaining influence in the Middle East. Syria, a "client regime" of Iran was re-arming Iran's surrogate in Lebanon, Hezbollah, at an alarming pace. Hamas, a puppet regime of Iran in Gaza, periodically fires rockets at Jewish school buses in Israel without even a whisper of protest from the rest of the world. Egypt, a former enemy of Iran, is sending an ambassador to Tehran.

Will Israel be "wiped out" as Iran threatens? There may be wars involving Israel, however, I do not believe that Israel will be wiped out by Iran. Perhaps the opposite may occur.

Why do I believe this?

> "Thus says the LORD God: 'Surely I have spoken in My burning jealousy against the rest of the nations and against all Edom, who gave My land to themselves as a possession, with wholehearted joy and spiteful minds, in order to plunder its open country. Therefore prophesy concerning the land of Israel, and say to the mountains, the hills, the rivers, and the valleys...I have raised My hand in an oath that surely the nations that are around you shall bear their own shame. But you, O mountains of Israel, you shall shoot forth your

branches and yield your fruit to My people Israel, for they are about to come. For indeed I am for you, and I will turn to you, and you shall be tilled and sown. I will multiply men upon you, all the house of Israel, all of it; and the cities shall be inhabited and the ruins rebuilt...I will make you inhabited as in former times, and do better for you than at your beginnings. Then you shall know that I am the LORD. Yes, I will cause men to walk on you, My people Israel; they shall take possession of you, and you shall be their inheritance; *no more shall you bereave them of children*" (Ezekiel 36:5–12) (my emphasis added).

In 1948, the Lord partially fulfilled this prophesy and restored the people of Israel to their native land. The Lord says unequivocally that He will preserve His Holy Land for all of His people and *never again* will He deprive His children of it. Ezekiel prophesies in chapters 38 and 39 that the invaders including Persia (Iran) will be destroyed.

No, my brethren, Israel will not be wiped out! The mountains of Israel are filled with the "horses and chariots of fire" of God (2 Kings 6:17) (including anti-missile Iron Domes) that will shield it from the wrathful scorn of the surrounding nations, particularly Iran. Bring them on Lord that all may know You are the Lord of the universe! Amen.

JOY

"For the joy of the LORD is your strength" (Nehemiah 8:10).

THE JOY OF A FATHER

Two of the most joyful days in my life were the days on which my children were born. I can remember those days as vividly as yesterday, even down to the minute they were born. Even more joyful, however, were the days that I saw my children born again: the days in which they saw and heard Jesus Christ as their Savior and knew that their names were written by Him in the book of life in heaven. To me as their father, my children are unique: they have a very special place in my heart. My love for them as a father is limitless no matter what they do.

It is with this joy in my heart for my own children that I get just a glimpse of the endless joy and blessings our Father in heaven experiences knowing that His children see the things that they see and hear the things that they hear (Luke 10:23–24). The words of Jesus express my desire as a father that my children experience joy in their lives as they walk deeper with Him, "These things I have spoken to you, that My joy may remain in you, and that your joy may be full." (John 15:11).

The context in which Jesus said these things as a Father is recounted in Luke 10 and 11. In Luke Chapter 10, Jesus appointed seventy-two disciples and sent them out to spread the Good News. They went out in two's (Luke 10:1).Their assignment was to travel light (take no purse or bag or sandals), to heal the sick, and to tell the people about Jesus and that He would be coming. When the seventy-two returned, they "returned with joy saying, 'Lord, even the demons are subject to us in Your name.'" (Luke 10:17). But knowing what the pride of life would do to them, Jesus admonished them citing the pride by which Satan fell "like lightening from heaven" (Luke 10:18). Even though He'd given them "authority to trample on serpents and scorpions, and over all the power of the enemy," they were not to rejoice that the spirits submitted to them, but to rejoice that "your names are written in heaven," in the book of life (Luke 10:19–20).

Our Father gets indescribable joy, not in what we do for Him, but in knowing that we see and hear Him: "In that hour Jesus rejoiced in the Spirit and said, 'I thank you, Father, Lord of heaven and earth, that You have hidden these things from the wise and prudent, and revealed them to babes'" (Luke 10:21).

Our Father blesses us with His grace. He is even more blessed in knowing that we receive His grace seeing His love and hearing His Word. The religious leaders of the time, the Pharisees and the teachers of the Law, could not see or hear Him; but the Lord's children could.

The greatest gift God can give us is His love. As a Father, He gives us His love, His peace, His comfort, His food, His shelter and best of all, His grace. If we ask Him for a fish, He doesn't give us a snake; He gives us a fish! If we ask him for an egg, He doesn't give us a scorpion; we get an egg! (Luke 11:11–12). As parents who love our children, we know how to give good gifts to our children. Even greater than this, our Father in heaven gives to us, His children, His Holy Spirit! (Luke 11:13). All we need to do as His children is ask Him and He will give us His greatest gift, heavenly grace through His Holy Spirit, for He is our Father and we are His children. It is His greatest joy!

KINDNESS

"That I am the LORD, exercising lovingkindness, judgment, and righteousness in the earth, For in these I delight" (Jeremiah 9:24).

A PICTURE OF KINDNESS

In our daily morning devotions, it is very important to read and study the entire Bible, for the Scriptures, "The Old Testament," are pictures of the teachings of Jesus Christ as written in The New Testament. To the two men on the road to Emmaus "beginning at Moses and all the Prophets, He expounded to them in all the Scriptures the things concerning Himself" (Luke 24:27). The Bible is all about Jesus—all of it.

The story of Joseph in Genesis is an example of the principle that The Old Testament is a picture of the teachings of Jesus Christ as written in The New Testament. Joseph is a picture of Jesus.

Joseph was one of the twelve sons of Jacob (renamed by God as "Israel"). "Now Israel loved Joseph more than all his children, because he was the son of his old age...when his brothers saw that their father loved him more than all his brothers, they hated him and could not speak peaceably to him" (Genesis 37:3–4). Jesus "came to His own, and His own did not receive Him" (John 1:11). Joseph's brothers were hostile to him and not only rejected him, but sold him into slavery. Jesus' brethren were hostile to Him and caused Him to be crucified by the Romans.

Israel sent Joseph to see if all was well with his brothers who were at Shechem tending the flock, but his brothers, being jealous of Joseph "conspired against him to kill him" (Genesis 37:14, 18). When Joseph arrived at Shechem, his brothers "stripped [him] of his tunic, the tunic of many colors that was on him" (the one given to him by his father) "and cast him into a pit" (Genesis 37:23–24). Thereafter they sold him to slave traders "for twenty shekels of silver" (Genesis 37:28). In like manner, Judas Iscariot, one of the twelve disciples, betrayed Jesus to the Jewish authorities in exchange for a payment of "thirty pieces of silver" (Matthew 26:14–16). As a result of Judas' betrayal, Jesus was arrested and while in the custody of Roman soldiers "they stripped him and put a scarlet robe on Him" (Matthew 27:28). The cruel treatment of Joseph by his brothers is a picture of what was done to Jesus by the leaders of Israel, His brethren, as written in The New Testament.

The slavers sold Joseph to Potiphar, the Egyptian captain of the guard. Joseph initially suffered in Egypt, but the Lord showed him kindness, granted him favor and gave him success in all that he did. For example, Pharaoh had dreams which troubled him, but no one could interpret the king's dreams, that is, no one but Joseph. Giving glory to God the Father, Joseph used his God-given gift and interpreted Pharaoh's dreams (Genesis 41:16–28). Joseph explained that Pharaoh's dreams foretold of great abundance in the land for seven years followed by seven years of famine (Genesis 41:29–30). He advised Pharaoh to store up food for seven years. Pharaoh was delighted with Joseph's insight and rewarded him by making him second in command over the whole land.

Joseph was thirty years old when he entered the service of Pharaoh (Genesis 41:46). Jesus was thirty years old when He began His ministry (Luke 3:23). Joseph's fame spread throughout the land of Egypt. At the start of His ministry, news about Jesus spread throughout Galilee. "And He taught in their synagogues, being glorified by all" (Luke 4:14–15).

As foretold by Joseph, after seven years of plenty, a famine engulfed all the lands except Egypt where "there was bread" (Genesis 41:54). During the famine, Joseph's brothers came to Egypt to buy food. When they appeared before him, Joseph's brothers did not recognize him but when Joseph saw his brothers, he wept over them—twice (Genesis 42:24; 43:30). Like Joseph's brothers, many of Jesus' brethren did not acknowledge who He was nor did they believe in Him as the Messiah (John 7:5). Like Joseph, "Jesus wept" over His people, on two occasions (Luke 19:41; John 11:35).

Instead of seeking revenge for the evil that his brothers had done to him, Joseph bestowed great kindness upon them. Jesus bestowed great kindness upon His people even though many didn't believe in Him. The Bible describes thirty-five miracles which Jesus performed upon His people. Jesus' apostle Paul wrote about the kindness of our Lord, kindness that was illustrated by the story of Joseph, "See that no one renders evil for evil to anyone, but always pursue what is good both for yourselves and for all" (1 Thessalonians 5:15).

Joseph forgave his brothers for all they'd done to him. He entreated them not to feel guilty for their heinous actions toward him. He said to them that God sent him ahead to preserve a remnant on the earth and to save their lives "by a great deliverance" (Genesis 45:7). Jesus said on His Cross, "Father, forgive them, for they do not know what they do" (Luke 23:34). God sent His Son Jesus Christ to save the world. "Whoever believes in Him should not perish but have everlasting life" (John 3:16).

God uses the Scriptures (The Old Testament) to enable us to see a vivid picture of the loving kindness of our Lord and Savior Jesus Christ as written in The New Testament. One of those pictures, the story of Joseph, shows that God is delighted when we are kind to others, "That I am the LORD, exercising lovingkindness, judgment, and righteousness in the earth, For in these I delight" (Jeremiah 9:24).

His kindnesses "are new every morning; Great is Your faithfulness!" (Lamentations 3:23).

KINGDOM

Jesus Christ said, "Repent, for the kingdom of heaven is at hand" (Matthew 4:17).

IMAGINE A PERFECT WORLD

God created the heavens and the earth in six days and He saw that it was good (Genesis 1). If it was good to God, it was perfection because God is perfect. Just imagine what a perfect place the world was when God created it!

The book of Genesis paints a picture of a beautiful plush garden "eastward in Eden" (Genesis 2:8), a rain forest where God placed His creations, man and woman. Picture it: The days are warm and the nights are cool with gentle breezes. Food is abundant. Pure cool water is plentiful. Disease is non-existent. Peace and tranquility prevail and all of creation lives in harmony. There is an eternal bond of truth and integrity between the people, for the Lord is with them and His Spirit is upon them. He is their God and they are His people. Truth, righteousness and justice are the standards by which they live. There is no war, just peace; no crime, just honesty; no sin and no death, just love. The Prophet Isaiah describes how it will be on the day of the Lord and it was presumably that way in the beginning when God created it, "The wolf also shall dwell with the lamb, The leopard shall lie down with the young goat, The calf and the young lion and the fatling together; And a little child shall lead them" (Isaiah 11:6). It was paradise!

But then Genesis 3 describes the fall of man where man abused the free will given to him by God. In his pride, man committed what is called "original sin." In defiance of the Father, man (Adam) declared himself free from God. Now, instead of paradise, all that was in the world were "the lust of the flesh, the lust of the eyes, and the pride of life," things not of the Father, but of the flesh (1 John 2:16). What was left after the fall of the first worldly person was a life filled with fleshly lust, idol worship, and pride. By the time of the judges of Israel, things got so bad that "everyone did what was right in his own eyes" (Judges 21:25).

Today's world is a consequence of man's rebellion against God. Truth is no longer determined by what corresponds to reality, that is, the revelation of God to His creation, or the resurrection of His Son, Jesus Christ, but by man's power of reason and by empiricism, that is, the senses of man. In the worldview of many, what they cannot see, hear, touch, smell, taste, or test scientifically, does not exist and is untrue. That rules out God! Now, war, not peace is the norm; famine and pestilence the rule; and greed, crime, and dishonesty a way of life. Righteousness and truth is what is so in one's own mind. Commitment and accountability are passé. The attitude is, "What is good for me is good for the world." To the unbeliever in God, the world is a dark and depressing place, without hope.

When viewing these two worldviews, that is, the "Garden view" and the "unbeliever's view," it is apparent that the main difference between them is *the presence or absence of God*. As the prophet Jeremiah recorded the words of God spoken to him, man lost his way "Because you have forgotten Me and trusted in falsehood" (Jeremiah 13:25). Today, the unbelieving person is as defiant of God as Adam was at the time of the fall of man of Genesis 3. As time passes, more and more of mankind seeks to eliminate God from their world. The postmodern secularists have even declared God dead!

In our contemporary world where disbelief in God is in vogue, it is easy for believers to become discouraged. It almost seems as if wickedness is winning. The apostle Paul was a prophet when he wrote in his letter to Timothy how perilous the world would be in the last days. When I read this prophetic letter, I see our culture described to a tee, "For men will be lovers of themselves, lovers of money, boasters, proud, blasphemers, disobedient to parents, unthankful, unholy, unloving, unforgiving, slanderers, without self-control, brutal despisers of good, traitors, headstrong, haughty, lovers of pleasure rather than lovers of God" (2 Timothy 3:2–4). Using Paul's description of culture as a measure, we indeed are in the last days of this world as we know it!

But Christian believers—do not lose sight of the Lord's plan. The promise of the perfect world of God's kingdom on earth is assured, "The LORD will guide you continually, And satisfy your soul in drought,

And strengthen your bones; You shall be like a watered garden, And like a spring of water, whose waters do not fail" (Isaiah 58:11).

Jesus Christ comforted His disciples about the troubled world,

> "Let not your heart be troubled; you believe in God, believe also in Me. In My Father's house [in the kingdom of heaven] are many mansions; if it were not so, I would have told you. I go to prepare a place for you. And if I go and prepare a place for you, I will come again and receive you to Myself; that where I am, there you may be also" (John 14:1–3).

So Christian brethren, be encouraged, but also be watchful. It's just a matter of time before the Garden of Genesis 2 is restored by the Lord. He is coming back and the world will once again be a perfect place. Justice will prevail over wickedness. Righteousness will be the measure of the world, for righteousness and justice are what God is. The Lord will be with us. He will be our God and we will be His people (Leviticus 26:12; 2 Corinthians 6:16). Be patient. Just wait on the Lord. "Those who wait on the LORD Shall renew their strength; They shall mount up with wings like eagles, They shall run and not be weary, They shall walk and not faint" (Isaiah 40:31).

Imagine such a perfect world!

A TIME TO BE BORN AND A TIME TO DIE

Birth is easy to understand: we were born and we're alive now. But even though dying is as much a part of life as birth, it's difficult to understand what death is, why it occurs, and what happens when we die. The issues raised by death are different for a person who believes in Jesus Christ than for a person who does not. To the nonbeliever, death is something to fear—it is the final extinction of a person's worldly existence. In his or her mind, life is over—there's nothing more. What a futile outlook!

For the Christian believer, death is not something to fear since life and death are "two different states of existence." Death is not extinction of one's existence. No it is simply a transformation to "a different mode of existence." Millard J. Erickson, *Christian Doctrine*, 376.

Recently, our family experienced the death of our beloved mother. She was a Christian and though in her final days she physically suffered, in the end she was in the Lord's arms as He carried her over the threshold of physical death into His Kingdom. Her funeral was not a somber occasion. The service was a celebration of life, both here on earth and in heaven where we know Mom is now, free of all pain and suffering and filled with the great joy of Him.

Since her death, we've pondered what Mom's life must be like now as she continues her existence with the Lord forever. We turned to the Bible, the inerrant Word of God, for some answers.

<u>Where is Mom now</u>? She is with Jesus in the kingdom of heaven, the place of everlasting bliss: "And I heard a loud voice from heaven saying, 'Behold, the tabernacle of God is with men, and He will dwell with them, and they shall be His people. God Himself will be with them and be their God'" (Revelation 21:3).

<u>Is her suffering over</u>? Absolutely! "And God will wipe away every tear from their eyes; there shall be no more death, nor sorrow, nor crying. There shall be no more pain, for the former things have passed away" (Revelation 21:4).

<u>What is her life like now</u>? It is a life of joyful worship at His throne: "You have come to Mount Zion and to the city of the living God, the heavenly Jerusalem, to an innumerable company of angels, to the general assembly and church of the firstborn who are registered in heaven, to God the Judge of all, to the spirits of just men made perfect, to Jesus the Mediator of the new covenant, and to the blood of sprinkling that speaks better things than that of Abel" (Hebrews 12:22–24).

<u>Where does she live in heaven</u>? With our Father in a room in His house in the kingdom of heaven: "In My Father's house are many mansions...I go to prepare a place for you. And if I go and prepare a place for you, I will come again and receive you to Myself; that where I am, there you may be also" (John 14:2–3).

<u>What is she doing</u>? She is "before the throne of God...serving... Him day and night in His temple" (Revelation 7:15).

<u>What is she like?</u> She is Christ-like! "For whom He foreknew, He also predestined to be conformed to the image of His Son...whom He predestined, these He also called; whom He called, these He also justified; and whom He justified, these He also glorified" (Romans 8:29–30).

For us Christians, the apostle Paul had it right: "For to me, to live is Christ, and to die is gain" (Philippians 1:21).

God has blessed you Mom as you continue your eternal life in heaven, forever! We look forward to joining you in His kingdom when it is our time.

KNOWING THE LORD

Words of the LORD: "Let not the wise man glory in his wisdom, Let not the mighty man glory in his might, Nor let the rich man glory in his riches; But let him who glories glory in this, That he understands and knows Me, That I am the LORD, exercising lovingkindness, judgment, and righteousness in the earth. For in these I delight" (Jeremiah 9:23-24).

COME NOW, AND LET US REASON TOGETHER

God commands us to love Him. "Hear, O Israel: The LORD our God, the LORD is one. You shall love the LORD your God with all your heart, with all your soul, and with all your strength" (Deuteronomy 6:4–5). The first part of this wonderful command of God is known to the Jewish people as the *Shema* (pronounced, *Shmah*), the Hebrew word for *hear*. It is recited at the beginning and the end of most synagogue services. It is a sacred prayer. Coupled with the Shema is God's commandment to love. But, what is the love God speaks of?

Jesus Christ spoke about God's love. He called loving Him as the first and greatest commandments of God. He said, "You shall love the Lord your God with all your heart, with all your soul, and with all your mind" (Matthew 22:37). Then Jesus said, "And the second is like it: 'You shall love your neighbor as yourself'" (Matthew 22:39). By loving God, loving others becomes easy.

The apostle John wrote about the kind of love God speaks of in the Shema. He wrote, "God is Love, and he who abides in love abides in God, and God in him...because as He is, so are we in this world" (1 John 4:16–17). The apostle Paul described the Godly concept of love,

> "Love suffers long and is kind; love does not envy; love does not parade itself, is not puffed up; does not behave rudely, does not seek its own, is not provoked, thinks no evil; does not rejoice in iniquity, but rejoices in the truth; bears all things, believes all things, hopes all things, endures all things. Love never fails" (1 Corinthians 13:4–8).

It is our purpose in life to love God who is love. King Solomon wrote, "Let us hear the conclusion of the whole matter: Fear God and keep His commandments, For this is man's all" (Ecclesiastes 12:13).

But how do we love God? By knowing Him and understanding

Him; by knowing who He is. "And this is eternal life, that they may know You, the only true God, and Jesus Christ, whom You have sent" (John 17:3).

How do we know God? We know Him by using our mind; our soul. God's command is to love Him "with all your soul." That means He wants us to think about Him, to reason with Him, to listen for Him, to see Him in all of His creation (John 10:38), and to understand who He is (Jeremiah 9:23–24).

But even if we come to know God, it is not easy to understand Him for He is limitless. He is everywhere at once. He is within us and without us, all at the same time. He holds all things together with His power and knowledge—from neutrons, protons and electrons to the axis of the earth, and beyond. He is infinite in time and space. He is constant. He is consistent. He is Spirit that begets the material things of the world. He speaks all things into existence. He is the Creator of all creators. He is all knowing. He is personal. He is holy, righteous, and just. He is truth. He is merciful, forgiving, compassionate and full of grace. He is generous and giving. He transcends all that is, was and will ever be. He is complex, but above all, He is love.

Because God is a complex Being, Christians must think and use their minds to reason with Him to understand Him and His Word. "And He opened their understanding, that they might comprehend the Scriptures" (Luke 24:45).

God uses prayer as the means by which His Holy Spirit within us communicates with Him in an effort to know and understand Him. "The LORD will command His lovingkindness in the daytime, And in the night His song shall be with me—A prayer to the God of my life" (Psalm 42:8). "Now we have received...the Spirit who is from God, that we might know the things that have been freely given us by God" (1 Corinthians 2:12).

Along with prayer, He has provided us with another valuable tool to understand and know Him: the Bible. The Bible is God's spoken Word inspired by Him (2 Timothy 3:16). It is all about Jesus Christ (Luke 24:27). "As we search and think deeply on the Word of God asking God to speak to our hearts, He will work in such a way to help us understand His will." Charles Stanley, *The Glorious Journey*, 231–32.

Our God-given ability to reason enables us by His grace to ascertain the meaning of His Word and to know Him. He desires that we reason together. The Holy Spirit within us urges us to seek Him through prayer, to understand who He is, and to emulate Him. "My soul longs, yes, even faints, For the courts of the LORD; My heart and my flesh cry out for the living God" (Psalm 84:2). As we reason and come to understand Him, exhilaration fills our soul and we feel great love for Him—and others.

To know God is to love Him!

"'Come now, and let us reason together,' Says the LORD" (Isaiah 1:18).

LORD

Let us stand in awe of the LORD, the living God, the Creator of the universe: "Oh come, let us worship and bow down; Let us kneel before the LORD, our Maker. For He is our God, And we are the people of His pasture, And the sheep of His hand" (Psalm 95:6–7). "Every tongue should confess that Jesus Christ is Lord" (Philippians 2:11).

LET US BOW DOWN AND WORSHIP THE LORD FOR HE IS MAGNIFICENT

Our Lord, our Father, our Creator—He is to be regarded with great love, honor and reverence for all that He has done for us, is now doing for us, and will forever do for us. He is to be worshiped. We worship and adore Him because His Word tells us that He is Lord (Philippians 2:11). Our Lord Jesus Christ is true to His Word for He blesses us with life and all that we need: the air we breathe, food on our table, the roof over our head, and the clothes on our back. Most of all, He gives us the free will to choose Him, to love Him, to worship Him, and to adore Him.

The psalmist tells us that we are to shout for joy to the Lord and worship Him. We are to "Serve the LORD with gladness; Come before His presence with singing" (Psalm 100:2). We are to exalt Him "at his holy hill; For the LORD our God is holy" (Psalm 99:9).

Why do we worship the Lord? We worship Him because He is our wondrous and awesome Creator. Think about it! By just <u>speaking</u>, He created all that was, is and is to come, including you and me! (See John 1:3–4). In just six days, He created all that is just by His spoken word.

He <u>said</u>, "'Let there be light;' and there was light...and God divided the light from the darkness" and there was day and night—"the first day" (Genesis 1:3–5). He <u>said</u>, "'Let there be a firmament in the midst of the waters, and let it divide the waters from the waters'...And God called the firmament Heaven. So the evening and the morning were the second day" (Genesis 1:6, 8).

He <u>said</u>, "Let the waters under the heavens be gathered together into one place, and let the dry land appear" (Genesis 1:9). Thus the land and the seas were created.

He <u>said</u>, "'Let the earth bring forth grass, the herb that yields seed, and the fruit tree that yields fruit according to its kind, whose seed is in itself, on the earth;' And it was so" (Genesis 1:11). He provided (and continues to provide) abundant food for us, "the third day" (Genesis 1:13).

He <u>said</u>, "Let there be lights in the firmament of the heavens to divide the day from the night; and let them be for signs and seasons, and for days and years; and let them be for lights in the firmament of the heavens to give light on the earth" (Genesis 1:14–15). There was created by Him the sun and the moon and the stars, "the fourth day" (Genesis 1:19).

He <u>said</u>, "Let the waters abound with an abundance of living creatures, and let birds fly above the earth across the face of the firmament of the heavens" (Genesis 1:20). "So the evening and the morning were the fifth day" (Genesis 1:23).

He <u>said</u>, "Let the earth bring forth the living creature according to its kind: cattle and creeping thing and beast of the earth, each according to its kind" (Genesis 1:24).

He <u>said</u>, "'Let Us make man in Our image' ...male and female He created them" (Genesis 1:26–27).

Then He blessed all that He created and said, "Be fruitful and multiply; fill the earth and subdue it" (Genesis 1:28). "Then God saw everything that He had made, and indeed it was very good. So the evening and the morning were the sixth day" (Genesis 1:31).

Look around at His creation. It's no wonder that we stand in awe of Him, the living God, the Creator of the universe. So much of it is still a great mystery to us, mere humans. It's just wondrous!

"Oh come, let us worship and bow down; Let us kneel before the LORD, our Maker. For He is our God, And we are the people of His pasture, and the sheep of His hand" (Psalm 95:6–7).

How magnificent is He!

LOVE

Jesus said to His disciples, "This is My commandment, That you love one another as I have loved you. Greater love has no one than this, than to lay down one's life for his friends" (John 15:12–13).

LOVE THY NEIGHBOR AS THYSELF

Jesus summed up all of the teachings of the Law and the Prophets when He replied to the question posed to Him as to which is the most important commandment. He said,

> "The first of all the commandments is: 'Hear, O Israel, the LORD our God, the LORD is one. And you shall love the LORD your God with all your heart, with all your soul, with all your mind, and with all your strength'...And the second, like it, is this: 'You shall love your neighbor as yourself.' There is no other commandment greater than these" (Mark 12:29–31). (See also Leviticus 19:18).

The commandment to love your neighbor is a difficult commandment to fulfill. Daily, we all face temptations of life which challenge this Godly principle. For example, how do I love the other driver who cuts me off or is going too slow on a highway? How do I love the person in front of me in the checkout line who seems to be taking forever to checkout? How about the person who is taking a long time to complete his or her banking transaction? How do I deal with a family member who condemns me for believing in Jesus? How do I love my landlord who just told me that my rent is being increased to an amount that I cannot afford? How do I love my wife of many years who has told me that she is leaving me and getting a divorce? How do I love my boss who constantly treats me with unkindness? How do I love a person who is impolite or rude towards me? How does an Israeli parent love their Palestinian neighbor whose son has just killed 23 people (including the Israeli's child) while blowing himself up in a crowded pizza store in Jerusalem? Finally (and the list is endless), how do I love a person who hates me because I believe in Jesus Christ? We all face hostile situations in our everyday lives which test our ability to follow the Lord's commandment to love our neighbor.

At times in the face of adversity, rather than feeling love toward the offensive person, I find myself angry, resentful, hostile, impatient, and unforgiving while sensing a need to fight and lash out at my adversary. I feel this way notwithstanding all that I have learned and know from the teachings of Jesus. I don't feel like a very good Christian when I have this attitude towards my neighbor. In those situations, why can't I just love my neighbor as Jesus tells me to do?

The apostle Paul wrote in Romans 3:9–18 that we are all under sin. He wrote quoting Psalm 14:1, "There is none who does good, no, not one" (Romans 3:12). According to Paul, we are all wretches and live lives of wretchedness.

But knowing that I've got lots of no-goodniks for company doesn't solve my dilemma. How do I love in the face of adversity if I am so wretched (as Paul described himself in Romans 7:24)? How do I learn to change my sinful ways? How do I get right with God? M.R. DeHaan wrote in his commentary *Studies in First Corinthians*, "Every thing God wants us to know is in this Book and there is no need for additional revelation or evidence." God gave us His gospel so that we may know how to live life in the right way.

In my quest to know how I can overcome my negative feelings in the face of adversity and love my neighbor, I followed Dr. DeHaan's advice and checked my Bible for some answers. There follows some of the principles the Word of God sets forth about how to overcome the whispers of Satan and love our neighbor.

Paul says, "Imitate me, just as I also imitate Christ" (1 Corinthians 11:1). Notice the order of teaching advocated by the apostle:

1. Christ is the supreme example for all of us. The apostle Peter also stated this teaching: "For to this you were called, because Christ also suffered for us, leaving us an example, that you should follow His steps" (1 Peter 2:21).
2. Christ's apostles followed His example.

3. Like His apostles, we are to follow Christ's example. (See also 1 Corinthians 4:16).

With the God-given words of the apostles, the Bible provides guidance as to how I can grow out of my wretchedness, become more like Christ, and love my neighbor. The apostles spoke from authority. They experienced the same challenges that you and I experience, and they overcame these challenges. They learned well from the Master how to love their neighbor.

In reading the apostles' teachings, we are told what it means to love. John described Jesus as Light and Love: "God is Light and in Him there is no darkness at all...if we walk in the light, as He is in the light, we have fellowship with one another, and the blood of Jesus Christ, His Son, cleanses us from all sin" (1 John 1:5, 7).

In his letter to the Corinthians Paul described what it means to love. He wrote, "Love...is kind...does not envy...is not puffed up... does not behave rudely...bears all things, believes all things, hopes all things, endures all things" (1 Corinthians 13:4–5, 7).

It is sometimes difficult for people not to judge others. God is the one who will judge righteously in the end. It is not our place to judge. Thus in loving my neighbor, I must remember that God, not me, will decide who is righteous (1 Peter 2:23).

Peter further wrote, "Finally, all of you be of one mind, having compassion for one another; love as brothers, be tenderhearted, be courteous; not returning evil for evil or reviling for reviling, but on the contrary blessing, knowing that you were called to this, that you may inherit a blessing" (1 Peter 3:8–9).

The Bible makes it clear that there is hope for all of us in this dilemma of loving your neighbor: "Then they came and laid hands on Jesus and took Him. And suddenly, one of those who were with Jesus stretched out his hand and drew his sword [John 18:10 indicates this was Peter], struck the servant of the high priest, and cut off his ear" (Matthew 26:50–51). If we compare Peter's actions in Matthew 26 with his words as spoken in 1 Peter 3:8–9, we see the maturation of a follower of Christ and realize that there is hope for all of us as we walk deeper in His Spirit and fill our lives with the Word of God.

So what does Peter's progression in his walk with the Lord teach us in our quest to learn how to love our neighbor and not lash out or judge as we may have done in the past? The words of the apostles tell us how to do it, that is, how to learn to love our neighbor. We are to be strong in the Lord and in His mighty power. We are to put on the full armor of God so that we can take a stand against the wiles of the devil. What is the armor of God the apostles instruct us to wear? It is the daily immersion of our minds in the Word of God. They exhort us to pray often, especially in the moment when we are facing our adversaries. They urge us to see others as the Lord sees us, as His children. They ask us to look at everyone and know that God created something in the nature and character of Himself in each one of us. As we look into our neighbor's eyes, they teach us to see God's creation in him or her. They remind us that it is God's place to judge evil, not ours. They encourage us to fill our lives with thoughts that are true, noble, right, pure, lovely, admirable, excellent or praiseworthy (Philippians 4:8). They testify that God loves us and that His Holy Spirit lives within us.

If we follow the examples given to us by Jesus Christ and spoken by Him through His apostles; if we immerse our minds in the Holy Word of God; if we pray often, especially in the face of adversity; if we truly love our neighbor as Jesus loves us; if we do all of this, the fruit of His Spirit within us will instill in us the things of life for which we all strive: "Love, joy, peace, longsuffering, kindness, goodness, faithfulness, gentleness, self-control. Against such there is no law" (Galatians 5:22).

Lord, may Your grace be upon us when we strive to follow the example of Your Word in loving our neighbor. Amen.

MARRIAGE

"A man shall leave his father and mother and be joined to his wife, and they shall become one flesh" (Genesis 2:24). Marriage is love and respect. "Let each one of you...so love his own wife as himself, and let the wife see that she respects her husband" (Ephesians 5:33).

THE PATIENCE OF A SAINT

I'm sure you've heard the expression *the patience of a saint.* But did you know its origin? The apostle John used this phrase to describe Christians who endure the onslaught of suffering at the hands of worldwide wickedness and are rewarded with eternal life by Our Lord and Savior Jesus Christ. He wrote, "Here is the patience and the faith of the saints...here are those who keep the commandments of God and the faith of Jesus" (Revelation 14:12). Revelation is a book of hope to those of us who have faith in Jesus Christ. By writing to his fellow believers, the saints, John encouraged them to be patient, to persevere, to be of good courage, and to know that through faith in Jesus Christ, they would overcome persecution, even death, and be filled with joy. (See 1 John 1:4).

The great test for Christians is whether through patient endurance of suffering they will remain loyal to Jesus and not fall prey to the deception of Satan. They do this by serious attention to God's Word and by faithfulness to Christ Jesus. The apostle Paul wrote in his letter to Roman Christians,

> "Therefore, having been justified by faith, we have peace with God through our Lord Jesus Christ, through whom also we have access by faith into this grace in which we stand, and rejoice in the hope of the glory of God. And not only that, but we also glory in tribulations, knowing that tribulation produces perseverance; and perseverance, character; and character, hope" (Romans 5:1–4).

In a footnote to Romans 5:3–4, the *Life Application Bible, New King James Version* (Tyndale), explains these statements by Paul: "For first century Christians, suffering was the rule rather than the exception. Paul tells us that in the future we will *become*, but until then we must *overcome*. This means we will experience difficulties that help us grow. We rejoice in suffering not because we like pain or deny its tragedy, but because we know God is using life's difficulties and Satan's attacks to build our character. The problems we run into will develop our perseverance—which in turn will strengthen our character, deepen our trust in God, and give us greater confidence about the future."

I have come to believe that the greater the difficulties, the deeper the joy will be when I've passed the test. But passing the test sometimes takes great patience; pressing on in the face of adversity requires strong perseverance and fortitude. My personal testimony is but another illustration of Paul's words in Romans 5:3–4.

In 1978, my marriage of fifteen years was falling apart. Without detailing the issues facing my wife and I, there was a deep schism in our relationship. We'd separated for a short time. We'd drifted away from Judaism, the religion of our youth. We weren't practicing religion, although we both had strong beliefs in God. We were lost souls searching for answers. We didn't know Christ. But in spite of our divisiveness, we both knew that there was love between us, that fifteen years of life history together was something not to be discarded lightly, and that we needed to work through the issues facing us since if we didn't, we'd merely carry that baggage elsewhere.

We weren't done with each other. It wasn't God's plan for us. Our choices were limited: (1) divorce or (2) stand our ground together and work through the issues. We chose the latter path. It wasn't easy— it was hard. There were times when the going seemed impossible, but we persevered. We drifted into New Age. We both started doing human potential retreats such as Est, Lifespring, and Human Factors. We were hurting. Yet we were both searching for answers.

On a September evening in 1983, while at a seven-day introspective retreat held in an 1899 one-hundred room mansion on the shores of beautiful Lake Champlain in Shelburne, Vermont, I experienced Jesus Christ being crucified on the cross at Golgotha. In a vision as real as the book you are holding, with my eyes shut (in my mind's eye) I saw a man with a beard and dressed in just a loin cloth being crucified on the cross. It was as if I was one of the witnesses of His crucifixion at Golgotha. His body was enveloped by a brilliant oval of white light that sizzled on its edges. I was overwhelmed. I felt great sorrow and sadness, and at the same time great joy when I realized that I was seeing Christ crucified on His cross. The joy came from the realization of what He was doing for me on that cross—He was sacrificing His life for me, a sinner amongst sinners. I cried for a long while. I felt weak—I had no strength to stand up. But yet, I experienced a peace like I'd never experienced in my life.

When Paul experienced the light that flashed around him on the Damascus Road "he fell to the ground" (Acts 9:4). Similarly, the prophet Daniel fell on his face (Daniel 8:17) as he watched the vision of "one having the appearance of a man" (Daniel 8:15). Daniel wrote regarding the man he saw in the vision, "Now, as he was speaking with me, I was in a deep sleep with my face to the ground; but he touched me, and stood me upright" (Daniel 8:18). I note these incidents to parenthetically illustrate what could happen to us, mere mortals, when one has a direct experience with God.

For a long time after my vision of the Christ, I was unable to recount my experience with the Lord without shedding tears. After Shelbourne, I was a changed man. My family and friends knew from my demeanor that something wonderful had occurred in my life. I smiled more than I frowned. I was relaxed rather than up-tight. I was at peace with my world. My personality went from an A+ to a C-.

Wanting to share this wondrous experience with my wife, I encouraged her to attend the next introspective seminar (held in Molokai, Hawaii) and to seek the truth. Miraculous as it may seem, while attending that seminar, Jesus appeared to her in a vision. I don't ascribe these experiences to the particular seminar nor do I mean to suggest (or boast) that we are special. We were at bottom in our relationship and our lives were in shambles. We were ready for a miracle and the Lord answered our prayers—He saved our marriage!

With Christ in our lives, the crumbled foundation of our marriage began to strengthen and the difficulties we thought insurmountable grew dimmer. Jesus guided us in His path of righteousness and truth. Openness, truth, love, respect, and communication (in my case, listening) became important concepts in our lives. As the days went by, the work of restoring our marital bonds became easier and easier. We began studying God's Word in morning devotions and started attending a church. There we found that we shared common bonds with other believers and found our family of God.

Today, our Lord and Savior Jesus Christ is our closest Friend. My wife and I are best friends. The joy we experience today as husband and wife can only be measured by the indescribable joy we experience in knowing the Lord. Paul summed it up when he wrote, "Be anxious for nothing, but in everything by prayer and supplication, with thanksgiving, let your requests be made known to God; and the peace of God, which surpasses all understanding, will guard your hearts and minds through Christ Jesus" (Philippians 4:6–7).

We just celebrated our fifty-fourth wedding anniversary and our thirty-fourth year knowing Jesus Christ our Lord and Savior! Praise God!

MATURITY

A mature Christian is one who doesn't just talk about his or her faith, but lives it; who practices the truth; who prays to the Lord in the face of troubles; and who seeks to be wise. A mature Christian with wisdom from above "is first pure, then peaceable, gentle, willing to yield, full of mercy and good fruits, without partiality and without hypocrisy" (James 3:17).

ON THIS ROCK I WILL BUILD MY CHURCH

Jesus Christ said, "And I also say to you that you are Peter, and on this rock I will build My church" (Matthew 16:18).

The life of the apostle Peter is a story of a man on a path to spiritual maturity. When we are first introduced to Peter in the Bible, we find anything but a rock. He was unschooled, impulsive, and impatient; a man of little grace. Pastor Warren Wiersbe in his book, *Be Alert*, 9, describes Peter as one that "had a tendency in his early years to feel overconfident when danger was near and to overlook his Master's warnings. He rushed ahead when he should have waited; he slept when he should have prayed; he talked when he should have listened. He was a courageous, but careless, Christian." Yet, when we read Peter's letters written toward the end of his life to Jewish and Gentile Christians in Asia Minor, we find a pillar of the early church—enlightened, courageous, humble, loving and full of grace.

Peter's first steps as a Christian were truly baby steps. Peter may have figured that if Jesus could walk on water, so could he. He said to Jesus, almost double daring Him, "Lord, if it is You, command me to come to You on the water." "Come." [Jesus said]. "And when Peter had come down out of the boat, he walked on the water to go to Jesus. But when he saw that the wind was boisterous, he was afraid; and beginning to sink he cried out saying, 'Lord, save me!'" Like a Father tending to his helpless child, Jesus grabbed Peter's hand and saved him. Jesus then reprimanded Peter for his petulance, "O you of little faith, why did you doubt?" (Matthew 14:28–31).

Although he grew steadily as a believer in Christ, Peter stumbled many more times. For example, Jesus had predicted His death on the cross. To this Peter impetuously took the Lord aside and rebuked Him, "Far be it from You, Lord; this shall not happen to You!" (Matthew 16:22). Imagine rebuking God! That's when Jesus "turned and said to Peter, 'Get behind Me, Satan! You are an offense to me, for you are not mindful of the things of God, but the things of men.'" (Matthew 16:23).

Have you ever been scolded by a person of authority such as a teacher or a spiritual leader? Imagine how Peter felt being reprimanded by the Creator of the Universe. At best, such an experience would be disheartening, enough to turn one away from that person. But not Peter! He persevered.

Peter continued on in his walk toward spiritual maturity. After denying three times that he even knew Jesus, Peter saw the folly of his pride and wept bitterly (Matthew 26:75). Alas, the Holy Spirit thereafter came upon him at Pentecost and tongues of fire rested upon him, so much so that when he spoke of Jesus before a crowd, three thousand people gave their lives to Christ (Acts 2:3, 41). How powerful is the Spirit of the Lord!

The words Peter wrote in his second epistle truly reflect a mature Christian believer:

> "But also for this very reason, giving all diligence, add to your faith virtue, to virtue knowledge, to knowledge self-control, to self-control perseverance, to perseverance godliness, to godliness brotherly kindness, and to brotherly kindness love. For if these things are yours and abound, you will be neither barren nor unfruitful in the knowledge of our Lord Jesus Christ" (2 Peter 1:5–8).

Peter spoke with authority for he'd lived through the rough spots of life and had stumbled over them on his spiritual journey to God.

His words of encouragement were spoken with the confidence of a man with deep spiritual conviction. He wrote, "Therefore, brethren, be even more diligent to make your call and election sure, for if you do these things you will never stumble; for so an entrance will be supplied to you abundantly into the everlasting kingdom of our Lord and Savior Jesus Christ" (2 Peter 1:10–11).

Indeed, just as Jesus had foretold to him early on, Peter became the rock upon which the Lord built His church.

SPIRITUAL MATURITY: STRIVING TO BE LIKE JESUS CHRIST

When I think of maturity, I think of such things as experience, good sense, patience, perseverance, understanding, competence, knowledge, truth and most importantly, wisdom. Why do I believe that wisdom is the most important mark of maturity? Because the Word of God says that "The fear of the LORD is the beginning of wisdom; A good understanding have all those who do His commandments" (Psalm 111:10). The only One who fulfills all of God's commandments and who is Wisdom personified is Jesus Christ. He is our ideal of spiritual maturity. He is the Wisdom we strive to emulate.

God's Word provides the standards for believers to be spiritually mature. He instructs us how to be like Him. In his letter to strife-ridden believers, the apostle James wrote about the spiritual immaturity that was occurring in the early church, and in so doing, outlined some ways that believers can work toward spiritual maturity. In James' day the church was experiencing problems that worked against the principles upon which the Lord had established His church. Dr. Warren W. Wiersbe in his commentary on The Epistle of James entitled *Be Mature*, describes at page 12 some of the issues facing the early church,

> "...these Jewish Christians were having some problems in their personal lives and in their church fellowship. For one thing, they were going through difficult testings. They were also facing temptations to sin. Some of the believers were catering to the rich, while others were being robbed by the rich. Church members were competing for offices in the church, particularly teaching offices. One of the major problems in the church was a failure on the part of many to live what they professed to believe. Furthermore, the tongue was a serious problem, even to the point of creating

wars and divisions in the assembly. Worldliness was another problem. Some of the members were disobeying God's Word and were sick physically because of it; and some were straying away from the Lord and the church."

James wrote about these issues to emphasize a common cause for these problems in the church—spiritual immaturity. His letter describes the means by which a believer could overcome these faults, that is, to become spiritually mature.

James wrote that a mature Christian is one who is patient (perseveres) when he or she is being tested by trials allowed by the Lord and when he or she is being tempted by temptations offered by Satan. James wrote, "My brethren count it all joy when you fall into various trials, knowing that the testing of your faith produces patience" (James 1:2–3). When faced by life's trials, do I say, "It is God's will that is causing this to occur; all will be fine in the end?" Or do I say, "I can't take it anymore; it's all going to end in disaster; I give up; I'm no good; it's my fault?" The mark of a mature Christian is one who doesn't lose his or her faith in Jesus in the face of life's trials. "Blessed is the man who endures temptation" (James 1:12). Spiritual maturity is achieved when we are patient and persevere with the knowledge that in times of difficulty God is with us.

Dr. Wiersbe further wrote (*supra* at 13), "God is looking for mature men and women to carry on His work, and sometimes all He can find are little children who cannot even get along with each other." Do you contribute to the lack of spiritual maturation of other Christians by engaging in idle talk, or do you listen and participate knowing that God is the reason for what is occurring? "So then, my beloved brethren, let every man be swift to hear, slow to speak, slow to wrath; for the wrath of man does not produce the righteousness of God" (James 1:19–20). When dealing with church affairs, keeping a tight rein on one's tongue is a sign of one who walks with the Lord. The Lord should be our reason for doing anything, not our judgmental opinions of others.

A mature Christian listens and serves the Lord; spiritual speech without action is but fruit of spiritual immaturity.

> "For if anyone is a hearer of the word and not a doer, he is like a man observing his natural face in a mirror; for he observes himself, goes away, and immediately forgets what kind of man he was. But he who looks into the perfect law of liberty and continues in it, and is not a forgetful hearer but a doer of the work, this one will be blessed in what he does" (James 1:23–25). James concluded, "Pure and undefiled religion before God and the Father is this: to visit orphans and widows in their trouble, and to keep oneself unspotted from the world" (James 1:27).

A mature Christian is one who practices the truth. Wiersbe, *Be Mature, supra,* 85. In Chapter 2 of his epistle to Jewish Christians, James enunciates his well known statement that "faith without works is dead" (James 2:26). Our faith in Jesus Christ naturally leads us to do good deeds. Jesus said, "Do not do according to their [the scribes' and Pharisees'] works; for they say, and do not do...But all their works they do to be seen by men" (Matthew 23:3, 5). A mature Christian works for the Lord, not just to be seen or approved by others. No matter what response one receives from others regarding spiritual works, the focus should always be that the work is for the Lord and no others.

A mature Christian is one who doesn't just talk about his or her faith, but lives it. "What does it profit, my brethren, if someone says he has faith but does not have works? Can faith save him?" (James 2:14). The reason a mature Christian lives his or her faith is that he or she is focused on the true object of their faith: Jesus Christ. A mature Christian has faith in Jesus; that faith creates a desire to bear good fruit (e.g. by tending to widows and orphans, as the early elders did in Acts 6); and the rewards of such good deeds are crowns in heaven.

A mature Christian is one who seeks to be wise. "The fear of the LORD is the beginning of wisdom. And knowledge of the Holy One is understanding" (Proverbs 9:10). James speaks of two kinds of learning in life: wisdom from heaven, and knowledge from below. The knowledge from below is "earthly, sensual, demonic" (James 3:15). A spiritually immature person who disseminates worldly knowledge is one who harbors "bitter envy and self-seeking" in his or her heart, who boasts about it, and lies against the truth (James 3:14). A mature Christian is one who is "pure; then peaceable, gentle, willing to yield, full of mercy and good fruits, without partiality and without hypocrisy"(James 3:17). These traits reflect wisdom from heaven.

Oh, how I pray that I could be a person with wisdom from heaven to do what is right as a spiritually mature Christian, for "The work of righteousness will be peace, And the effect of righteousness, quietness and assurance forever" (Isaiah 32:17).We should all seek that as a goal of our lives, that is, a harvest of righteousness and peace. Could there be a better epitaph on one's grave than, "He bore a harvest of righteousness?"

Finally, a mature Christian is a person who prays to the Lord in the face of troubles. The troubles in our world manifested on September 11, 2001 drew thousands of non-church-goers into houses of worship. But a true sign of the spiritual immaturity of many has been the subsequent return to their old ways—many have once again turned away from the Lord and gone back to their material idols. James was prophetic about our times when he wrote concerning materialistic people, "Your riches are corrupted, and your garments are moth-eaten. Your gold and silver are corroded, and their corrosion will be a witness against you and will eat your flesh like fire" (James 5:2–3).

What about other troubles? James asked, "Is anyone among you suffering?" (James 5:13). "Is anyone among you sick?" (James 5:14). A mature Christian is one who "call[s] for the elders of the church and let[s] them pray over him, anointing him with oil in the name of the Lord. And the prayer of faith will save the sick, and the Lord will raise him up" (James 5:14–15). James concludes his letter by exhorting his

Christian brethren to pray, because "The effective, fervent prayer of a righteous man avails much" (James 5:16).

In summary, a mature Christian is one who doesn't lose his or her faith in the face of life's trials, who reins in his or her tongue, who practices the truth, who fears the Lord in everything he or she does and is thus seeking to be wise, and is one who prays "without ceasing" (1 Thessalonians 5:17). God bless you in your walk towards Wisdom. May you become like Jesus Christ, our Lord and Savior. Amen.

MEEKNESS

"Blessed are the meek, for they shall inherit the earth" (Matthew 5:5).

MEEKNESS—HUMBLE STRENGTH

Imagine—it's a lovely spring day. You are seated on soft green grass on a steeply sloping hillside overlooking a large lake—the Galilee in Israel. Even near the top of the hill, you can hear the lapping sounds of the lake hitting the rocks along the shore. About half-way down the hill, there's a Rabbi who calls Himself *Jesus*. He is sitting amongst the crowd and is teaching about the kingdom of Heaven. Because of the acoustics of the hillside, all can hear His words. He describes nine declarations of blessedness which are called the *Beatitudes*. Of the nine, one is somewhat puzzling: "Blessed are the meek, For they shall inherit the earth" (Matthew 5:5). What does Jesus mean by *meek*? Does He mean *weak*, that is, those easily acted upon or submissive as the secularists define it? Does He mean those who are humble but act with strength in their ways—lovers of God?

In the worldly sense, it isn't the weak that usually prevail on the earth. It's usually the powerful, the rich, or often the wicked who rule the ways of the world. So what could the Lord mean that the "meek... shall inherit the earth?" The Lord sees meekness in a person as a good trait. If being meek is being weak, how could the weak inherit the earth? How could they overcome those who act without principles, without moral reference?

In His lesson plan, the great Teacher was quoting from the writings of the psalmist, His ancestor David, who wrote in Psalm 37:10–11, "For yet a little while and the wicked shall be no more; Indeed, you will look carefully for his place, But it shall be no more. But the meek shall inherit the earth, And shall delight themselves in the abundance of peace." In a note to Psalm 37:11, *The NIV Study Bible*, 1046, defines the *meek* as, "Those who humbly acknowledge their dependence on the goodness and grace of God and betray no arrogance toward their fellowman."

Meekness is closely linked with the word *humility*. *Vine's Complete Expository Dictionary*, 401. In the same work, *humble* is defined as "poor, meek." *id* at 118. A humble heart is a meek heart which does not resist God. *Self* (selfishness) gets in the way of God. Meekness gets out of the way of God.

In *The Imitation of Christ*, 94, Thomas A' Kempis defined *meekness* as if Jesus Himself was speaking and defining the term, "Jesus: A person is highly valued by God, if he is grounded in true humility and filled with love, if he always seeks God's honor with purity and integrity, if he has a humble opinion of himself, if he sincerely dislikes his selfish nature, and even if he does not mind being looked down upon and belittled by others, instead of being honored."

Defining meekness by what it is not leads to such terms as pride, pretense, and fear of man. An example of a prideful man versus a meek man was given by Jesus in the parable of the Pharisee and the Tax Collector:

> "Two men went up to the temple to pray, one a Pharisee and the other a tax collector. The Pharisee stood and prayed thus with himself, 'God, I thank you that I am not like other men—extortioners, unjust, adulterers, or even as this tax collector. I fast twice a week; I give tithes of all that I possess.' And the tax collector, standing afar off, would not so much as raise his eyes to heaven, but beat his breast, saying, 'God, be merciful to me, a sinner!'" (Luke 18:10–13).

The Pharisee's pride, *self*-love, is a burden to him. A sinner who tries to prove he is perfect (without sin) lives a *self*-life in conflict because he'll never shake the binds of pride. The labor of *self*-love is an impossible burden. The Pharisee in the parable was comparing himself to another man. He was measuring his life by the life of another rather than God. Although supposedly a man of God, God was not part of his *self*-imposed test for determining what was perfection in life. He was the judge and jury of his own life.

On the other hand, the humble man, the tax collector, sought God's approval of his life and actions rather than man's approval. To him, God's opinion of his life was the ultimate test. The tax collector didn't view seeking God as a weakness. Instead, his worldview was a Godly one—a view from strength.

One who seeks God's approval and not that of man, is a person standing on a firm foundation. He is a man of "strength under control." *Jon Courson's Application Commentary, New Testament*, 25.

A meek man is one who has lived enough in this world to know that it is not his *self* that is guiding his life, but a Designer, One who has planned his life for him and is guiding him as he lives that life. He no longer deludes himself that he is strong, immortal, all-knowing, *self*-driven—no longer confident in all that he is, does, and has. No, a meek man is one who has found the One in his life that is All-knowing, All-loving, All-righteous, and All-just, and he is humbled by this knowledge. No longer does he look to earthly others to determine whether he is worthy. No, he is aware that he will never be seen by the world as the Lord sees him—and he is unconcerned that he isn't approved by earthly others. He looks to God for everything in his life, and is blessed.

How does the meek man get his strength? He takes the advice of the Great Rabbi, Jesus Christ, who beckoned him, "Come to Me, all you who labor and are heavy laden, and I will give you rest" (Matthew 11:28).

The burden Jesus speaks about is life itself. He knows all of our hearts and the trials and tribulations which life presents to us from time to time. But why do we have to bear burdens in this life? Why do we have to be "heavy laden" from time to time? We have to bear burdens because as Adam's progeny, we have his DNA—the DNA of sin. Sin is rebellion against God. There is no way that man can rebel against God and succeed in life. Satan, the author of sin, tries to attract our attention away from God, but he is without power to do so. He cannot overcome the power of God and God will always prevail. However, as the battle for our souls ensues throughout our lives, it wears us out. That's the "weary" part.

The prophet Isaiah describes this process in beautiful terms,

> "The everlasting God, the LORD, The Creator of the ends of the earth, Neither faints nor is weary. His

understanding is unsearchable. He gives power to the weak, And to those who have no might He increases strength. Even the youths shall faint and be weary, And the young men shall utterly fall, But those who wait on the LORD Shall renew their strength; They shall mount up with wings like eagles, They shall run and not be weary, They shall walk and not faint" (Isaiah 40:28–31).

The meek get their strength from the Lord. They are like little children who, in their daily lives, do not compare themselves to others. That is why Jesus said that little children are the greatest in the kingdom of heaven. He said,

"Assuredly, I say to you, unless you are converted and become as little children, you will by no means enter the kingdom of heaven. Therefore, whoever humbles himself as this little child is the greatest in the kingdom of heaven. Whoever receives one little child like this in My name receives Me" (Matthew 18:3–5).

Jesus' desire for you and me is that we become more and more like Him. He urged us, "Take My yoke upon you and learn from Me, for I am gentle and lowly in heart, and you will find rest for your souls. For My yoke is easy and My burden is light" (Matthew 11:29–30).

Pastor Ray Stedman wrote in *Adventuring Through the Bible*, 221, "Our goal should be to have a humble opinion of ourselves and an exalted opinion of God...But the attitude God wants to build in us is one of humble dependence upon His infinite resources." This pastoral advice was also given by another pastor, the apostle Paul, "For I say, through the grace given to me, to everyone who is among you, not to think of himself more highly than he ought to think, but to think soberly, as God has dealt to each one a measure of faith" (Romans 12:3).

Be meek—with humble strength, and be blessed, for "I can do all things through Christ who strengthens me" (Philippians 4:13).

MIRACLES

"Many believed in His name when they saw the signs [miracles] which He did" (John 2:23).

THE MIRACLE WORKER:
JESUS IS OUR HOPE

Hope expresses absolute certainty, not a mere wish or desire. When we have hope, we have confidence that something <u>can</u> occur, not whether something will occur. The apostle Paul wrote that the Lord Jesus Christ <u>is</u> "our hope." He didn't say, "Jesus will be our hope," or "Jesus was our hope." He said with confidence, "Paul, an apostle of Christ Jesus by the commandment of God our Savior and the Lord Jesus Christ, our hope" (Timothy 1:1).

Do you have any doubt that Jesus is alive or that He is with us in every breath we take? Do you have any doubt that in His own time, we who believe in Him, who believe that He died for our sins, and who believe that He rose from the grave and was resurrected, will be with Him forever in the New Jerusalem? Do you wonder why Paul was so absolutely certain that Jesus would give us the gift of eternal life? Why was Paul so certain that we would be so blessed?

Paul spoke from authority that Jesus is our hope, for he had a direct living experience with the Lord on the road to Damascus,

> "As he journeyed he came near Damascus, and suddenly a light shone around him from heaven. Then he fell to the ground, and heard a voice saying to him, 'Saul, Saul, why are you persecuting me?' And he said, 'Who are you, Lord?' Then the Lord said, 'I am Jesus, whom you are persecuting'" (Acts 9:3–5).

Paul experienced a miracle in which God appeared to him in a vision. With his eyes and ears, Paul saw and heard God speaking to him. Without being disrespectful to Paul, I wish to raise a question. Was Paul so unique in experiencing a miracle, the result of which was that he knew Jesus Christ was alive and had spoken to him? Is Paul unique in being in a special category of Biblical characters who were blessed to see and hear a miracle performed by Jesus? Or are you and I, who believe in Jesus, of the same mode as Paul: that even though we are not in the Lord's Bible, we experience Jesus' miracles every moment of our lives? I submit that the answer to this question is a resounding YES!

The late Julie A. Link, writing in *Our Daily Bread* (RBC Ministries, May 22, 2001), said, "...sometimes I get the idea that God stopped working in people's lives when He finished writing the Bible. Now that He's *less visible*, I conclude that He's also less involved. But that's not true. Even though God has finished His book, He hasn't finished telling the story; He's simply using a different form of media to tell it." (my emphasis added).

Paul said with certainty that Jesus *is* our hope. When Paul said "is," there was no uncertainty as to his meaning of the word. In his view, Paul meant that Jesus is with us now. He wrote in Romans 1:20, "For since the creation of the world His invisible attributes are clearly seen, being understood by the things that are made, even His eternal power and Godhead, so that they are without excuse."

Do you see, hear, feel, touch and smell the "invisible things" that Jesus is creating at this very moment? YOU BET YOU DO!

In his commentary on Romans 1:20, *Thru the Bible*, Vol. IV, 652, Pastor J. Vernon McGee wrote, "How can invisible things be seen? Paul makes this a paradox purposely to impress upon his readers that the 'dim light of nature' is a man-made falsehood. Creation is a clear light of revelation. It is the primary revelation."

You can just see David before he was a king—just a lowly shepherd—awe inspired by the creation of God. In his mind there was no uncertainty about the visibility of God when he wrote, "When I consider Your heavens, the work of Your fingers, The moon and the stars, which You have ordained" (Psalm 8:3). He also wrote, "The heavens declare the glory of God; And the firmament shows His handwork" (Psalm 19:1).

So how can I be absolutely certain—how can I be sure that Jesus Christ is alive and is my hope? By looking around at the miracles He IS performing this very millisecond and being aware of them with the same realization that Paul had on the Damascus Road. Jesus Christ said, "Though you do not believe Me, believe the works, that you may know and believe that the Father is in Me, and I in Him" (John 10:38). In other words, believe His good works.

Here's just a few of His miracles (works) which are happening as you read this, and I'm sure you can add to my feeble attempt to inventory the miracles that Jesus Christ our Lord *is* performing this very minute:

1. The air we breathe.
2. The temperature range on earth—just right for us to exist.
3. The balance between day and night and how evenly and slowly one transitions into the other.
4. The elevation of the land we live on above the ocean—it rises above it.
5. The food that grows with the light of the sun and the rain that He gives us from the sky.
6. The plants and animals that He has provided to sustain us and/or to be our companions.
7. The water to sustain us.
8. The work He provides for us.
9. The freedoms that we enjoy to express ourselves, to worship Him, and to live our lives.
10. The ability to know right from wrong.
11. Being chosen by Him and being able to see and hear Him.
12. The intelligence we have to be aware of Him and His miracles.
13. The miraculous works He has done in creating our bodies, gigantic miracles in and of themselves and how they work.
14. The birth of our children.
15. His healing power.
16. The science of medicine He has created and made known.
17. Our families.
18. Our happiness and contentment.
19. The power and balance of the natural forces that He has set in motion and holds together: wind, fire, rain, sunlight, electricity, radio and television waves, etc.

20. Life and death.
21. Freedom from pain.
22. Long life.
23. Courage to do that which is right in the eyes of God.
24. The laws of nature.
25. How an airplane flies.
26. The balance of the universe.
27. The orbits of the planets and how they stay in place in relation to all other bodies in space.
28. Space.
29. Gravity.
30. Prayer and the answers He gives.
31. The ability to know Him and that HE IS.
32. His love for us.
33. Our ability to love and receive love.
34. The Bible—His Word.
35. Peace on earth.
36. Godly parents.
37. The five senses.
38. Grace.
39. The beauty and balance of His creations.
40. Time.
41. Music.
42. Our church.
43. Sleep and the ability to rest and restore our bodies.
44. Life-giving blood that flows through us.
45. Our ability to appreciate Him and to give thanks.
46. Our innate gifts.
47. The judgment of God when it is our time to be judged by Him.
48. The blessings He has given us.
49. Fear of the Lord.
50. Our redemption from bondage of the world, from sin and death, and the gift of eternal life.

You can certainly add to this list and I urge you to do so. It is a fulfilling experience to think about the wonders of God as they are occurring in our lives.

Do you still have any doubt that Jesus Christ is our hope? If so, read Psalm 104 where God, placing words in the mouth of the psalmist, has prepared His own inventory of the "invisible things" of creation. These are the miracles that He has, is, and will continue to perform. He is indeed Immanuel, God with us!

Oh Lord, how manifest are your works! In wisdom have you made them all: the earth is full of your riches. Jesus you are our hope! Amen.

OVERCOMING

"These things I have spoken to you, that in Me you may have peace. In the world you will have tribulation; but be of good cheer, I have overcome the world" (John 16:33).

SOME THOUGHTS ON OVERCOMING

Doesn't the world seem like it's in turmoil these days? From my small window on the universe, it seems as though peace and goodwill amongst humanity will never occur. As a person keenly interested in world events and history, I often find myself reading, watching and listening to every source of news of the world that I can get my hands on: newspapers, news programs, the internet, talk-radio programs, and the like. At times, I find myself getting caught up in the world's seemingly never-ending conflicts between the left and right in our country.

I get discouraged by the "self-interest" (not special interest) groups who seem bent on eliminating God from our society in the guise of protecting their individual rights, the alleged "fundamental" rights of those opposed to God. At times, I feel the negative emotions of anger and resentment rising within me at those whose intent seems to be to undermine everything I've been taught and believe in. I ask: Where are my individual rights to have my grandchildren pray in school if they want to? Where are my individual rights to use the words *under God* when reciting the pledge of allegiance? Each day I find a new attack on Christ or a court decision restricting my right to worship the Lord as I see fit and where ever I see fit.

How is it, I ask, can people honestly believe that removing Saddam Hussein from power was a disservice to his people and the world in general? How is it, I ask, that taking the war on terror to the terrorists, is wrong? Where is it written that the random slaughter of innocent women and children in the guise of terrorists' rights is justified under any circumstances? How is it, I ask, that the appeasers have not learned from history that appeasement doesn't work in a world of injustice? How is it, I ask, that people cannot see the justice and truth in opposing those who apparently hate our country and everything it stands for?

Where does the argument for individual rights of the self-interested end? Does it end in the death of an unborn child? Does it end in undermining the family unit? Does it end in the condemnation of those who believe in God? Does it end when those who speak their opinion are suppressed in their views? Does it end when the rule of law is disregarded? Does it end when God is completely eliminated from our society? Is that the goal of the self-interested? Where does it all end? When is enough, enough? The urge to engage in battle with those who oppose my beliefs sometimes gets me fighting mad!

But then, as this downward emotional spiral of frustrating conflict between what I see as the age-old battle between good and evil reaches a crescendo, the Holy Spirit brings me back to my senses and reminds me that God is in control. He reminds me of what is really important in this world: His Word. As a Christian, I seek His Word and He immediately enables me to overcome my negative emotions. I thank God that each time I find worldly anger arising within me, He enables me, no, He arms me with the weapon to overcome the temptation to fight the battle on the adversary's level: His Word, the Bible. When I turn to His Word, I quickly realize that the world's turmoil is but the Lord's plan unfolding before my very eyes! I recall the words of Jesus in John 16:33, "These things I have spoken to you, that in Me you may have peace. In the world you will have tribulation; but be of good cheer, I have overcome the world." He has overcome the world and will continue to do so until the end of time. I am so thankful that I have Jesus Christ in my life!

As a believer in Jesus Christ, I take great comfort in knowing that the wicked ways of the world are but foolish ways of people who cannot see or hear beyond their flesh. The Lord enables me not to feel anger toward them, but compassion, for they too have the opportunity to be God's children and to be part of His family. It's a matter of choice. I feel compassion because He tells me through the words of his King David in Psalm 37 to think Godly wisdom, not worldly "wisdom" (that is, knowledge from darkness). He says, "Do not fret because of evildoers, Nor be envious of the workers of iniquity. For they shall soon be cut down like the grass, And wither as the green herb" (Psalm 37:1–2).

In Psalm 37, He gives me great assurance that enables me to

overcome my fleshly, worldly tendencies toward anger and resentment for our contemporary world condition. David wrote,

> "For yet a little while and the wicked shall be no more; Indeed, you will look carefully for his place, But it shall be no more. But the meek shall inherit the earth, And shall delight themselves in the abundance of peace" (Psalm 37:10–11). "Trust in the Lord, and do good... Delight yourself also in the LORD, And He shall give you the desires of your heart" (Psalm 37:3–4). "Cease from anger and forsake wrath; Do not fret—it only causes harm. For evildoers shall be cut off; But those who wait on the LORD, They shall inherit the earth" (Psalm 37:8–9).

By His Word, He shows me how to overcome my anger toward those who in their lack of knowledge of Him, seek to undermine my world. He lets me get a glimpse of His big picture, of heaven itself. He brings me full circle to a remembrance of hope, optimism and peace. He enables me to love, not hate. Our Lord is a wonderful God of righteousness and justice! (Psalm 89:14).

Oh Lord, thank You for being in my life. Thank You for showing me the Way to overcome this world. Thank You for delighting in my way. Though I shall stumble, because of You I shall not fall prey to the darkness of this world for You uphold me in your hand (Psalm 37:23–24). Amen.

PEACE

"The work of righteousness will be peace, and the effect of righteousness, quietness and assurance forever" (Isaiah 32:17).

Jesus is Righteousness.

Jesus is Justice.

Jesus is Peace.

PEACE CAN ONLY BE ACHIEVED BY GOD

A sign along the road reads, "War is not the answer." If war is not the answer, then one must infer that there is a peaceful means of overcoming sinful human acts that cause war such as oppression, dictatorship, and genocide. But peaceful means only work if everyone involved has peaceful intentions. Unfortunately we live in a world of sinners. "There is none righteous, no, not one...for all have sinned and fall short of the glory of God" (Romans 3:10, 23). In certain instances in our fallen world, the wicked must be met with force to overcome their evil intentions. For example, is it even reasonable to assume that Hitler could have been persuaded by peaceful means to desist from his wicked ways?

There is abundant authority in the Bible that in the presence of great evil, God uses war to achieve His purposes. See for example Deuteronomy 20:17 wherein God commanded Moses regarding the Canaanites, "you shall utterly destroy them...as the LORD your God has commanded you." In Jeremiah 5 the Lord used war to punish the Israelites for their sinful ways by sending the Babylonians to kill or capture them. Jesus Christ said, "When you hear of wars and rumors of wars, do not be troubled; for such things must happen...nation will rise against nation, and kingdom against kingdom" (Mark 13:7–8).

War is conflict between right and wrong and good and evil. The foundation of the Lord's throne is mercy (love), truth (faithfulness), righteousness and justice (Psalm 89:14). Righteousness and justice require that evil be forcefully resisted. King Solomon wrote, "To everything there is a season, A time for every purpose under heaven...A time of war, And a time of peace" (Ecclesiastes 3:1, 8).

Just as God by His righteousness causes man to forcefully resist evil in war, He ultimately brings about peace through His justice, for His Word will prevail in the end.

> "These [ten evil kings and the beast] will make war with the Lamb, and the Lamb will overcome them, for

He is the Lord of lords and King of kings; and those who are with Him are called, chosen, and faithful" (Revelation 17:14). "In righteousness He judges and makes war" (Revelation 19:11).

But how does one reconcile the words of Jesus Christ ("Love your enemies, do good to those who hate you, bless those who curse you, and pray for those who spitefully use you. To him who strikes you on the one cheek, offer the other also" (Luke 6:27–29)) with the words of the Father who told the Israelites to annihilate the Hittites, Amorites, and Canaanites and take possession of the promised land? One explanation offered is that in teaching His disciples to love their enemies, Jesus was giving instructions to *individuals*, not nations. On the other hand, Godly commands to avenge evil are directed at *governing authorities* established by Him to serve as His "avenger to execute wrath on him who practices evil" (Romans 13:1–4).

Yes, there will come a time when peace and security will be achieved in the world. But that won't be until Jesus Christ returns. Peace can only be achieved by God. "He shall judge between the nations, and rebuke many people; They shall beat their swords into plowshares, And their spears into pruning hooks. Nation shall not lift up sword against nation, Neither shall they learn war anymore" (Isaiah 2:4). He will make everything new. The dwelling of God will be with men. "He will dwell with them, and they shall be His people... And God will wipe away every tear from their eyes; there shall be no more death, nor sorrow, nor crying. There shall be no more pain, for the former things have passed away" (Revelation 21:3–4; Isaiah 25:8). Then and only then will there be true peace and security in the world and—war will not be the answer.

To Jesus Christ be the glory forever!

JESUS CHRIST: PRINCE OF PEACE OR SWORD-BEARER

The prophet calls Him the "Prince of Peace" (Isaiah 9:6). And yet, Jesus Christ said (citing Micah 7:6),

> "Do not think that I came to bring peace to earth. I did not come to bring peace but a sword. For I have come to 'set a man against his father, a daughter against her mother, and a daughter-in-law against her mother-in-law'; and 'a man's enemies will be those of his own household'" (Matthew 10:34–36).

Throughout the Bible, the Lord teaches peaceful things, yet here He states that He is the bearer of a sword, not peace. Is this an inconsistency in His Word? By no means!

Christ came to earth to establish peace on earth (John 14:27). However, the peace Jesus speaks of in Matthew 10:34 is the peace between His believers and God. For those who do not believe in Him, there will be a price to be paid for their non-belief, for they will be caught up in the conflict between Christ and Satan, the so-called "ruler of the world." That conflict is between light and darkness and between good and evil. For those who believe in Christ, there will be everlasting life with the Lord in His kingdom of heaven (John 3:16). For the unbelievers, there will also be eternal life, but one of damnation, separate from God, in a place where there is eternal weeping and gnashing of teeth (John 3:18)(eternal condemnation).

In Matthew 10:33–35, Jesus, speaking to His twelve apostles told them that there will be conflict with those who do not accept Him as Savior. Instead, Jesus' sword, the Word of God, would cause conflict between the Lord's children and unbelievers; between men and their unbelieving fathers; and conflict between believing mothers and their unbelieving daughters (Matthew 10:35). The conflict is whether to believe in Him or not and that conflict usually occurs between family members. I can attest to that latter point. When I told my Jewish parents that I believed that Jesus was the Messiah, they turned me out. The sword of which Jesus spoke in Matthew 10:34 split our family in two.

But why is there such conflict?

To the unbelieving world, there are no moral absolutes. In the secular atheistic world, everybody and everything is OK no matter what one does "as long as it doesn't harm anyone." You've heard it said: "Is it any of your concern what I do in private?" or "It's my body to do with as I please." Everyone who thinks this way does what's right in his or her own eyes (Judges 21:25).

In the world's view, wrong is right and right is wrong, depending on one's self-interest. Everywhere we look in our society, our precious right to exercise our religious freedom is being eroded: in schools, in government, and soon, if it continues the course it is taking, in our churches. Unbelief is permeating our national institutions.

Our country is split down the middle on every issue: between those who believe that they have a right to do anything without limitation (licentiousness) and those who love Jesus Christ; and between those whose moral base is their own mind and those whose moral reference is the Lord's righteousness and truth. The Father intended that Jesus be His standard-bearer for us. It's the ancient battle between good and evil, and between God and Satan. The consequence of such a battle may be the downfall of our nation, for Jesus Christ said, "Every kingdom divided against itself is brought to desolation, and every city or house divided against itself will not stand" (Matthew 12:25).

Jesus came to this world to cast His light on the darkness of a vain and wicked world (John 3:19–21). He set a high moral base against which our lives are to be measured. He taught love, righteousness, justice, truth, kindness, patience, purity—things which are admirable, excellent and praiseworthy. He is the Prince of Peace. However, He didn't come to the world to bring peace to those who have disdain for Him, but to set a high standard against which the prince of darkness shall be defeated. Satan will be defeated by the Lord's great and wondrous sword: His Word (Revelation 19:19–21).

But even to the unbeliever, there is great hope if he or she will change his or her way and believe in the words of our Lord. Jesus said,

> "I am the way, the truth, and the life. No one comes to the Father except through Me" (John 14:6). "I am the resurrection and the life. He who believes in Me, though he may die, he shall live. And whoever lives and believes in Me shall never die" (John 11:25– 26). "Most assuredly, I say to you, he who hears My word and believes in Him who sent Me has everlasting life, and shall not come into judgment, but has passed from death into life" (John 5:24).

Brothers and sisters, members of households, believers or unbelievers—rejoice, for He is with us! He watches over us. He guards us against the forces of evil in this world. He is the bearer of the sword against all evil and in wielding the sword in our behalf He is our Prince of Peace. He is the only way to eternal life. All we need to do is believe in Him! In so doing we shall overcome with Him the forces of evil and our sinful nature and receive eternal life in His heavenly kingdom.

It is written in the prophets, "All your children shall be taught by the LORD, And great shall be the peace of your children" (Isaiah 54:13). "The peace of God, which surpasses all understanding, will guard your hearts and minds through Christ Jesus" (Philippians 4:7).

PRAISE

"The heavens declare the glory of God; and the firmament shows His handiwork" (Psalm 19:1).

Hallelujah! Praise the Lord!

LET EVERYTHING THAT HAS BREATH PRAISE THE LORD

"Blessed be the God and Father of our Lord Jesus Christ, who has blessed us with every spiritual blessing in the heavenly places in Christ" (Ephesians 1:3). Thus wrote the apostle Paul in his epistle to the Ephesians. Paul explained why we should praise and give thanks to the Lord. He has blessed us with every spiritual blessing "in Christ." Before the creation of the world (John 17:5), He put us who believe in Christ in the Book of Life and chose us to be holy and blameless in His sight (See Romans 8:29). By His grace we are forgiven for all of our sins. He has adopted us as His children through His Son Jesus Christ. He has given to us freely His grace and glory. He provides everything we need in life. In Him, we have redemption from our sins through the blood of His Son. He has graciously made known to us the mystery of His will. He has enabled us to hear His Word of Truth, the gospel of our salvation, and to believe in Him (Ephesians 1:4–13). Having believed, He has marked in us His seal, His Holy Spirit, "the guarantee of our inheritance until the redemption of the purchased possession, to the praise of His glory" (Ephesians 1:14). As believers "in Christ" our salvation is assured—thanks be to God!

The Book of Psalms, a book of praise, emphasizes that we are to praise God for His great works in us, namely, our creation and redemption. The five books of The Book of Psalms each conclude with either the words, "Praise the LORD," " Blessed be the LORD God of Israel," or words of similar import. See Psalms 41:13; 72:18–19; 89:52; 106:48; and 150:6.

"Praise the LORD," said the psalmist in Psalm 150, the final great *Hallelujah* (Hebrew for "Praise the LORD"). Psalm 150, the last Psalm in the Psalter, is the crescendo, the mountaintop of The Book of Psalms. It answers the questions *where* God should be praised (Psalm 150:1), *why* God should be praised (His acts of creation and redemption) (Psalm 150:2), *how* He should be praised (with symphony and dancing) (Psalm 150:3–5), and *who* should praise God ("Let everything that has breath praise the LORD") (Psalm 150:6).

As the Psalmist describes his excitement with the Lord, the setting of praise becomes electrified. He wrote,

1. "Praise the LORD! Praise God in His sanctuary; Praise Him in His mighty firmament!
2. Praise Him for His mighty acts; Praise Him according to His excellent greatness!
3. Praise Him with the sound of the trumpet; Praise Him with the lute and harp!
4. Praise Him with the timbrel and dance; Praise Him with stringed instruments and flutes!
5. Praise Him with loud cymbals; Praise Him with clashing cymbals!
6. Let everything that has breath praise the LORD. Praise the LORD!"

We are to praise the Lord because He breathed the breath of life into our nostrils (Genesis 2:7; Acts 17:25) and He wants everything that has the breath of life to praise Him for the miracle He graciously gave us: life.

We are to praise Him in the mighty firmament, His sanctuary (Psalm 150:1), for "The heavens declare the glory of God; And the firmament shows His handiwork" (Psalm 19:1).

We are to glorify Him for His mighty acts according "to His excellent greatness" (Psalm 150:2). Jesus said, "Believe the works, that you may know and believe that the Father is in Me, and I in Him" (John 10:38). Some of the miracles of life created by His hand are the air we breathe, the food He provides, the clothes on our backs, the roof over our heads, the majesty of the earth we live in—the list is endless (see essay: *The Miracle Worker: Jesus is Our Hope*).

We are to praise Him with wind, string and percussion (Psalm 150:3–5). Imagine a choir of millions of voices accompanied by every musical instrument that ever was, all singing, dancing and playing in unison, praising His Name.

All are to praise Him, "Let everything that has breath praise the LORD. Praise the LORD!" (Psalm 150:6). "Nor is He worshiped with men's hands, as though He needed anything, since He gives to all life, breath, and all things" (Acts 17:25).

What a precious gift our Lord has given us! It's no wonder the psalmist shouts from the highest mountain,

> "Oh, sing to the LORD a new song! Sing to the LORD, all the earth. Sing to the LORD, bless His name; Proclaim the good news of His salvation from day to day. Declare His glory among the nations, His wonders among all peoples. For the LORD is great and greatly to be praised" (Psalm 96:1–4).

PRAYER

Our response to adversity, like our Lord, is to be in prayer with a gentle spirit. "Pray without ceasing" (1 Thessalonians 5:17).

PRAYER WITH A GENTLE SPIRIT

"Christ also suffered for us, leaving us an example, that you should follow His steps...who, when He was reviled, did not revile in return; when He suffered, He did not threaten, but committed Himself to Him who judges righteously" (1 Peter 2:21, 23). After hearing the false testimony against Him, "He kept silent and answered nothing" (Mark 14:61). In the face of extreme adversity, our Lord displayed quiet strength, yet at the same time, meekness and gentleness.

On the one hand, our Lord's "eyes were like a flame of fire" (Revelation 19:12). "Now out of his mouth goes a sharp sword, that with it He should strike the nations. And He Himself will rule them with a rod of iron. He Himself treads the winepress of the fierceness and wrath of Almighty God" (Revelation 19:15). At the same time, He is meek, humble, no burden, loving, considerate, peace-loving, submissive, full of mercy, as a child, respectful, least, obedient, of quiet Spirit, not resentful, slow to anger, kind, sensitive, speaks in a gentle whisper and is like the South wind.

The Lord is a gentle Spirit. "Gentleness is a most necessary feature of the inner man [the spirit]. It is the opposite of harshness. God requires us to cultivate a gentle spirit." Watchman Nee, *The Spiritual Man*, Vol. II, 176.

Not much has changed in the world since Jesus was attacked by His enemies. He said that people would insult us, persecute us, and falsely say all kinds of evil against us because we believe in Him (Matthew 5:11). Daily, we read about attacks on Christians in the world. Prayer has been banned in the schools and now there is a movement to ban prayer in public. Licentiousness is the rule rather than the exception. God's commandments are considered inappropriate displays in public places. Selfishness, rather than generosity, prevails. Freedom of religion is under attack in our culture under the guise of political correctness. Our nation has drifted toward secularism in all aspects of life.

Our fleshly tendency is to lash out in righteous anger at those who seek to suppress our beliefs. But, though we perceive those who oppose us to be sinners, we are reminded by the Scriptures that we too are sinners and that none are righteous, "There is none who does good" (Psalm 14:1). God deals with all of us with an even hand because we are all sinners (Romans 3:9). "He makes His sun to rise on the evil and on the good, and sends rain on the just and the unjust" (Matthew 5:45).

Despite the persistent attacks on Christianity by secularism, Jesus taught, "But whoever slaps you on your right cheek, turn the other to him also" (Matthew 5:39). He exhorted us to be peace-loving and to pray for our oppressors with a gentle spirit as He did, even on His cross. As He was dying, He cried out, "Father, forgive them, for they do not know what they do" (Luke 23:34).

Revenge is not ours, but the Lord's (Deuteronomy 32:35; Romans 12:19). Having learned well from the Lord's teachings, the apostle Paul wrote to the Roman Christians,

> "If it is possible, as much as depends on you, live peaceably with all men. Beloved, do not avenge yourselves, but rather give place to wrath; for it is written, 'Vengeance is mine; I will repay,' says the Lord. Therefore 'If your enemy is hungry, feed him; If he is thirsty, give him a drink; For in so doing you will heap coals of fire on his head.' Do not be overcome by evil, but overcome evil with good" (Romans 12:18–21).

It is written in the Bible that in His timing, Jesus Christ will return with blazing fire in His eyes to judge the world with equity and justice. In the meantime, He teaches that we should live as gentle children of God. He said, "Blessed are the meek, For they shall inherit the earth...Blessed are the merciful, For they shall obtain mercy... Blessed are the peacemakers, For they shall be called Sons of God" (Matthew 5:5, 7, 9). He also teaches that we should give our coat willingly to one who is suing us, to pray for those who persecute us, and offer our left cheek to one who has already struck our right cheek

(Matthew 5:40, 44, 39). Yes, it's very hard to do this. Our flesh tells us to hate our enemies. But our Lord taught us to do otherwise. He said,

> "You have heard that it was said, 'You shall love your neighbor and hate your enemy.' But I say to you, love your enemies, bless those who curse you, do good to those who hate you, and pray for those who spitefully use you and persecute you, that you may be sons of your Father in heaven" (Matthew 5:43–45).

> Our response to adversity, like our Lord, is to be in prayer with a gentle spirit. "[T]hough it has the power of revenge and the protection of the law, [the gentle spirit] nevertheless has no wish to avenge itself with the arm of flesh. It is a spirit which in suffering harms no one. The one who can boast such a spirit as this lives righteously himself but never demands righteousness from others. He is full of love and mercy; wherefore he can melt the heart of those around him." Nee, *The Spiritual Man*, Vol II, 177.

Live life as Jesus taught, with wisdom and patience and prayer in a spirit of gentleness. With meekness, we shall inherit the land in peace.

PRESENCE

"[I]t is necessary to always be aware of God's presence by talking with Him throughout each day. To think that you must abandon conversation with Him in order to deal with the world is erroneous. Instead, as we nourish our souls by seeing God in His exaltation, we will derive great joy at being His." *

---

* Brother Lawrence, *The Practice of the Presence of God*, 8.

NOTES FROM AN EXPERIENCE WITH THE CHRIST

Have you ever been to Israel, Jesus' homeland? Have you ever walked where Jesus walked? Have you seen the mountains, valleys, and villages where He lived, worked and changed the world? Have you ever waded into water upon which He walked? If you haven't, you must. I have been blessed to visit His Holy Land twice and I pray that I may be blessed to go there again. His Word promises that one day all believers will be with Him in His New Jerusalem (Revelation 21). But for now, I can best describe the experience as if one was walking in another Person's shoes. You will see what I mean when I say that being in someone's home is truly the way to get to know that Person.

It was 4:00 a.m., September 1, 1999. My wife Cheryl and I were at Nof Ginosar Kibbutz on the Sea of Galilee in Israel. Nof Ginosar is both a working kibbutz (collective farm) and a resort on the western shore of the Galilee. The Sea of Galilee (also known as Lake Kinneret) is really a fresh water lake about 8 miles wide and about 14 miles long. It is surrounded by mountains on the west, the north and the east. Looking up the lake from Nof Ginosar to the Northeast are the Golan Heights and beyond that, Syria. Across the lake to the east are the mountains of Gilead and Jordan.

I was restless and excited about the coming day. I couldn't sleep. So I got up, dressed, and went out into the dark early morning. The path from our hotel building to the dock on the lake was lit by low lights along the path. I followed the path until I came to the dock and cautiously walked out to the end of the unlit dock.

The setting was grand! The moon was almost full and the stars twinkled softly in the moonlit sky. I could hear the lapping of the water against the rocks on the shore below—the same sound Jesus may have heard. The lake was quiet and a warm gentle breeze was coming from behind me from the west (offshore winds). To my right, I could see the lights of Tiberias in the south on the western shore of the Sea of Galilee. It is said that Tiberias is a city that Jesus never stepped into since it was a Roman city built by Herod Antipas. At the time of Jesus, Tiberias was a place of pagan gods, a city dedicated by Herod to the Roman Caesar Tiberias. When we toured it, Tiberias still seemed very worldly. I looked northeast towards the Golan Heights and I could see the lights of country/mountain villages blinking in the high places of the Golan. That view seemed more serene, more peaceful, more Godly, than the lights of the city built by Herod.

The grandeur of it all overwhelmed me. I felt the presence of the Lord Jesus all around me. I began to sing worship songs about our Lord, and prayed on my knees. Tears came to my eyes. It was so glorious being in a land where Jesus lived. I felt the overwhelming sense that nothing had changed in this place in two thousand years. Oh yes, there were modern buildings such as the kibbutz. Yet God's creations of the night, the moon, the stars, the mountains, the lake— all of these had been there when Jesus walked the earth mere miles north in Capernaum. Perhaps he had experienced a similar setting when He lived as a Man.

After a while, I could sense that the sky was getting brighter in the east—the first light. As the sky brightened ever so gradually, I observed how gently the Lord changes night into day. At 6:18 a.m. (I looked at my watch and noted the time in my journal), the sun was ready to burst over the mountains of Gilead. The only sounds I heard besides the waters of the lake lapping on the rocks were sparrows feeding on food that apparently was on the dock. I suspected that they were feeding on insects. Could it have been that the ancestors of these sparrows chirped near Jesus' ear?

"There it is," I thought to myself, as the sun rose over Gilead across the Sea of Galilee. It cast an orange glow on the gently rippling water. The eastern mountains took on an indistinct gray and served as a wall over which the sun was climbing. I started to hear the sounds of different birds as they arose for the new day. Crows and blackbirds hearkened to the newly risen sun. All was happening so gradually kind of like the Grand Canyon Suite (it starts out very faint and then ends in a grand crescendo). It was all so glorious, so powerful—all so magnificent! How wonderful to experience this splendor as the apostle did. "The glory of the celestial is one, and the glory of the terrestrial is another" (1 Corinthians 15:40). I knew in my heart that what I was seeing, hearing, sensing and experiencing had to be what Jesus saw, heard, and experienced when He lived and prayed nearby.

Nof Ginosar is about four miles south of Capernaum on the shore of the Sea of Galilee where Jesus lived, taught, and spoke as One who had authority. "Then they went into Capernaum, and immediately on the Sabbath He entered the synagogue and taught. And they were astonished at His teaching, for He taught them as one having authority, and not as the scribes" (Mark 1:21–22). Today, Capernaum contains the ruins of a synagogue, the foundation of the home of Simon (Peter) and Andrew (over which is now built a Catholic Church), and many remnants of the days when Jesus was there.

That early morning in Jesus' Holy Land I enjoyed the solitude of a time of prayer and worship on the Sea of Galilee. I had a splendid time! I knew He was with me. I knew in my heart that my Lord was showing me many of the things that He'd created and enjoyed: the stillness of early morning, the serenity of the setting, the warm gentle breezes and soft sounds all around me, the blazing orange reflection of the rising sun, the mountains of Gilead, and His Father's splendor. What a joyous time I had—my time all alone with my Host, Jesus!

After completing our tour of Israel and experiencing the Spirit of the Lord everywhere we went, we returned home. A few weeks later before dawn, while doing my early morning devotions, prayer and Bible readings, I came across this passage from Mark 1:35,

> "Now in the morning, having risen a long while before daylight, He went out and departed to a solitary place; and there He prayed."

When I read this, my heart leaped for joy! I knew in my heart that the solitary place where Jesus prayed while it was still dark had to be on the shore of the Sea of Galilee where He could see the mountains of Gilead, hear the lapping of the water on the rocks on the shore, take in the moon and the stars, and best of all, be with His Father. I was and continue to be so blessed having been with my Lord in His home where He shared with me the splendor of all that He is. Amen.

PRIDE

"Better to be of a humble spirit with the lowly, Than to divide the spoil with the proud" (Proverbs 16:19).

HUMILITY—THE ABSENCE OF PRIDE

"For all that is in the world—the lust of the flesh, the lust of the eyes, and the pride of life—is not of the Father but is of the world" (1 John 2:16). As the apostle John wrote in his epistle, the three basic sinful acts against God are lust of the flesh, lust of the eyes, and the pride of life. These are also the temptations that Satan offered to Eve (Genesis 3:6) and to the Lord Jesus Christ (Matthew 4:1–11). *Thru the Bible*, J. Vernon McGee, Vol. IV, 22. In the Garden, Adam and Eve failed the test. But in the wilderness, Jesus was immutable in resisting Satan's evil offers.

Of the three temptations of Satan, pride is especially abhorrent to God. This is stressed in the Bible by Jesus' teachings about humility. Pride is the absence of humility. "Humility expresses a genuine dependency on God and others. Humility recognizes that we live the Christian life in the same manner we become a Christian—by the grace of God...God hates pride so much that He is willing to allow adversity into the lives of His children to root it out." *The Glorious Journey*, Pastor Charles Stanley, at 306, 307.

Pride is self-exaltation rather than God-exaltation. Pride has no place in the life of the godly, since "A man's pride will bring him low, But the humble in spirit will retain honor" (Proverbs 29:23). Jesus said it another way, "Whoever exalts himself will be humbled, and he who humbles himself will be exalted" (Luke 14:11).

Adam and Eve showed a lack of humility before God when they defied Him and listened to Satan. In Genesis 2:17, God commanded Adam not to eat from the tree of the knowledge of good and evil "for in the day that you eat of it you shall surely die." But Satan knew their weakness—pride. By appealing to their desire to gain the wisdom possessed only by God, he convinced them to disobey the Lord's command not to eat the fruit of the tree. "So when the woman saw that the tree was good for food, that it was pleasant to the eyes, and a tree desirable to make one wise, she took of its fruit and ate" (Genesis 3:6). She knew that she was disobeying God, that is, committing sin since her husband had presumably told her about God's command not to eat of the tree (Genesis 3:17). Sin likes company, so Eve offered some of the fruit to Adam and he ate it. Perhaps she thought there is strength in numbers and that she would have a protector if God confronted them. Pride of life caused Adam and Eve to reject God's command. The apple of the tree tasted good to their flesh, was pleasing to their eyes, and gave them forbidden knowledge of the world. But the world they chose was the world of Satan referenced by the apostle in 1 John 2:16, that is, the realm of sin.

In His anger at their defiance, God banished Adam and Eve from the Garden. Suddenly, life became very difficult for them. No longer would they live free from the burden of getting or growing food, shelter, or the necessities of life that God had provided. Now, Eve would not bear children without the pain of child birth. Adam would have to work by the sweat of his brow to survive and would return to the ground, that is, die. "For the wages of sin is death" (Romans 6:23).

Unlike Adam, Jesus was steadfast when it came to His love and obedience to His Father. In everything, He showed great humility and respect for His Father. His power was made perfect in meekness. Emulating the Lord, His apostles strived to do everything with "tender mercies, kindness, humility, meekness, long suffering" (Colossians 3:12). They also taught us that we are to "be clothed with humility, for 'God resists the proud, But gives grace to the humble'" (1 Peter 5:5). Finally, the apostle Paul's words exhort us "to walk worthy of the calling with which you were called, with all lowliness and gentleness, with longsuffering, bearing with one another in love" (Ephesians 4:1–2), for humility is the absence of pride.

PROSPERITY

"Blessed is the man who fears the LORD, who delights greatly in His commandments...wealth and riches will be in his house, and his righteousness endures forever" (Psalm 112:1, 3)

PROSPERITY: HAVING FAITH IN JESUS CHRIST

We Americans tend to have a sense of well-being from the things we *do* and *have*. It is not just a roof over our heads, a good job, having food on the table, or clothes on our back that convince us that we are prosperous. No, we measure our sense of success or prosperity by other things: material wealth, status in society, intellect, and even beauty. These are all very nice to *do* and *have*, but they are not things that cause us to *be* better people. They have little significance to who we are as human beings.

What is prosperity? What is meant by being prosperous? Is it important that I *do* and *have* things? Sure, it's important that I have a roof over my head, food on the table, and clothes on my back. But how much do I need? The answers to these questions become apparent when we face challenges to what we *do* and *have*—challenges which usually occur in times of trouble.

When I think of the times in my life when I have faced troubles, whether financial, family, or health issues, the things of the world became irrelevant. It was then that "who I *am*" was tested. Tested by whom? By the only meaningful Source of prosperity in our lives: our Lord and Savior Jesus Christ. It was in those times of testing that I was able to get perspective on what was really important in my life. It was in those times when I experienced spiritual growth.

King Solomon wrote with wisdom when he concluded that good times teach us less spiritually than times of trouble (Ecclesiastes 7:1–6). In times of trouble, what was the nature of my spiritual growth? Solace for my soul. What were the means of spiritual growth? I began to rely on the Word of God on a regular basis (daily), I prayed to the Lord often, and I cherished the fellowship with Jesus Christ in His body, the Church.

As I have lived my life, it has become clear to me that real prosperity in life comes from faith in the Lord, knowing Him more intimately, and going deeper in the living waters He provides. His

Word, the Bible, tells us that He is "the bread of life" (John 6:35), "the light of the world" (John 8:12), and "the good shepherd" (John 10:11). Knowing God is true prosperity. It is truly fulfillment in life. It is the gift of His grace to us.

In commenting on Psalm 23:1, Matthew Henry wrote in his *Concise Commentary of the Whole Bible*, 473, "The greatest abundance is but a dry pasture to a wicked man, who relishes in it only what pleases the senses; but to a godly man, who by faith tastes the goodness of God in all his enjoyments, though he has but little of the world, it is a green pasture."

Jesus spoke of true prosperity when He addressed the people of the church at Laodicea. He said, "You say, 'I am rich, have become wealthy, and have need of nothing'" (Revelation 3:17). The people who made up the church at Laodicea regarded themselves as prosperous. Laodicea (now Pamukkale in modern day Turkey) was the wealthiest city in the Roman Province of Phrygia. It was known for its banking institutions, fine textiles, a medical school, and its famous eye salve. The Laodiceans believed they were well-off and successful, two of the definitions used to define prosperity. But Jesus redressed them for this. He excoriated them when He said, "[you] do not know that you are wretched, miserable, poor, blind and naked" (Revelation 3:17). Jesus told them that if they really wanted to be wealthy, they should "buy from Me gold refined in the fire, that you may be rich; and white garments, that you may be clothed, that the shame of your nakedness may not be revealed; and anoint your eyes with eye salve, that you may see" (Revelation 3:18). What was the Lord actually saying to these "wealthy" people?

The Beatitudes lend insight into the Lord's admonition to the Laodiceans,

> "Therefore I say to you, do not worry about your life, what you will eat or what you will drink; nor about your body, what you will put on. Is not life more than food, and the body more than clothing? Look at the birds of the air, for they neither sow nor reap nor gather

into barns; yet your heavenly Father feeds them. Are you not of more value than they?" (Matthew 6:25–26). "Therefore do not worry, saying 'What shall we eat?' or 'What shall we drink?' or 'What shall we wear?'... For your heavenly Father knows that you need all these things. But seek first the kingdom of God and His righteousness, and all these things shall be added to you" (Matthew 6:31–33).

Jesus' definition of prosperity is not being well-off materially or being successful in a worldly sense. To Jesus, it is not *doing* or *having*. It is *being*. It is who we are in Christ. It is being unconcerned about worldly things by acknowledging in faith that He lives His life in and through us. The apostle Paul affirmed this when he wrote, "I have been crucified with Christ; it is no longer I who live, but Christ lives in me; and the life which I now live in the flesh I live by faith in the Son of God, who loved me and gave Himself for me" (Galatians 2:20).

If I truly examine what it means to me to be prosperous, it is, through my faith in Jesus Christ, being unconcerned about things of the world so that "the peace of God, which surpasses all understanding" guards my heart and mind "through Christ Jesus" (Philippians 4:7). If I think about all the wonderful things the Lord freely gives to us, namely truth, righteousness, things that are pure, lovely, noble, excellent or praiseworthy, the world around me loses much of its importance and all my worldly cares, concerns, anxieties and worries fade away leaving that for which I groan and long for (Romans 8:23)—the peace of God, as my true prosperity..

Our Lord delights in our well-being. He said, "Let the LORD be magnified, Who has pleasure in the prosperity of His servant" (Psalm 35:27). He assures us that if we love Him, obey Him and serve Him—if we seek Him—we'll enjoy true prosperity and contentment for the rest of our lives (Job 36:11). Seek the Lord, not worldly things and you will be prosperous. You will "not lack any good thing" (Psalm 34:10). "Seek first the kingdom of God and His righteousness" and all things He freely gives will, by His grace, be given to you as well (Matthew 6:33).

PURITY

"The fear of the LORD is clean, enduring forever" (Psalm 19:9).

PURIFY YOUR HEART WITH THE WORD OF GOD

In His Sermon on the Mount, the Lord Jesus Christ said, "Blessed are the pure in heart, For they shall see God" (Matthew 5:8). The Psalmist wrote, "Who may ascend into the hill of the LORD? Or who may stand in His holy place? He who has clean hands and a pure heart" (Psalm 24:3–4). God teaches that we should live a clean life with a pure heart. Purity of heart speaks of perfection, of clarity, and of ultimate refinement. Christ set the standard. He said, "Therefore you shall be perfect, just as your Father in heaven is perfect" (Matthew 5:48).

Dr. Charles Stanley defines *heart* as it is used in the spiritual sense as "your innermost being where motivation and desire reside." Pastor Stanley wrote, "If your heart is right, your character is right...Jesus modeled a consistent character. His character validated His mission and ministry. The key to Christ's character was purity of heart." *The Glorious Journey*, 23.

But, as J. Vernon McGee wrote in his commentary *Thru the Bible*, Matthew 5:8, Vol IV, 30, "No honest man can say his heart is pure. How can the heart of man, which is desperately wicked, be made clean?" How can we who are not without sin be pure in heart? A pure heart sounds like something that's impossible. Pastor McGee addressed this issue in his *Thru the Bible*, commentary of John 15:3, Vol IV, 467, "We were born again by the Word of God, washed from our sins. Then in our walk down here we get dirty and need the Word of God to cleanse us continually. That is one reason to study the Bible—to be cleansed."

The dross of yesterday's living sometimes hangs over us like the morning after. Yet in spite of this, every morning we awake to a new day, a new opportunity to live life, to work, to create, to do that which is right and good, but most of all to love with a pure heart (Lamentations 3:23). Morning is the perfect time to "be renewed in the spirit of your mind" (Ephesians 4:23). "How can a young man cleanse his way? By taking heed according to Your word" (Psalm 119:9). The Lord Jesus Christ said, "*You* are already clean because of the word which I have spoken to you" (John 15:3). Jesus did as He preached. "Now in the morning, having risen a long while before daylight, He went out and departed to a solitary place; and there He prayed" (Mark 1:35).

I find that early morning is a wonderful time to spend in the Bible, to pray to the Lord and study His Word. It is a quiet time, free of distractions. The first time doing it may seem like a sacrifice (that is, giving up some sleep time), however, after some time, it becomes second nature to be alone with God. It is the time of the day when my mind is the clearest. Reading the Bible and saying prayers to God quiets me down and prepares me for a day of interaction with the world. It almost always shows me something that can be improved, changed, or hopefully made purer in my life. It is doing as Jesus did when He prayed at Capernaum, early in the morning (Mark 1:35).

Perhaps I shall not achieve absolute purity of heart while on this earth, but what I do know is that I shall ask the Lord for it every morning in a prayer, "Create in me a clean heart, O God, And renew a steadfast spirit within me" (Psalm 51:10).

GOD'S PURPOSE FOR US IS THAT WE BE PURE IN HEART

"Finally, brethren, whatever things are true, whatever things are noble, whatever things are just, whatever things are pure, whatever things are lovely, whatever things are of good report, if there is any virtue and if there is anything praiseworthy—meditate on these things" (Philippians 4:8). The virtues described by the apostle Paul are wholesome and inspire us to lead a life of moral and spiritual purity.

Jesus Christ taught on a hill overlooking the Sea of Galilee, "Blessed are the pure in heart, For they shall see God" (Matthew 5:8). Being pure is being without fault; perfect; sinless. There is only One who has these traits: our Lord. Jesus Christ is pure for "in Him there is no sin" (1 John 3:5). He is perfection. He "is love" (1 John 4:16).

> "Love suffers long and is kind; love does not envy; love does not parade itself, is not puffed up; does not behave rudely, does not seek its own, is not provoked, thinks no evil; does not rejoice in iniquity, but rejoices in the truth; bears all things, believes all things, hopes all things, endures all things. Love never fails" (1 Corinthians 13:4–8).

The purity of Jesus Christ is all of these and more.

When Jesus teaches us to be pure in heart, He is saying that we should be like Him. We are His children and as children of God, we must strive to be Christ-like.

> "Behold what manner of love the Father has bestowed on us, that we should be called children of God... and it has not been revealed what we shall be, but we know that when He is revealed, we shall be like Him, for we shall see Him as He is. And everyone who has

this hope in Him purifies himself, just as He is pure"
(1 John 3:1–3).

"God is determined to have His child as pure, clean and white as driven snow [like Him]...God is determined to make you pure, holy and right...God is going to bring you out pure, spotless and undefiled..." Oswald Chambers, *My Utmost for His Highest*, July 1.

Becoming pure in heart is a lifetime process. Of ourselves we cannot become pure like the Lord. We need His Holy Spirit to mold us and refine us as He does with pure silver—it is purified in a furnace of clay seven times (Psalm 12:6). "...when the Holy Spirit comes in, He brings into the center of my personal life the very Spirit that was manifested in the life of Jesus Christ, *viz*, the Holy Spirit, which is unsullied purity." Oswald Chambers, *id* at July 26.

One example of the process by which the Holy Spirit refines or purifies our hearts is found in Matthew 18:15 wherein Jesus said, "Moreover if your brother sins against you, go and tell him his fault between you and him alone. If he hears you, you have gained your brother." Has a brother or sister in the Lord ever done anything that offended you or caused you pain? I'm sure the answer is a resounding *yes* for all of us. In the face of such an offense, what action, if any, did we take? Did we speak out and confront our brother or sister with love, or did we let it sit and fester? The easy route in such circumstances would be to remain silent or not say anything. But that's repaying dishonesty with dishonesty. It's not what Jesus would do. It takes courage to speak the truth to your brother or sister by telling him or her how they've been inconsiderate, or judgmental, or selfish, or dishonest etc. Jesus instructs us to tell our brother his fault. In so doing, we not only clear up the hidden agenda between us and our brother (or sister), but a purification process occurs by which our own hearts are cleansed and enables us to know He is with us. It's the Holy Spirit at work molding us and refining us like the Potter at the wheel. See the essay entitled *Resolving a Dispute: Lawsuit or Christian Mediation* for a discussion of the blessings that come from speaking the truth in the context of a "Matthew 18 Mediation" and how the truth, when uttered, purifies our hearts.

It is God's purpose that His children be pure in heart and by so doing, be like Him. It may take a lifetime of purification by the Holy Spirit, but He wants us to know Him and not obstruct His life in us so that, in the end, we are one with Him just as He and the Father are One. That is purity.

PURPOSE OF LIFE

According to the Word of God, our purpose in life is not to be God, but to emulate Him in every way: "Then God said, 'Let us Make man in Our image, according to Our likeness'" (Genesis 1:26). "For whom He foreknew, He also predestined to be conformed to the image of His Son" (Romans 8:29). "Let us hear the conclusion of the whole matter: Fear God and keep His commandments, for this is man's all" (Ecclesiastes 12:13.

THE PURPOSE OF LIFE QUESTIONS

Recently, I retired from my profession of forty-three years. It's been quite a run: education, marriage, family, work, church and community have filled my days. Where did all the time go? I remember the day I turned thirty. I exclaimed, "I'm not a teenager anymore!" One day I am young and setting goals for my future, and then before I know it, most of the goals have been fulfilled and I'm approaching the twilight of my life.

As the initial excitement and freedom of retirement wears down and the days become routine, unsettling purpose of life questions come to the fore: Why was I born? What's my purpose in life? What is the meaning of my life? Is there something else God intends for me before my flesh returns to dust? Why do I have to die? Have I done right by God in my lifetime? Have I been a good person? What has been my moral reference in life? Has it been God or have I acted from self? The list of questions is endless. Only God knows the answers.

I love the Bible, God's Word, because it always answers any question I have in life! The Bible is the inerrant Word of God. It says, "All Scripture is given by inspiration of God, and is profitable for doctrine, for reproof, for correction, for instruction in righteousness" (2 Timothy 3:16). The Bible was written by Holy Spirit-inspired men of God for our instruction so that as we endure life we might be assured of the hope of God and "be complete, thoroughly equipped for every good work" (2 Timothy 3:17). The apostle Paul wrote, "For whatever things were written before were written for our learning, that we through the patience and comfort of the Scriptures might have hope" (Romans 15:4).

King Solomon, the wisest of all kings, asked purpose of life questions as he contemplated his final years in this world. He questioned what gain a man got from all of his years of toil on the earth. He observed that as the sun comes up and goes down day by day, generations come and go—but the earth continues as if a man never existed. Whatever has been on earth will again be repeated.

Solomon concluded that "there is nothing new under the sun...no remembrance of former things...[or]...of things that are to come" (Ecclesiastes 1:9, 11).

At first glance it appears that Solomon regarded life as meaningless and without purpose, but when he was about to face his Maker in his later years, he found the answer to all of his "purpose of life" questions. He wrote, "For I considered all this in my heart, so that I could declare it all: that the righteous and the wise and their works are in the hand of God" (Ecclesiastes 9:1). When all of his wisdom was spoken and done, Solomon concluded that there is only one answer to the purpose of life questions—God. He wrote, "Let us hear the conclusion of the whole matter: Fear God and keep His commandments, For this is man's all" (Ecclesiastes 12:13). Without God in one's life, there is no purpose for life and no purpose of life questions to be answered in seeking the truths of life.

After the five thousand had just been miraculously fed bread and fish, the Lord Jesus Christ answered a purpose of life question posed by some of them. "They said to Him, 'What shall we do, that we may work the works of God?' Jesus answered and said to them, 'This is the work of God, that you believe in Him whom He sent'" (John 6:28–29). In just a few words, the Lord explained what this life is all about. He said that we are to "seek first the kingdom of God and His righteousness, and all these things shall be added to you" (Matthew 6:33). In essence, belief in Jesus Christ as Lord and Savior is our purpose in life. By believing in Him, all our purpose of life questions will be answered and fulfilled both in this life in the flesh and throughout eternity—forever.

I am at the age of my life where the precious days given to me by God are coming to a close. It is a time of reflection, of examination of life's truths—a look at what it has been all about. It's amazing how the Holy Spirit places purpose of life questions in front of our minds at just the right times. God didn't create us to be able to answer these questions ourselves. However, I am greatly comforted by our Lord's answer in His Word, particularly as to what I'm to do the rest of my life— "seek first the kingdom of God and His righteousness"

(Matthew 6:33) and "...fill [my] thoughts with his desires...," mold my character as much as possible after Him, and "...serve and obey him in everything." Note at Matthew 6:33 (NKJV), *Life Application Bible*, Tyndale. He'll take care of the details.

I rest easy these days as I ponder the purpose of life questions that arise from time to time. As each day begins, it is my conscious desire to obey Him and look to Him for direction—He always comes through. Although retired, my life is so filled with Godly things that sometimes I could almost burst with excitement over the things I have to look forward to the rest of my days and beyond!

What a wondrous God we have in Jesus Christ!

SHIFTING SHADOWS

Life on earth is measured by two existential events: birth and death. King Solomon wrote, "To everything there is a season, A time for every purpose under heaven: A time to be born, And a time to die" (Ecclesiastes 3:1–2). As I go through the twilight of my life, these words have become more and more significant because our days are but "handbreaths...every man at his best state is but vapor...every man walks about like a shadow" (Psalm 39:5–6). Life in the flesh is temporary and fleeting and at some point in time, ends.

The apostle James, brother of Jesus, asked, "What is your life?" Then he answered his own question, "It is even a vapor that appears for a little time and then vanishes away" (James 4:14). The psalmist wrote, "LORD, what is man, that You take knowledge of him? Or the son of man, that You are mindful of him? Man is like a breath; His days are like a passing shadow" (Psalm 144:3–4).

> In the face of great tribulation, the prophet Job pondered the meaning of life in the flesh, "Man who is born of woman Is of few days and full of trouble. He comes forth like a flower and fades away; He flees like a shadow and does not continue...Since his days are determined, The number of his months is with You; You have appointed his limits, so that he cannot pass... But man dies and is laid away; Indeed he breathes his last And where is he?...If a man dies, shall he live again?" (Job 14:1–2, 5, 10, 14).

Even though Job stated that man's life is "like a shadow," Job's last question ("Shall he live again?") reflects his deep faith that God will call him, even from the grave, and that death in the flesh is not the end of life. As J. Vernon McGee wrote about these verses, "...God is not through with us at our death." *Thru the Bible*, Job 14:14, Vol II, 613.

Most people, at one time or another, ask the *meaning of life* questions. They ponder, "What is the meaning of my life? What is its purpose? Why was I born? What happens to me when I die? Why do I continually experience trouble as though I've done wrong? How am I to know right from wrong?" King Solomon wrote that God, and how He works, is incomprehensible to man, "Then I saw all the work of God, that a man cannot find out the work that is done under the sun. For though a man labors to discover it, yet he will not find it; moreover, though a wise man attempts to know it, he will not be able to find it" (Ecclesiastes 8:17). "The secret things belong to the LORD our God" (Deuteronomy 29:29).

Even with all of his Godly wisdom, Solomon struggled with the same existential questions that we struggle with in life. His initial conclusion, "'Vanity of vanities,' says the Preacher. 'Vanity of vanities, all is vanity.' ...I have seen all the works that are done under the sun; and indeed, all is vanity and grasping for the wind" (Ecclesiastes 1:2, 14). However, after thoroughly examining life's meaning as recorded in his Book of Ecclesiastes, Solomon concluded that everything under the sun is *meaningless without God.* He wrote a Proverb explaining how we must deal with life in the flesh, "Trust in the LORD with all your heart, And lean not on your own understanding; In all your ways acknowledge Him, and He shall direct your paths" (Proverbs 3:5–6).

To the atheist the supernatural doesn't exist. To him or her, only the material world exists. In his or her view, life is just an accident and has no purpose other than "gathering and collecting." Solomon concluded that "This also is vanity and grasping for the wind" (Ecclesiastes 2:26). To the secularist, there is no God, no Creation, no meaning, and no life after we die—it's over when it's over. But David thought such thinking was foolish. He wrote, "The fool has said in his heart, 'There is no God'" (Psalm 53:1).

In post-modern times, the evolutionist says, "I am here, not by design, but by a quirk of fate; an insignificant accident in time— evolved from an ooze, a materialistic cell slithering its way across a sea of slime." Even if this were so, the evolutionist can't explain where the ooze came from. In his or her view "it just happened," or "it came from outer space," or being honest, they say, "I don't know where it came from." The evolutionist doesn't see meaning or purpose for life. Perhaps the evolutionist's idea of the purpose of life is to evolve into something else—a purposeless meandering.

On the other hand, godly men such as David and his son Solomon believed that life was designed, planned, and created by a Supreme, Omniscient, Omnipotent, Omnipresent, Immanent, Immutable, Transcendent, Righteous, Loving Being—God (See Psalm 139:1–18). To Solomon, everything under the sun is from God. He saw God as the purpose for it all, "This also [eating, drinking, and working], I saw, was from the hand of God. For who can eat, or who can have enjoyment, more than I? For God gives wisdom and knowledge and joy to a man who is good in His sight" (Ecclesiastes 2:24–26).

God intended that our lives be lived *in His image*, to love Him as He loves us, to do His will and not ours, and to cherish Him and not our *self.* According to the Word of God, our purpose in life is not to be God, but to emulate Him in every way, "Then God said, 'Let Us make man in Our image, according to Our likeness'...So God created man in His own image; in the image of God he created him; male and female He created them" (Genesis 1:26–27). "For whom He foreknew, He also predestined to be conformed to the image of His Son" (Romans 8:29).

If we are to emulate God, that is, to live in His image, we need to clothe ourselves ("Put on the whole armor of God") (Ephesians 6:11) with the characteristics of God—His love, compassion, kindness, humility, gentleness, patience, forgiveness, righteousness, justice, holiness, strength, splendor, majesty, glory, power, honor and respect—and be conformed to His likeness (See Colossians 3:12–14). In conforming to the likeness of God, we should *be* and *do* "whatever things are true, whatever things are noble, whatever things are just, whatever things are pure, whatever things are lovely, whatever things are of good report, if there is any virtue and if there is anything praiseworthy—[we should] meditate on these things" (Philippians 4:8). We can *be* and *do* these things only by the grace of the Lord. He will provide us with His grace if we trust Him, believe in Him, have faith in Him, and are willing to die to ourselves.

God provided the means by which we can become aware of His character and emulate His image—the Holy Bible. "Faith comes by hearing, and hearing by the word of God" (Romans 10:17). When I study God's Word and think about things above, my spirit is uplifted. I feel totally congruous with Him when I am mindful of the presence of His Holy Spirit within me. It is the natural state of being for the human spirit to be completely congruous with the Holy Spirit of God. That had to be Adam's state of being before he was misled to sin by the evil spirit, Satan.

When I think of things above and act accordingly, the focus of my mind leads me to a purer state of being. But in my fleshly existence, there is something within me that prevents me from achieving the pure state of being taught by God: unclean or sinful thoughts which emanate within me out of *self*. Thoughts occur within me that are not in accord with God's teachings such as judgment of others, profanity, and other negative thoughts. Those dark thoughts interfere with my ability to act in accordance with the pure teachings of God.

The conflict between *self* and our ability to follow the directions of the Holy Spirit of God within us arises out of something else within us that is God-given—free will. Being free to choose of my own will, I often make wrong choices and act against the will of God. Just as our ancestor Adam made wrong choices in defiance of God, my wrong choices also defy the will of God. Defiant wrong choice against God is sin.

But why did God give us free will? A related question is whether free will is really volitional in view of Romans 8:29 (see above)? But that is part of the mystery of life in the flesh to be answered if we make the right choice. Perhaps God's thinking in giving us freedom of choice was that true love cannot be imposed; it has to be volitional to be real. Being our eternal Father, He loves us and wants us to love Him as He loves us. He wants us to do that freely, not by His imposition. God is a beneficent Person, not a dictator.

In the conflict between *self* and God which arises in the exercise of the alleged freedom to choose, our mind fluctuates back and forth—to God—to *self*—to God—to *self*—*ad infinitum*. While in our earth suits, we are like floating objects tossed to and fro in a stormy sea. "He who doubts [God] is like a wave of the sea driven and tossed by the wind" (James 1:6). We change like "shifting shadows" (James 1:17 NIV).

What could be God's objective for us to be in constant conflict in this life in the flesh? Perhaps He wants our attention. For sure He wants our love. There's no question that He wants our faith and He wants us to walk deeply with Him as we mature in life—as we approach the *opposite* existential gate—death. How does He accomplish that? He allows life's troubles into our lives. He tests us. "The LORD your God is testing you to know whether you love the LORD your God with all your heart and with all your soul" (Deuteronomy 13:3). God wants us to see life's troubles as tests and to recognize them as such. In this context, life's purpose becomes clear. "My brethren, count it all joy when you fall into various trials, knowing that the testing of your faith produces patience. But let patience have its perfect work, that you may be perfect and complete, lacking nothing" (James 1:2–4). The apostle Paul said it another way,

> "Therefore, having been justified by faith [i.e., as believers in Christ, God pronounced us righteous in His sight], we have peace with God through our Lord Jesus Christ, through whom also we have access by faith into this grace in which we stand, and rejoice in hope of the glory of God. And not only that, but we also glory in tribulations, knowing that tribulation produces perseverance; and perseverance, character; and character, hope. Now hope does not disappoint, because the love of God has been poured out in our hearts by the Holy Spirit who was given to us" (Romans 5:1–5).

While on earth, God wants to draw us closer to Him. When troubles occur in life, most people naturally reach out to God. The

Psalmist provided an explanation for this, "God is our refuge and strength, A very present help in trouble" (Psalm 46:1). But when things seem to be going well, the tendency is to forget about God. An example of this is the tragedy of "9/11." The churches filled during the troubling months following the tragedy of September 11, 2001. People sought the hope and comfort of God. Thereafter, as time passed and memories of that tragic event dimmed and started to fade, many drifted back in their spiritual walk—away from God—and resumed their earthly lives, as shifting shadows.

As we grow older and approach the end of earthly life, I believe that it is the Lord's intent that the conflict between *self* and Him diminishes and that more and more, He becomes the focus of our life. As stated above, God designed us to be in His image; in His likeness (Genesis 1:26). God is holy (John 6:69). Becoming more like God's holiness as we near the final border of life in the flesh is called *sanctification*—becoming holy or good. It is the work of all three Persons of the Trinity, but especially the Holy Spirit within us that we are redeemed and become more holy, more blameless, more Jesus-like, as our life progresses (1 Peter 1:1–2).

On the other hand, even though God desires that as we progress in life we draw closer to Him and love Him as He loves us, he created in us a mechanism that seeks to protect *self* at all costs. Psychologists call the mechanism *ego* which means *self*. Ego is *self*-love—a state of being opposed to God. The more free-will is exercised to choose things opposed to God, the more ego grows. The more ego, the less there is of God in our life; the more *self*, the less God is part of our life. So if ego is a God-given mechanism to protect *self* and the protection of *self* is opposed to God, why would God give us ego? Like all things of God, it is a mystery, another issue in life that causes us to be in a state of undulation, shifting back and forth between *self* and God—a shifting shadow.

Regarding ego, when we are born in the flesh, our spirit is dormant; at low ebb. Look at a new-born baby. Its sole purpose for existence is survival. He or she cries out for food, clean diapers, and warm loving comfort from mother and father. The baby is almost in pure *self.* Its prime existential purpose is to sustain its own life. As we mature, we begin to see that there is more to life than empirical things. Our spirit begins to reach out ("groan") for more in life than just material things. If it is God's will for us, He touches our groaning spirit, aligns it with His, and causes us to be reborn with His Holy Spirit within us and become one of His *elect.*

Our ego causes us to seek things that we think we need to sustain our human fleshly life, but in our misdirected desire to fulfill fleshly needs, we often end up doing that which we don't want to do—ignoring God and His moral law, that is, sinning. Sinning is the act of ignoring, doubting or defying God. Paul wrote about this in his letter to the Roman believers in Christ,

> "I am carnal, sold under sin. For what I am doing, I do not understand. For what I will to do, that I do not practice; but what I hate, that I do. But now, it is no longer I who do it, but sin that dwells in me. For I know that in me (that is, in my flesh) nothing good dwells; for to will is present with me, but how to perform what is good I do not find. For the good that I will to do, I do not do; but the evil I will not to do, that I practice. Now if I do what I will not to do, it is no longer I who do it, but sin that dwells in me" (Romans 7:14–15, 17–20).

Peter had good intentions when he started walking on the water towards the Lord Jesus. "But when he saw that the wind was boisterous, he was afraid, and, beginning to sink he cried out, saying, 'Lord, save me!'" (Matthew 14:30). His focus had quickly shifted—from God to *self.* When this occurred, doubt crept into his mind. Believing that only his *self* could save him and doubting that Jesus was who He said He was, Peter started to drown. Jesus saved him from drowning and said to him, "O you of little faith, why did you doubt?" (Matthew 14:31). Peter started out from the boat focusing on the Lord and then shifted back to *self* and became but another shifting shadow.

But why did God design us with free will? Why did he create *ego* in us? Why did he create the need in us to protect our *self* at all costs? These purpose-of-life questions are plaguing to us humans who cannot totally comprehend who or what God is. Indeed, the answers to these questions are the secret things of God (Deuteronomy 29:29).

All of these questions deal with life-in-the-flesh issues. Perhaps these non-material earthly mechanisms are designed by God in order to enable us to survive in the flesh. What's ironic is that we ultimately do not survive in the flesh. We are all sinners and the penalty for sinning is death, death of the flesh.

But why do we need to survive in the flesh? Why do we need to have fleshly life in the first place? In the vast concept of time, life on earth is but a blink of the eye. Determined just by its brevity, it could not have been intended to be a permanent home for us. Perhaps it's because God placed us in a testing laboratory (earth) (See Deuteronomy 13:3, above) to see if we'd ultimately choose Him— or not. In that laboratory, perhaps God gave us an opportunity to participate in the decision of where we shall spend eternity: in heaven with God, or in condemnation with his fallen angel, Satan.

"He shall not return by way of the gate through which he came, but shall go out through the opposite gate" (Ezekiel 46:9). The prophet's statement is a metaphor of life in the flesh. As a loving Father, the Lord wants us to come back to Him in His heavenly realm by way of the gate (the "Spirit-gate") opposite the gate (the "*flesh/self*-gate") through which we entered the world. He wants us to see Him, hear Him, need Him, and obey Him while we are on the earth. He doesn't want us to reject Him as Adam and Eve did in His garden.

Like Adam, God started us out and gave us but one command as to how to live on the earth: obedience to Him. Earthly life is a temporary place in which God has given us the free right to choose— Him or otherwise. The prime issue is whether we will choose rightly within the brief time He's allotted or whether we will choose wrongly like Adam who was left in the dust of the earth, banned from God's heavenly garden? That's a presumption on my part about Adam. Only God knows whether he ultimately repented of his sinful ways once he was ejected from God's garden. It raises interesting questions about the effect on mankind if he did repent—but that's for another day's question about the purpose of life.

God placed the first man in a majestic garden—He called it "the garden of Eden" (Genesis 2:15). In God's garden, He provided everything man needed to live his life on earth. However, God told Adam, "Of every tree of the garden you may freely eat; but of the tree of the knowledge of good and evil you shall not eat, for in the day that you eat of it you shall surely die" (Genesis 2:16–17). But in exercising his God-given free will, Adam defied God's command and ate the fruit from the forbidden tree. This was the original sin of man. Before Adam committed sin against God by defying His command, death may not have been a part of God's plan for creation. In Genesis 3:19, death of fleshly man as a consequence of his sin is the prescribed penalty, "For dust you are, And to dust you shall return." Perhaps until he ate of the tree, Adam may have been living an eternal life with God in His eternal garden.

Note that a very important word in Genesis 2:16 is *freely.* God gave Adam free will with one limitation: he was free to eat, drink and live as he desired, but he was not free to disobey God, that is, to commit sin without consequence. Above all else, God created us to love and obey Him.

Jesus Christ said,

> "'You shall love the LORD your God with all your heart, with all your soul, and with all your mind.' This is the first and great commandment. And the second is like it: 'You shall love your neighbor as yourself.' On these two commandments hang all the Law and the Prophets" (Matthew 22:37–40).

Jesus said this in response to a question from a teacher of the law who asked Him, "Teacher, what shall I do to inherit eternal life?" (Luke 10:25).

"God is love" (1 John 4:8). He loves us with all His heart, soul and mind and He wants us to love Him in the same manner. But Adam wasn't content with just loving God. He wanted to be like God, not just in His image, but *to be as a god himself.* Satan led the way for he'd done the same thing with respect to God and had been thrown out of heaven (Luke 10:18). In his desire to make *self* the center of his universe, Adam did that which he shouldn't have done (or perhaps, didn't want to do): he defied God's command. In exercising free will, he didn't love God back, but loved *self* more than God. Like a shifting shadow, when he came to the Tree of the Knowledge of Good and Evil Adam chose wrongly. In his brief earthly life, he failed God's test. What was the consequence? The consequence was death, "For the wages of sin is death" (Romans 6:23). In God's Word in Genesis 3 the Lord has described how and why mankind suffered a great fall from the grace of God to a life of sin (disobedience of God in favor of *self*). It was here that the sinful nature spoken of by Paul in Romans 7 entered into the earthly life of man. It was here that death came into being.

In our search for the meaning of life we start out as babies in pure *self* and like a hamster, we go back and forth, up and down, side to side trying to find a way through the maze of fleshly life. In this process, our ego-centered *self* wills that we focus on empirical things: what we see, hear, taste, touch and smell—the material things of life. C. S. Lewis in his first book, *The Screwtape Letters*, called this going back and forth *undulation.* Just as the world moves in cycles, so do we shift back and forth, between flesh (*self*) and Spirit (God). Our life goes up and it goes down. When life seems to be good, we focus on the world; when life's down, we seek God. We undulate!

God is in everything, both spiritual and material. Neither is meaningless. However, in our earthly journey, we should ultimately conclude that the material things of earth are not as important as the spiritual. Spiritual is on a higher plain than material for in the beginning spiritual begot material. Material was created from the spiritual (John 1:1). God is Spirit (John 4:24). Therefore from His point of view, it is the heavenly things that He wants us to see and choose as our purpose of life. He desires that after life in the flesh, we rejoin Him in heaven.

Without God, life is meaningless. "The only things we can keep are the things we freely give to God." C. S. Lewis, *Mere Christianity*, 213. As described above, King Solomon ultimately discovered this truth late in his life (See Ecclesiastes 2:24–26; 12:13–14).

In his heart and soul, man knows about God. The Lord designed it that way. At one time or another in life, we groan to be with God. "As the deer pants for the water brooks, So pants my soul for you, O God. My soul thirsts for God, for the living God" (Psalm 42:1–2). Inwardly, we long to know Him as a Father, for Him to adopt us, to love us, and to answer our cries to be saved from our sinful nature (Romans 8:23). Why do we long for God? His Word tells us that He will save us. He says, "Call upon Me in the day of trouble; I will deliver you, and you shall glorify Me" (Psalm 50:15).

Like the shifting shadow we cast as we walk under the sun, so too does our spirit shift to and fro. It is when we willingly and freely choose to shift our focus upon God that we discover a Life that stays firm, like a Rock in the swift current of a flooded river in spring. In contrast to us who are but wisps of air on the wind while in the flesh, God is the Rock that endures forever. God is the "anchor of the soul, both sure and steadfast" (Hebrews 6:19). It is so important for our eternal lives that while in the flesh, we willingly and knowingly choose to stop our shifting shadows and attach our anchor to the "anchor of the soul."

God's purpose for us is good (Romans 8:28). "Every good gift and every perfect gift is from above, and comes down from the Father of lights, with whom there is no variation or shadow of turning" (James 1:17). God does not change (Malachi 3:6; Hebrews 13:8). He is the Standard Bearer against which all things are measured. He is the ultimate moral reference for the universe. He is consistency in a world of inconsistency. He is our Rock, our Fortress, and our Deliverer (2 Samuel 22:2). What possible reason could there be to choose other than Him? What possible other purpose could there be for life?

Jesus said, "If anyone desires to come after Me, let him deny himself, and take up his cross daily, and follow Me" (Luke 9:23). To be more like Christ (that is, in God's image), our God-given *daily* choice must be to deny our flesh (our *self*), take up the gift of the cross that He, by His grace, has given to us, and choose Him. In so doing, we shall become less changeable and more like Him, unchangeable. We'll no longer be shifting shadows, but children of the Light. "If then you were raised with Christ, seek those things which are above, where Christ is, sitting at the right hand of God. Set your minds on things above, not on things on the earth" (Colossians 3:1–2). By so doing, "you have put off the old man [self] with his deeds, and have put on the new man, who is renewed in knowledge according to the image of Him who created him" (Colossians 3:9–10).

Live in the image of God to carry out His purpose for our lives—eternal life with Him. Don't undulate like a shifting shadow, but emulate the Lord in all ways. Study His Word each day and by doing so, mature and deepen your faith in Him. Spend time with Him in His presence thus deepening your relationship and faith in Him. "Do not look at the things which are seen, but at the things which are not seen. For the things which are seen are temporary, but the things which are not seen are eternal" (2 Corinthians 4:18).

The universe I live in is the Lord's place. I am just an invited guest in His world. It is but a temporary visit. While I am here, He *allows* me the limited freedom to shift back and forth—between *self* and God—a spiritual shifting shadow—so that I can learn to fulfill His purpose for my life. What is that purpose? That purpose should be to think like Jesus Christ, to live as Jesus Christ taught, and to make the right choice in life: not *self*, but God. King Solomon summed it up in a few words of wisdom: "Fear God and keep His commandments, For this is man's all" (Ecclesiastes 12:13).

The lyrics of a popular hymn, *Empty Me, * written and composed by John Comer and Gene Way, succinctly set forth what our prayer in this earthly life should be,

> "Holy fire, burn away
> My desire for anything
> That is not of you and is of me
> I want more of you
> And less of me.
> Empty me, empty me, fill me
> With you, with you."

Oh Lord, this is our prayer: Permit us to seek less of *self* and more of You. As we go through this fleshly life, assist us in our quest not to be shifting shadows, but to choose to be like You.

B. NEIL SHAW

RECONCILIATION

Jesus is the Great Reconciler. He said, "No one comes to the Father except through Me" (John 14:6). "I am the Alpha and the Omega, the Beginning and the End, the First and the Last" (Revelation 22:13). He connects the beginning with the end. He reconciles all.

THE GREAT RECONCILER

Reconcile: to bring together; to understand how the beginning relates to the end.

In a recent study of the book of The Revelation of Jesus Christ, it occurred to me that there is a special connection between the beginning of the Bible and the end of the Bible. I thought, "Is the beginning of the Bible tied in to its end? How does one reconcile the entire Bible?" A clue to this question occurs in Revelation 22:13 wherein Jesus says, "I am the Alpha and the Omega, the Beginning and the End, the First and the Last." He makes this statement as recorded by the apostle John in the last chapter of the last book of the Bible.

The Bible has a definite order to it—an order set over many centuries by many God-inspired theologians. Its order is perfectly logical, chronologically describing the creation process in the beginning and the destruction of all things of earth at the end. In Genesis 1 (the first book), creation of the universe is described in great detail. In Revelation (the last book), the Lord describes how it will all end and even how it will be after the end of things. In His Holy Bible the Lord reconciles the beginning with the end. He brings it all together from the Alpha to the Omega and from the first to the last. He is the Great Reconciler. He brings it together from the beginning to the end.

Let's take a closer look as to the overall theme of the Bible and how the Lord reconciles the beginning with its end.

The first words of the Bible are, "In the beginning God created..." (Genesis 1:1). He created the heaven and the earth, light and darkness, the sea and the land, and the plants and animals. But His most important creation was man. Why is man God's most important creation? Because man was the only living being that He created in His own image. He gave man dominion over all the earth and all of its creatures as His divinely appointed steward (Genesis 1:26). He loved man, His fondest creation, and as our loving Father, He wanted us to be with Him from the start.

"And the LORD God formed man of the dust of the ground, and breathed into his nostrils the breath of life; and man became a living being" (Genesis 2:7). Man was intended by God to have a special place in His heart. He placed him in a special place close to God's heart: in a garden which God Himself had planted (Genesis 2:8). This tells us that God created us outside His garden and then put us into His Garden where He could watch over us with His infinite wisdom and with His love and grace as a loving Father. In the beginning, it was His plan that we live with Him eternally, in peace, love and righteousness. He wanted us to be with Him in His kingdom, His Garden of Eden, and He wanted us to love Him as He loves us.

But something went awry. He'd planted all kinds of trees in His garden, trees that are "pleasant to the sight and good for food" (Genesis 2:9). He'd also planted special trees in the middle of His garden—the tree of life and the tree of the knowledge of good and evil. These trees bore fruit that contained the most vital secrets of life and death, Godly secrets—secrets which revealed the powers of the Lord Himself (See Deuteronomy 29:29). The tree of life gave life to those who ate of its fruit (an existence that God intended for man) whereas the tree of the knowledge of good and evil gave Godly knowledge, both moral and ethical, of good and evil to those who ate of its fruit. God knew that if Adam and Eve ate the forbidden fruit of the tree of the knowledge of good and evil, they would do so at Satan's urging against God's will in order to be gods themselves, that is, on the same level of spiritual being and power as God. They wouldn't need God and like Him, would have great power and authority over all things, a power and authority that might be misused as it was by Satan.

Because of the sacredness of the Godly secrets of good and evil, the Lord told Adam that he was forbidden to eat of the tree of the knowledge of good and evil (Genesis 2:17). He told Adam that he was free to eat of every tree and plant in His garden, but that he must not eat from the forbidden tree or he would die. By implication it follows that if Adam obeyed the Lord and didn't eat of the special tree, he wouldn't die, that is, he'd have eternal life with God and would be with Him in His garden forever. This part of the Bible infers that God gave Adam a choice: to obey Him or not (free will).

"'Knowledge of good and evil' refers to moral knowledge or ethical discernment." *The NIV Study Bible*, 11, note to Genesis 2:9. Eve (and through her, Adam) was tricked by Satan into believing that if they ate of the special tree they would not die (Genesis 3:4), but that they would have a "creaturely source of discernment in order to be morally independent of God." *id*. Satan, the prince of liars, told Eve that if she ate of the tree she would not die, her eyes would be opened, and that she would be as God, knowing all things good and evil (Genesis 3:4, 5). Violating God's admonition, Adam and Eve defied God and chose to eat of the tree. They'd had a cushy life with God in His special garden. What did they do to show their appreciation for His grace and love? They exercised (abused) the free will graciously given to them by God and chose evil. They chose to follow the lie of the serpent and disobey God. They chose to sin.

God was angry at His creations and as punishment (with God there are consequences for one's sins), God not only banished Adam (and consequently Eve, as well) from the garden, but made Adam toil for his survival and made the birth process of Eve painful. In essence, the Lord threw Adam and Eve out of His kingdom. They were doomed to live in Satan's world, the earth, and as a consequence they became subject to the ultimate end of that life—death.

Just as Adam and Eve wrongly defied God (in Genesis), as incredulous as it seems, in Revelation 20:7–9, after being in the presence of Jesus Christ for a thousand years, what did some of the people in Christ's kingdom (garden) do when Satan was loosed for a little while? They chose to go with Satan; with evil, and not with God.

Why the similar stories in Genesis and Revelation? What is God telling us by these lessons?

In his inherent *free* nature, man has the right to choose to follow God—or not. God gave us free will because He wants us to love Him freely. Compulsory love is not love. But by choosing not to follow

God, we are choosing evil. Evil is the serpent's way on earth. It is sin—rebelling against God. The result of choosing evil is to be outside of the garden of God, to be outside of His kingdom. The effect of choosing evil is denying that God exists. The psalmist wrote,

> "The fool has said in his heart, 'There is no God.' They are corrupt, They have done abominable works, There is none who does good. The LORD looks down from heaven upon the children of men, To see if there are any who understand, who seek God. They have all turned aside, They have together become corrupt; There is none who does good, No not one" (Psalm 14:1–3).

Citing this Psalm and Psalm 53:1–3, the apostle Paul wrote, "For all have sinned and fall short of the glory of God" (Romans 3:23).

Being inherently evil in our hearts, God threw man out of His garden because of Adam's wrong choice. But out of His great love for us, He still wanted us to be with Him in the garden: "For all this His anger is not turned away, But His hand is stretched out still" (Isaiah 5:25). So God did a wondrous thing to assuage His wrath for man's defiance: He cast upon His own Son all of man's sins. "Without shedding of blood there is no remission" (Hebrews 9:22), no remission of sins. He sacrificed His Son so that notwithstanding our inherited sinful nature, we could have eternal life with Him in His garden, His kingdom. "For He made Him who knew no sin to be sin for us, that we might become the righteousness of God in Him" (2 Corinthians 5:21).

The sacrifice of God's Son enables us to come back to Him in His garden. It reconciles (brings together) us to Him. All we have to do is to make the right choice this time, that is, to have faith in our Lord and Savior Jesus Christ, God's only begotten Son (Romans 10:9; John 3:16). He will freely give us His grace, grace to be free from the bondage of sin, grace to be redeemed from sin and to be the objects of His love and care for eternity (Romans 3:21–26). The promise of

His eternal grace comes by faith in Him. If we have faith in Jesus, we are declared guiltless (our sins are forgiven). Christ's righteousness is thus imparted to us.

In His final book of the Bible (Revelation), the Lord Jesus Christ reconciles us to Him. He brings those who have faith and believe in Him back into the garden, His kingdom. In Genesis 3, He banished all mankind. In Revelation 21, as a loving Father He brings His faithful back into the garden. In Revelation 21:2, we who have faith in Jesus are brought back into His new heaven and new earth and are "prepared as a bride adorned for her husband." Once again, the dwelling of God is with men who believe in Him, who listen and obey His Word, and who seek His righteousness and truth. Restored to His garden, we shall be His people and He will be our God (Revelation 21:3). He will wipe every tear from our eyes. Death will be no more, "nor sorrow, nor crying...or...pain" (Revelation 21:4). The earth will be restored to its original glory as existed at the time He first created Adam and placed him in His garden ("a new earth" Revelation 21:1). In His new garden, the animal kingdom will be tamed (Isaiah 11:6-8), the biosphere will be lush (Isaiah 35), we shall have perpetual good health (Isaiah 35:5), we'll enjoy eternal life (Isaiah 65:20), and world peace will prevail forever (Isaiah 2:4). Skip Heitzig, *Revelation Study Guide*, 218.

From beginning to end, from alpha to omega, from first to last, Christ, our loving God intended to be our Great Reconciler (2 Corinthians 5:18–19). The thousands of verses of the Bible between Genesis and Revelation are brought together in the same final lesson: we can choose Him and live, or choose Satan and die. "If anyone is in Christ, he is a new creation; old things have passed away; behold, all things have become new" (2 Corinthians 5:17). In Revelation 22:12–13, Jesus brings it all together (reconciles) and sums it up: "And behold, I am coming quickly, and My reward is with Me, to give to every one according to his work. I am the Alpha and the Omega, the Beginning and the End, the First and the Last."

RESOLVING A DISPUTE: A LAWSUIT OR CHRISTIAN MEDIATION?

No matter how careful we are in life, disputes happen. The proper question is not whether a dispute will come into our life, but *when* it will happen.

Society in general is geared to settle disputes applying man-made laws in man-created courts of law. However, are Christians to use non-believing judges to resolve differences between them? How did God intend that we settle disputes amongst ourselves?

The Bible provides the answer: we are to resolve disputes with our Christian brothers and sisters under the cloak of the Lord's church and not before judges appointed by the king (secular government).

The apostle Matthew recorded what Jesus Christ said regarding the issue of disputes between His brethren. He wrote in Matthew 18:15-17,

> "...if your brother or sister sins against you, go and tell him his fault between you and him alone. If he hears you, you have gained your brother. But if he will not hear, take with you one or two more, that by the mouth of two or three witnesses every word may be established. And if he refuses to hear them, tell it to the church. But if he refuses even to hear the church, let him be to you like a heathen and a tax collector."

In a footnote to Matthew 18:15-17, the *Life Application Bible* (NKJV) explains the application of these passages: "These are Jesus' guidelines for dealing with those who sin against us. They were meant for (1) Christians, not unbelievers, (2) sins committed against you and not others, and (3) conflict resolution in the context of the church, not the community at large...They [Jesus' words] are designed to reconcile those who disagree so that all Christians can live in harmony."

In essence, Jesus teaches us not to sue in the king's court, but to seek reconciliation with our brothers or sisters in the loving arms of our church brethren. The apostle Paul explains this in 1 Corinthians 6:1–7 by pointing out that we have the Holy Spirit and the mind of Christ within us—so why would we turn to those (the secular courts) who may not necessarily be aware of God's wisdom in applying the laws made by man? The apostle says that if we go to law against our brother in the king's court, we have already failed, no matter what the outcome.

I personally participated as one of four mediators in a *Matthew 18 Mediation*, the other two human mediators being pastors from my church. We three men served as the earthly mediators. There was another chair at the table—it was purposely left "empty," physically that is. It was the chair of the Holy Spirit.

After commencing the proceeding with much prayer by all present including the adversaries, we then listened to the facts and arguments of each of the parties. Periodically, someone would stop and ask for prayer about a particular issue raised by one of the parties. In the context of prayer, it was much easier (and less adversarial) to work our way through the facts and contentions of each of the parties. There developed a common bond of prayer amongst those present.

After hearing both sides' positions interspersed with prayer, a solution became apparent. This enabled the parties to reach a reasonable compromise of their differences. By the session's end there was reconciliation and the adversaries were hugging each other. There literally wasn't a dry eye in the house. We all felt the presence of the Lord working His wondrous ways in reconciling the parties. When we left the mediation, I along with the others knew we'd experienced a part of heaven—God's kingdom now. How blessed we were!

REPENTANCE

Repentance is changing one's mind from following *self* to living life in accordance with the Lord's way. It requires acknowledgment of a sinful act, remorse for such an act, a genuine intent to abandon a life of evil (rebellion) against God, and pure contrition. True repentance occurs when we turn from a rebellious life against the Lord, change our mind about how we want to live, and turn to Him (faith) in every aspect or our life. Repentance and faith in the Lord leads to salvation of the soul, knowledge of God's truth, and life in God's kingdom, now. Jesus said, "Repent, for the kingdom of heaven is at hand" (Matthew 4:17).

CONFESSION PURIFIES THE SOUL

We are God's children and He is our Father. He only wants the best for us. As our Father, He requires that we do that which is right and true. He is omniscient. He spoke through the hand of His prophet, "For my eyes are on all their ways; they are not hidden from My face, nor is their iniquity hidden from My eyes" (Jeremiah 16:17; see also Hebrews 4:13).

When we speak untruths or do wrongful acts, they are not against the person to whom we have lied or committed an offensive act, but against the Lord. "Against You, You only, have I sinned, and done this evil in Your sight" (Psalm 51:4). But even knowing this, we still try to hide things from God, from others, even from ourselves (denial). In fact, some actually believe that they can get away with their sins.

When we hide the truth (a sinful act), the result of this evil act is a dormant conscience. We fall into a state of passivity, that is, we allow our minds to sink into a coma-like suppressed state, ceasing to exercise conscious control over the mind and inactivating the proper functions of the will, conscience and memory. Satan acts upon man when he is in a passive or numbed-down-conscience state. It is in such a vacuous state that Satan moves in. In his book, *The Spiritual Man*, Vol. III, 96–97, Watchman Nee describes this process,

> "God calls man to choose actively, consciously and willingly to do His will so that his spirit, soul and body may be free; Satan coerces him to be his passive slave and captive: God appoints man to be autonomous, free to be his own master; Satan forces man to be his puppet, a marionette altogether manipulated by him: God never requires man to cease his activities before He can work; Satan bids man to be utterly passive and inactive...Satan charges man to obey him passively...to cease all his activities, including the functioning of his soul, so that his [Satan's] minions can act in place of man..."

Unfortunately, this is what happened to King David. Regarded by the Lord as a man after His own heart, David fell into Satan's spell of passivity. He was at the top of his game. He was king, invincible as a warrior, and reigned over a greatly expanded land (2 Samuel 8:15). But just like Adam, when he should have been elsewhere doing God's work, David was in an inappropriate place when he spotted forbidden fruit, namely, Bathsheba. Even though he knew she was married to one of his faithful warriors, Uriah the Hittite, and ignoring all that he knew and had written about God and his righteousness and justice, David summoned Bathsheba to his palace and committed adultery with her. In his dormant evil-minded state, he ordered that Uriah, her husband, be killed in battle (2 Samuel 11:14–15). In the process of suppressing his conscience, he eventually broke the sixth, seventh, ninth and tenth commandments (see Exodus 20:13–14, 16–17). By the wrongful use of his God-given will, he dulled his mind so that he wouldn't feel the pain of the guilt of his heinous acts.

But God, being the forgiving Father that He is, knew that David, with prompting, would awaken from his spiritually passive state. Thus He sent a divine message to David through the prophet Nathan, "Then Nathan said to David, 'You are the man...You have killed Uriah the Hittite with the sword; you have taken his wife to be your wife'" (2 Samuel 12:7, 9). By the prophet's mouth, the Lord convicted David and aroused his dormant conscience. All that the Father wanted from David was contrition: an acknowledgment of his sins, sorrow and remorse for the pain he'd inflicted on others, repentance from his dastardly ways, and humility from his prideful attitude. The Lord wanted David to confess his sins before Him, speak the truth, and thus be cleansed of the evil that had taken hold in him.

The words that David spoke to the Lord are powerful and moving. They are recounted in two of the seven penitential or confessional Psalms, Psalms 32 and 51 (the other penitential Psalms are Psalms 6, 38, 102, 130 and 143). The two Psalms describe the process by which David threw himself at the mercy of a gracious and forgiving Father, how the Father forgave him, and how David became upright in heart even though he eventually paid dearly for his sins (his family suffered much due to his wayward acts). "Psalm 51 was the confession of his great sins and the prayer for forgiveness. [Psalm 32] is the record of the confession made and the forgiveness obtained, and the conscious blessedness of his position as a son restored to his Father's house." J. J. Stewart Perowne, *Commentary on the Psalms*, 289. *

In the beautiful Psalm 32, David became aware of the passivity (numbness) of his conscience and confessed his sin, purifying his soul before God, "I acknowledged my sin to You, And my iniquity I have not hidden. I said, 'I will confess my transgressions to the LORD,' And You forgave the iniquity of my sin" (Psalm 32:5). The Lord responded to his confession by pointing out his previously passive state of mind, "Do not be like the horse or like the mule, Which have no understanding, Which must be harnessed with bit and bridle, Else they will not come near you. Many sorrows shall be to the wicked; But he who trusts in the LORD, mercy shall surround him" (Psalm 32:9–10).

John the Baptist cried in the Desert of Judea, "Repent, for the kingdom of heaven is at hand!" (Matthew 3:2). Repentance is like a summer thunderstorm. It purifies the land just as repentance cleanses a contrite spirit. Jesus Christ said, "If you abide in My word, you are My disciples indeed. And you shall know the truth, and the truth will make you free" (John 8:31–32). David, a contrite sinner, found the truth of the Lord and was set free from the binds of Satan when he spoke these words, "Create in me a clean heart, O God, And renew a steadfast spirit within me. Do not cast me away from Your presence, And do not take your Holy Spirit from me. Restore to me the joy of Your salvation, And uphold me by Your generous Spirit" (Psalm 51:10, 12). David's contrition purified his soul before God.

---

* Taken from *Commentary on the Psalms*, © Copyright 1989, by J. J. Stewart Perowne. Published by Kregel Publications, Grand Rapids, MI. Used by permission of the publisher. All rights reserved.

B. NEIL SHAW

A CRY IN THE WILDERNESS

Then the Lord stretched out His hand and touched the mouth of the prophet Jeremiah and he courageously spoke the words of the Lord to the unrighteous people of Jerusalem, "What injustice have your fathers found in Me, That they have gone far from Me, Have followed idols, And have become idolaters?...The prophets prophesied by Baal, And walked after things that do not profit. Therefore I will yet bring charges against you" (Jeremiah 2:5, 8–9).

When Jeremiah spoke these words, he was challenging the culture of Judah molded by Manasseh, the most evil of the Jewish kings. As recounted in 2 Chronicles 33, Manasseh defied the Lord in all that he did. His father Hezekiah, the most faithful of the Jewish kings, had devotedly followed the law of the Lord. Manasseh rebelled against his father's beliefs and God. Like the depraved Canaanites, Manasseh broke the Second and Third Commandments and rebuilt the high places wherein the Israelites worshipped man-made gods. He built altars for the craven images of the Canaanite gods. He sacrificed his sons who were consumed by fire in the Valley of Ben Hinnom. He practiced sorcery, divination and witchcraft and sought the counsel of mediums and spiritists. He provoked the Lord to anger. The Israelites followed the evil ways of their king. In spite of the Godly warnings uttered by the prophet, the people "refused to return [to the LORD]" (Jeremiah 5:3). The result: the destruction of Judah.

What is troubling about the biblical account of the sins of Manasseh is that Jeremiah's words ring true today. Like ancient Israel, many in our nation have abandoned God. Our country has banned Him from its culture and replaced Him with idols. Sports figures, movie stars, money and materialism are today's American idols. Lying, cheating and greed are becoming acceptable values to many. Christians are under attack by the politically correct secular culture. Prayer has been banned from our public educational institutions. Universities fire professors who dare to teach Intelligent Design or oppose their secular worldviews. As they were in Manasseh's kingdom, babies are killed—in the fire of abortion clinics. Since *Roe v Wade* became the law of the land, an entire generation has been killed. Body piercing, tattooing, spiritism, and permissive sexual mores are the norm. Just writing about the Manasseh-like apostasy in our land makes me feel the lamentations of the prophet.

Our Founding Fathers wrote on that fateful 4th of July in 1776, "...for the support of this Declaration, *with a firm reliance on the protection of Divine Providence*, we mutually pledge to each other our lives, our fortunes, and our sacred honor" (emphasis added). As a nation, we have abandoned that "firm reliance on the protection of Divine Providence." After 240 years of our nation's founding, America must acknowledge the dark direction it has taken and turn, as did our forefathers, to "the way, the truth and the life," words used by Jesus Christ to describe Himself (John 14:6).

The prophet of old cried out the words of the Lord in the wilderness, "Return, O backsliding children" (Jeremiah 3:14). To our non-believing fellow citizens, we too cry in the wilderness, Repent from your errant ways and seek the protection of Divine Providence, the Lord. For our Lord is a merciful and forgiving God and until He returns, there is still time to repent and turn to the Lord.

BE EARNEST AND REPENT
SAYS THE LORD

The Bible never ceases to amaze me in its wondrous teachings. Often, I find truths not necessarily hidden, but subtle in their presentation. For example, in His messages to the seven churches in the Book of Revelation, our Lord tells five of the seven churches to repent and commends the other two. What was the Lord teaching us about the churches, five of which He rebuked and two of which He commended? What were the two doing that the other five were not? That same issue of the Lord's message regarding His churches applies today just as it did in the time of the early churches.

Pastor J. Vernon McGee in his Bible commentary, *Thru the Bible*, discusses at length the dichotomy that exists between churches today. Churches that have a personal and loving relationship with Jesus Christ and remain true to His Word (the Bible) and similar in theology to the ancient Church at Philadelphia, are following His Way. Churches who have abandoned the Word of God and whose theology (lukewarm) is similar to that of the church at Laodicea, have lost their way and need to repent. Pastor McGee wrote,

> "There is a heart-searching message for this hour because we are living in the time of the Laodicean church and of the Philadelphian church. Both of them are side by side, and there is a great bifurcation in Christianity today. It is not in denominations, and it is not in Romanism and Protestantism. The great bifurcation consists of those who believe the Word of God and follow it, love it, obey it, and those who reject it." *Id*, Revelation 3:15–16, Vol V, 923.

Just as the Lord told the early (five) churches, the churches of today who do not follow the Word of God must repent. By repent, the

Lord means that they should change their mind and direction from following their own way and follow the Lord's Way.

The five churches who'd gone astray were: Ephesus (the *loveless church*)—they'd lost their personal and loving relationship with Jesus Christ; Pergamos (the *compromising church*) —they'd adopted heretic doctrines; Thyatira (the *corrupt church*)—they'd accepted a new morality, that is, accepted Christ but lived on a low moral plane; Sardis (the *dead church*)—they were spiritually dead and going through the motions of church; and worst of all, Laodicea (the *lukewarm church*)—they were neither hot nor cold for Jesus, that is, they were the apostate church which professed to be Christian but in reality were not.

In his letter to the Philippians, the apostle Paul said, "For to you it has been granted on behalf of Christ, not only to believe in Him, but also to suffer for His sake" (Philippians 1:29). It is our privilege as Christians to believe in Jesus Christ and to suffer just as He suffered for us on His cross. The churches at Smyrna and Philadelphia were commended by the Lord for their faith in Him. They were respectively the "suffering" and the "faithful" churches.

Smyrna was a center of emperor worship. There, the first temple in honor of Tiberius was built. Emperor worship was compulsory for every citizen on threat of death. Once each year a citizen had to burn incense on the altar to the godhead of Caesar and say, "Caesar is lord." Once said, the person would receive a certificate that presumably enabled him to engage in commerce with other citizens of Smyrna. Most Christians in Smyrna refused to worship Caesar and were severely persecuted. Pastor McGee wrote concerning the suffering Christians in Smyrna, "The Lord Jesus told the church in Smyrna not to fear suffering. Believe me, that is one thing that we in the church are frightened of today. We do not want to pay a price for serving the Lord Jesus, and yet that is His method." *Thru the Bible*, Revelation 3, Vol. V, 926.

I pray Lord that when the time comes, and it will come, that we Christians will have faith in You such that we shall be willing to suffer in your Name, just as the believers in Smyrna did.

The Christians in the Church in Philadelphia were missionaries. As the easternmost of the seven churches and an outpost of upper Asia, it was effective in evangelizing the area in the face of continual threats from the Barbarians. The Philadelphians like the believers in Smyrna, were persecuted for their beliefs in Christ and yet, they remained true to the Word of God, no matter what the circumstances. They faithfully and strictly followed the Word of God as it was determined by the doctrines of the early church and did not depart from their faith in Jesus Christ. Their faith was as strong as that of the apostolic church. They were deeply loyal to the Lord's Name and publicly confessed their belief in Him. Dr. John F. Walvoord, *Commentary on the Revelation of Jesus Christ*, 85.

The teachings of the Lord concerning His church hold true to this day. Unfortunately, there are still churches that are loveless, willing to compromise (political correctness), do not believe the Bible to be the inerrant Word of God, are corrupt, dead, and worst of all are lukewarm (neither here nor there). But glory be to God, there still are a multitude of churches that are faithful to His Word and who are willing to suffer for Him just as He suffered for us. With respect to a Laodicean church in our midst, do as the Lord says in Revelation 3:19, "be zealous and repent." Be on fire for the Lord, not lukewarm. Turn back to His Word and be willing to suffer for His Name.

"For the word of God is living and powerful, and sharper than any two-edged sword, piercing even to the division of soul and spirit, and of joints and marrow, and is a discerner of the thoughts and intents of the heart" (Hebrews 4:12).

THE PENITENT KING

There was in ancient days a mighty and powerful king. His name was David, the son of Jesse. God blessed him and regarded him as "a man after His own heart" (1 Samuel 13:14). He conquered many lands and acquired great wealth. He was a wise king and loved God.

One evening he went out onto the roof of his palace and there in his city below he saw a beautiful maiden bathing on her balcony. He sent his servant to inquire who she was. The servant learned that she was the wife of one of the king's warriors. Awed by her beauty, he sent for the woman and caused her to conceive a child.

Blinded by his lust for her and with evil intent, the king schemed to have the husband of the woman killed in battle so that she could be his to marry.

Shortly after this, Nathan, a prophet, said to the king, "Why have you despised the commandment of the LORD, to do evil in His sight?" (2 Samuel 12:9). Realizing that what he'd done was wicked, the king confessed to the prophet, "I have sinned against the LORD" (2 Samuel 12:13). Seeing that the king had genuine remorse for his sins, had honestly confessed them, and was contrite before God, the prophet declared, "The LORD also has put away your sin; you shall not die" (2 Samuel 12:13).

Repentance leads to salvation of the soul and the knowledge of truth. Emphasizing the importance of this Godly principle, Jesus' first words in His public ministry were, "Repent, for the kingdom of heaven is at hand" (Matthew 4:17). The Bible says that we are all sinners and that with the exception of God, no one is good, not one. Being sinners, the way in which we can seek God's forgiveness for those sins is to have a genuine intent to abandon a life of evil against our Creator. True repentance occurs when we turn from a rebellious life against God, "change our mind" and turn to Him in every aspect of our lives.

King David was humbled and genuinely contrite. After openly

confessing his sins and expressing honest remorse before his glorious God, he passionately prayed:

> "Have mercy on me, O God, According to Your lovingkindness;
> According to the multitude of Your tender mercies,
> Blot out my transgressions.
> Wash me thoroughly from my iniquity,
> And cleanse me from my sin.
> For I acknowledge my transgressions,
> And my sin is always before me.
> Against You, You only, have I sinned,
> And done this evil in Your sight—
> That You may be found just when You speak,
> And blameless when You judge...
> ...Hide Your face from my sins,
> And blot out all my iniquities.
> Create in me a clean heart, O God,
> And renew a steadfast spirit within me" (Psalm 51:1–4, 9–10).

Though he would live a long life, not without consequences for his sins, the king was restored to the joy of God's salvation and a willing Spirit sustained him all the days of his life, just as he had prayed, "Surely goodness and mercy shall follow me All the days of my life; and I will dwell in the house of the LORD Forever" (Psalm 23:6).

JESUS' BRILLIANT DESIGN FOR REPENTANCE AND FAITH

Can you imagine what it would be like to have a perfect mind, one where you are all knowing and all seeing? Jesus, being God in the flesh, the Creator of all creation, was brilliant in the way He brought people to faith in Him. To God, the process was easy. But we as mere mortals can learn much from the way He "witnessed" to us and brought us, His elect, to Him.

First, He focused on our recognizing responsibility for our own actions. He made us accountable. Next, He confronted us with a convicting issue. Once the convicting issue was realized by us, He pressed us (albeit gently) to experience regret for our prior or ongoing acts. The result, we repented (changed our mind) about continuing the sinful acts. He instilled in us, through His grace, a desire to reverse direction and a need to change our hearts toward God.

Once the Lord brought about repentance in the person's heart, the person embraced Him realizing the blessings He'd given, and with joy loved Him and believed that He was the Way, the Truth and the Life. In other words, he or she had faith in Him as Savior. So simple, yet brilliant!

The story of the woman at the well illustrates His brilliance in leading His elect to repentance and faith. Jesus knew it was not yet His time to confront the leadership of the nation of Israel. "He left Judea and departed again to Galilee" (John 4:3). There were three routes from Judea, the shortest of which was through Samaria on the west bank of the Jordan. Regarded by the Jewish people as a mixed race, part Gentile and part Jewish, the Samaritans were avoided by the Israelites. Thus rejected, the Samaritans established their own temple on Mount Garazim where they followed the first five books of Moses, but also practiced idol worship. Jesus intended to go through Samaria for a reason. He was going to bring more of His children into His sheepfold.

While His disciples went to a nearby village to obtain food, Jesus stopped by a well where a Samaritan woman was drawing water. It was mid-day, an odd time for a woman to be drawing water—the custom was to draw water for the day in the early morning hours. She was alone. Why was she alone? Pastor J. Vernon McGee explains that she was a "dissolute woman…She's rude and immoral." *Thru the Bible*, Vol. IV 389. She was probably shunned by the rest of the women of the village and sought to avoid them by drawing water at mid-day.

As the conversation between Jesus and the woman proceeds, we see the brilliance of the process by which He converts the woman. First, she responds to Him with hostility as if He were a Jew with a negative attitude towards Samaritans (John 4:9). Then she accuses Him of placing Himself above "our father Jacob" (John 4:12). Each time He speaks about the spiritual blessings He offers, she attempts to distract Him by changing the conversation back to worldly matters.

But then He spoke the zinger (the conviction) to her in John 4:16, "Go, call your husband, and come here." She replied, "I have no husband" (John 4:17). Turns out that she was living with a man who was not her husband and in fact, had been married to (and presumably divorced by) five husbands. Realizing that the Man with whom she was speaking was incredibly perceptive, the woman immediately changed her attitude toward Jesus. She said with new respect, "Sir, I perceive that You are a prophet" (John 4:19).

Being Omniscient, Jesus knew she didn't have a husband. Why therefore did He ask her to call her husband? Because without one's conscience being moved, there can be no rebirth. "The only way to prepare the soil of the heart for the seed is to plow it up with conviction." Jesus told her to get her husband because He knew she would be forced "to admit her sin." Pastor Warren W. Wiersbe, *Be Alive*, 49. "There must first be conviction and repentance…" before one can acquire faith that brings salvation. *Id.* Jesus knew what buttons to push to arouse the conviction of her conscience.

Not yet aware of who He was and still trying to get Jesus off her vulnerable life issue, the woman boasted (as if she knew) that once the Messiah came, He would straighten both her and Jesus out. She said, "I know that Messiah is coming (who is called Christ). When he comes, He will tell us all things" (John 4:25).

Then Jesus delivered the clincher. He declared, "I who speak to you am He" (John 4:26). Overwhelmed by the realization that she was talking with the Messiah, she left her water jar, forgot about drawing water from the well, and ran to the village to tell the people about Jesus. She was now part of His elect!

Simplicity, yet brilliant complexity! Our Lord is our Savior. He knows us inside and out. He knows all our good characteristics and all of our faults. Yet, as a loving Father does, he still sends His Holy Spirit to collect us and bring us under the protection of His wings.

As the psalmist wrote, "He who dwells in the secret place of the Most High Shall abide under the shadow of the Almighty" (Psalm 91:1). "He shall cover you with His feathers, And under His wings you shall take refuge; His truth shall be your shield and buckler" (Psalm 91:4). You can almost hear those words being uttered by the woman as she excitedly told the people in her village about Jesus. Her faith had become unshakeable!

RESTORATION

Biblical restoration is bringing back one's soul to spiritual health.* The LORD is the restorer of souls (Psalm 23:3). The Lord assures us of the restoration of our souls if we have faith in Him (Isaiah 42:16).

---

* Pastor Charles Stanley, *The Glorious Journey*, 42.

HE RESTORES MY SOUL

In the essay, *The Penitent King*, I wrote about David who, after being challenged by the prophet Nathan, repented for his sins against Uriah the Hittite and his wife Bathsheba (2 Samuel, chapters 11–12). The process by which Nathan brought David to repentance is called *restoration*. Dr. Charles Stanley defines *restoration* as returning "one to a former state;" bringing one "back to spiritual health." Charles Stanley, *The Glorious Journey,* 42. It is implicit in this definition that a person who is restored to spiritual health had been in good spiritual health, fell out of grace as a result of sin against God, repented of his ways, and then was reinstated back to good spiritual health. "Brethren, if a man is overtaken in any trespass, you who are spiritual restore such a one in a spirit of gentleness" (Galatians 6:1). The apostle Paul addressed this to Godly people in the churches of Galatia who walked with the Lord Jesus and lived their lives enabled by the Holy Spirit. They had the gift of restoration, a gift of bringing back a brother or sister who'd wandered off the path of righteousness.

A good example of restoration is Nathan's gentle nudging of David by which he brought him to repentance thus giving him the opportunity for restoration to good spiritual health. Instead of directly accusing David of murder, adultery and covetousness, sins that David had committed in connection with Uriah and Bathsheba, Nathan used allegory. He told David a story about two men in a certain town, a rich man and a poor man (See 2 Samuel 12:1–14). The poor man had little or nothing. However, he bought a little ewe lamb and raised it as if it were a daughter to him. The lamb was the family's pet. They nourished the lamb and loved it as it grew to maturity (2 Samuel 12:3).

A traveler came to visit the rich man. But even though the rich man had his own sheep and cattle, he took the poor man's lamb, had it slain, and fed it to his visitor. When David heard this story, he was outraged by the injustice of the rich man. "David's anger was greatly aroused against the man, and he said to Nathan, 'As the

LORD lives, the man who has done this shall surely die!'" (2 Samuel 12:5). Nathan's story was really about David's affair with Uriah's wife and how he had Uriah killed. Nathan then said to David, "You are the man!" (2 Samuel 12:7). When David saw that he was the "rich man" in Nathan's story, he repented and cried out, "I have sinned against the LORD" (2 Samuel 12:13). Instead of condemning him, Nathan gently restored David by saying, "The LORD also has put away your sin; you shall not die. However, because by this deed you have given great occasion to the enemies of the LORD to blaspheme, the child also who is born to you shall surely die" (2 Samuel 12:13–14). The child born in adultery to David and Bathsheba did die, but that was the Lord rendering David accountable for his sinful ways. It was God's form of justice.

David wrote a psalm of contemplation about his experience with sin, repentance, and God's forgiveness. He wrote,

> "Blessed is he whose transgression is forgiven, Whose sin is covered. Blessed is the man to whom the LORD does not impute iniquity, And in whose spirit there is no deceit...I acknowledged my sin to You, And my iniquity I have not hidden. I said, 'I will confess my transgressions to the LORD,' And You forgave the iniquity of my sin" (Psalm 32:1–2, 5).

With the gentle guidance of God's prophet, David was once again restored to a right relationship with God and continued his lifetime journey as "a man after God's own heart." His soul was restored by God (Psalm 23:3).

RESTORATION: THE HEALING OF THE SOUL

In his book *The Glorious Journey*, 42, Dr. Charles Stanley defines *restoration* as returning "...to a former state; to bring [one] back to spiritual health." Our Lord provides a perfect illustration of the process of restoration in *The Parable of the Lost Son* (Luke 15:11–32). In the parable, Jesus tells of a loving father who overlooks the reckless ways of his rebellious son and takes him back into the family as if he'd never sinned.

The father had two sons. "The younger of them said to his father, 'Father, give me the portion of goods that falls to me'" (Luke 15:12). Under the Law, if there were two sons, upon the death of the father the older son received two-thirds of the father's estate and the younger son, one-third. It was unusual that the estate would be divided before the father's death. In the parable, the younger son had the audacity to ask for his inheritance before his father died. Pastor Chuck Smith, *Commentary on Luke 14–15*.

The son's premature request tells us much about him. He was selfish, immature, impatient, foolish, rebellious, and worldly. The son's impatience rings a familiar note to many of us when we were in our youth. He was itching to *live* and show the world who he was.

On the other hand, the father was compassionate, gracious, *very* slow to anger, abounding in mercy and faithfulness, and forgiving of rebelliousness, wickedness and sin. In other words, he was a loving father. The father in the parable is a vivid picture of God the Father, our Father in heaven.

Notwithstanding the son's impetuousness and greed, with grace and love for his child the father generously divided his property and gave *both* his sons their inheritances. The younger son took all that was given to him and "journeyed to a far country, and there wasted his possessions with prodigal living" (Luke 15:13). The fallen boy soon found himself in desperation without means to provide himself with food or shelter. He fell so low that the only job he could get was feeding pigs, an abomination for a Jewish man (Luke 15:15).

He'd reached bottom and realized that even his father's servants had food to spare whereas he was starving to death. He came to his senses and turned back. In other words, he repented of his sinful and foolish ways and decided to go back home to his father. He planned what he would say to his father when he saw him, "Father, I have sinned against heaven and before you, and I am no longer worthy to be called your son. Make me like one of your hired servants" (Luke 15:18–19).

You might think that the father would be angry when he saw his wayward son. After all, in his later years, one-third of his estate had been foolishly squandered. But, no, being full of love, grace and mercy, the father "saw him and had compassion" (Luke 15:20). The father ordered his servants to put his best robe on his son (the robe of righteousness, Isaiah 61:10), a ring on his finger, and new sandals on his feet. Each of these had significance in times of old. The robe signified acceptance and a position in society. The ring was a symbol of authority and the sandals symbolized that he was a member of the family since servants weren't permitted to wear sandals. All of these symbols stood for absolute acceptance by the father just as the Lord would accept His children into His kingdom. The father even killed his best calf for a splendid homecoming meal for his prodigal son (Luke 15:22–23). The father exclaimed to all that could hear, "Let us eat and be merry; for this my son was dead and is alive again; he was lost and is found" (Luke 15:23–24).

The young man was restored to the family. He'd jumped into the world, fell as far as he could, and now was brought back into the comfort and rest of his father's home. He was restored to spiritual health.

The real story told here by our Lord is about our Father in heaven. When we fall in this world, God the Father restores us to the joy of His salvation and graciously grants us a willing spirit to sustain us. King David, another sinner who was restored back into the grace of God, wrote, "Restore to me the joy of Your salvation, And uphold me by Your generous Spirit" (Psalm 51:12). Peter, who denied the Lord three times, was restored to good spiritual standing by Jesus who asked him three times if he loved Him (John 21:15–17).

We are like baby birds in a nest yearning to fly out of the tree. God knows that at some point in our lives, we may fall out of fellowship with Him. But the Lord also knows that hitting bottom in the world is necessary to draw us back to the place of His blessings and protection. "The parable is not about how a sinner gets saved; it is about the heart of a Father who will not only save a sinner, but will also take back a son that sins." J. Vernon McGee, *Thru the Bible*, Vol. IV, Luke 15:14, at page 314.

Give thanks to the One "Who remembered us in our lowly state, For His mercy endures forever" (Psalm 136:23). He restores our souls (Psalm 23:3).

RESURRECTION

On the cross, Jesus Christ said with His last breath, "It is finished! And bowing His head, He gave up His spirit" (John 19:30). He died and was buried. But He overcame death and rose back to life again. He was resurrected to life!

An angel said to Mary Magdalene and the other Mary peering into the empty tomb, "He is not here; for He is risen, as He said" (Matthew 28:6). Jesus Christ was resurrected from the dead. He'd said, "With God all things are possible" (Matthew 19:26).

TO LIVE IS CHRIST AND TO DIE IS GAIN—THE GREAT HOPE OF THE RESURRECTION OF JESUS CHRIST

As I approach the eighth decade of my life, a recurring thought comes into my mind: the thought of my death. As a believer in Christ and the inerrant Word of God, I know in my heart that death of the flesh is not the end of my life. And yet, a voice occasionally whispers in my ear urging me to doubt the word of God and to fear death. When this occurs, for a slight moment my *self* listens to the urgings of the devil and takes me away from the assurances that Christ has given me that my faith in Him will resurrect me to the foot of His throne after I die. I have discussed this conflict between *self* and God at length in the essay entitled, *Shifting Shadows*.

I believe that the fear of death to the true Christian is not fear of *death*, but fear of the *act or process of dying*. The physical dying process usually involves pain or suffering. No human being looks forward to pain or suffering which may occur when his or her time on this earth is over. I can only say that when I was facing major surgery on my cervical spine (See essay entitled, *Our Hope Is In His Unfailing Love*), I experienced what it would be like to face death—I overcame those dark thoughts by focusing my mind on the Lord. In retrospect, I know now that as I was being wheeled into the operating room my fears were of unknown pain and suffering, and not of dying. I knew in my heart that even if I didn't make it through the surgery, that I'd be with the Lord in heaven. These days, if I have any lingering thoughts about the end of life and the process of dying, I focus on the glorious joy of knowing that Jesus Christ died a physical death, was buried, rose from the grave, and is sitting at the right hand of God the Father. I know that upon His return I shall be resurrected to join the multitude of His believers worshiping Him at the foot of His throne.

By His resurrection, Jesus Christ was victorious over death. That victory gives all who believe in Him everlasting life with Him in His kingdom. What joy it is to know that when I die, it will not be the end of life! The apostle Paul was right when he wrote, "To live is Christ, and to die is gain" (Philippians 1:21).

In this post-modern era there are many who, like the Sadducees of old, do not believe in anything supernatural such as resurrection, angels or spirits (Acts 23:8). As empiricists, they do not believe in anything that they cannot taste, see, hear, touch or smell. They say, "How can one die and come back to life?" Even though what may be known of God is manifest to them—God shows it to them all the time—they unwisely reject God and become fools (Romans 1:19–21). Jesus said to the unbelieving Jewish authorities that if they did not believe in Him, they must at least believe in His works (John 10:38). His works are His creation. He was saying to them, "Just look around." He was pointing to the land, the sea, the sky, the sun, the moon, the air we breathe, the miracle of our bodies and how they function, etc. The Lord was telling them that "with God nothing will be impossible" (Luke 1:37). The prophet Jeremiah wrote about the Lord when he said that God made the heavens and the earth by His great power, and that nothing is too hard for Him (Jeremiah 32:17). Yet, the Sadducees still didn't believe Jesus, nor do the post-modern secularists of today believe Him.

Paul wrote, "All Scripture is given by inspiration of God, and is profitable for doctrine, for reproof, for correction, for instruction in righteousness" (2 Timothy 3:16). The Bible, both the Old Testament and the New Testament, speaks of resurrection. In the Scriptures three of God's prophets and the psalmist wrote about resurrection and viewed it as a natural part of life. The prophet Isaiah wrote the words spoken to Him by God that the "dead shall live...they shall arise" (Isaiah 26:19). David wrote that God would "not leave my soul in Sheol" (Psalm 16:10). The prophet Ezekiel wrote the words of God spoken to him that He would cause people to come up from their graves (Ezekiel 37:12). The prophet Daniel wrote the words spoken to him by the angel of the Lord (some believe it was Jesus speaking to Daniel), "And many of those who sleep in the dust of the earth shall awake, Some to everlasting life, Some to shame and everlasting contempt" (Daniel 12:2). According to the angel of the Lord who spoke to Daniel, both believers and non-believers would be resurrected. Jesus confirmed this when He said to the Jewish leaders that there would be a resurrection of those who are good and those who are evil, the just and the unjust, the latter being doomed to a resurrection of condemnation (John 5:28–29; Acts 24:15). For the unjust, it too would be a life everlasting, but a life of weeping and gnashing of teeth separated from God.

Jesus Christ told His twelve apostles that He would be condemned by the chief priests and scribes and after three days He would rise in His body from the grave and be resurrected to life (Mark 10:33; Luke 18:31–33). He also said that all who believe in Him will have everlasting life and that He will raise them up at the last day (John 6:40, 44, 54). If we believe in Jesus Christ as Lord and Savior and that He died for us and rose again, He "will bring with Him those who sleep in Jesus" (1Thessalonians 4:13–16).

The Bible gives accounts of many eyewitnesses to Jesus' resurrection—hundreds who saw Him in bodily form after He'd died and was buried. Mary Magdalene first saw Him at the site of His grave (John 20:14–17). Then two of His disciples walked with Him on the road to Emmaus and had a meal with Him during which He explained the things concerning Himself in the Scriptures (Luke 24:13–32). Then He appeared to the eleven disciples at the Upper Room (Mark 16:14). While there He ate broiled fish and some honeycomb and showed them His wounds on His hands, feet and side (Luke 24:39–42). The apostle Paul recounted that Jesus was seen by Peter, then by over five hundred brethren, by James and by Paul himself (1 Corinthians 15:5–8). Jesus also spent time with His disciples at Galilee (John 21:5, 14).

In explaining why Jesus was resurrected from death, Paul wrote that Jesus "was delivered up because of our offenses, and was raised because of our justification" (Romans 4:25). Jesus assuaged the wrath of His Father towards sinful mankind by giving up "His life as a ransom for many" (Matthew 20:28). He "redeemed us from the curse of the law, having become a curse for us...that we might receive the promise of the Spirit through faith" (Galatians 3:13–14).

In the Scriptures it is written, "Without shedding of blood there is no remission" of sin (Hebrews 9:22 citing Leviticus 17:11). Jesus said to His apostles at the Last Supper (His last Passover sedar), "For this is My blood of the new covenant, which is shed for many for the remission of sins" (Matthew 26:28). God provided His only Son as the sacrificial offering to pay the ransom for the sins of the world. Jesus died so that we might live! Without the shedding of His blood, there would be no remission of sin in the world—no salvation for those who believe in Him. Because of His supreme sacrifice, His believers are forever pardoned (forgiven) of their sins (Hebrews 9:26) and can look forward to a resurrected life everlasting with Him in heaven.

I perceive that on a date certain to come I shall die and shall lie in my own grave. But I shall do so without any fear or trepidation concerning my future. For by His own death, burial and resurrection to life, Jesus Christ has given me great hope, hope for the glorious days when I shall be part of the multitude of believers standing in our resurrected bodies at the foot of His throne worshiping and praising our Lord and Savior, Jesus Christ. Amen and Amen.

REVELATION

"The Revelation of Jesus Christ, which God gave Him to show His servants—things which must shortly take place" (Revelation 1:1).

IMMANUEL: THERE IS GREAT HOPE IN THINGS YET TO COME

Does it seem like the world is growing darker spiritually, more evil, and more violent as it rejects the moral reference of God? The turmoil around us seems to grow in logarithmic proportions: nation threatens nation, weapons of mass destruction are stored by despots waiting to be used upon the unsuspecting, men threaten men, and discourtesy, lack of respect, and rudeness seem to be the practice rather than kindness and concern for fellow man. Concern for *self* is more important than graciousness towards others.

If elections are the true gauge of the pulse of the American people, our great nation under God is being torn from its very foundations. So many of our citizens are opposed to our government's stand against evil in the world. Belief in God is discouraged rather than encouraged by the very government established by Him. So many of our citizenry either do not know the Lord or have cast Him out in favor of "mute idols" (Habakkuk 2:18).

But is the inclination towards darkness and destruction really unique to our time or is the world merely the continuing battleground of the ongoing conflict posed by the evil one against God, a conflict which dates back to Genesis 3? I believe it is the latter.

But do not despair for there is great hope in things yet to come.

Sure there are better bombs available to destroy all of us. But always know that God has a plan. Joy is always preceded by pain, and the greater the pain, the deeper the joy we shall experience. Look at the Bible and see for yourself that even in Old Testament times before our Savior came to dwell amongst us in the flesh, righteous people suffered and died at the hand of evil. But God always stretched out His hand and defeated the evil tyranny.

The prophet Habakkuk wrote elegantly about this and gives us great hope in the face of a despairing world. Violence, injustice, destruction, strife and conflict abounded in his time. Habakkuk cried out to God, "O LORD, how long shall I cry, And You will not hear? Even cry out to You, And You will not save. Why do You show me iniquity, And cause me to see trouble? For plundering and violence are before me; There is strife, and contention arises" (Habakkuk 1:2–3). Do these words ring true for the culture that is becoming dominant in our country?

Habakkuk was a contemporary of the prophet Jeremiah and lived in Judah towards the end of Josiah's reign (640–609 B.C.) and at the beginning of Jehoiakim's reign (609–598 B.C.). King Josiah was one of Israel's good kings. He was righteous in the eyes of the Lord (2 Kings 22:2). But King Jehoiakim "did evil in the sight of the LORD" (2 Kings 23:37). It was during Jehoiakim's reign that Nebuchadnezzar, King of Babylon, invaded Judah and destroyed it, just as Habakkuk (Habakkuk 1:6) and Jeremiah (Jeremiah 4:6) had prophesied.

Habakkuk's questions reflect a man perplexed by God's seeming inaction in the face of overwhelming worldly wickedness, strife and oppression. He protested to God that justice was not prevailing, that the wicked had overtaken the righteous, and that worldly judgment of wicked acts was perverse (Habakkuk 1:4). In frustration, he *demanded* answers from God, "Why do You look on those who deal treacherously, And hold Your tongue when the wicked devours A person more righteous than he?" (Habakkuk 1:13). And just short of insolence to God, the prophet queried, "Shall they [the wicked ones] therefore empty their net, And continue to slay nations without pity?" (Habakkuk 1:17).

Do you find yourself asking similar questions about our contemporary world? Do you turn off the news in disgust, feeling like there is no end to the corruption around us? You are not alone! There are times when I find myself crying out, no, demanding almost disrespectfully of the Lord that it is time for Him to come back and clean out the madness around us. I often think of the Lord's return and the overcoming of evil by Him as a Hero overcoming the villain, the Humble defeating the bully, or the Silent Righteous One standing victorious over the oppressor. O, how I long and pray for that day to come! (These statements may reflect the fact that sometimes I forget that I too am a sinner!).

But Habakkuk received answers from the Lord and he wrote the Lord's answer to his complaints, "The vision is yet for an appointed time...at the end it will speak, and it will not lie. Though it tarries, wait for it; Because it will surely come" (Habakkuk 2:3). The Lord told his prophet that evil is puffed up and that it will not endure. He also told Habakkuk that the just who live by faith will prevail over the wicked (Habakkuk 2:4). In the face of all odds, when times seem to be the darkest, when the light of hope is almost gone, do not despair for the Lord will renew the righteous. Jesus came specifically to save us who love Him.

The Lord further answered Habakkuk's cry, "But the LORD is in His holy temple. Let all the earth keep silence before Him" (Habakkuk 2:20). The people of the world must be silent before the true God who is about to judge the evil corruption of the world. Habakkuk was then directed by God to record the vision wherein God spoke the five woes (warnings) against the wicked (Babylonians): Woe to those who hoard goods taken from others. Woe to those who covet unjust profit. Woe to those who build their city on the blood of others. Woe to those who ravage the victims of their conquest. Woe to those who worship gods of wood—idols (See Habakkuk 2:6, 9–12, 15, 18–19). In the face of impending disaster (the defeat of Judah by the Babylonians) and probable suffering and death of many, Habakkuk's faith is strengthened in the knowledge that the Lord will prevail over evil (Habakkuk 3:18–19).

As the Lord revealed His plan to overcome evil in the world to the prophet Habakkuk, so too He revealed it to the apostle John in a vision. In Revelation 19, John described his vision of Jesus Christ as "Faithful and True" who "in righteousness" will judge the people of the world and will prevail in war against unrighteousness (Revelation 19:11). John sees the battle that will be joined between the armies of angels led by the Lord Jesus Christ and the evil armies of the beast and the kings of the earth. In the end, the Lord will prevail over the armies of evil. Their evil leaders will be thrown "into the lake of fire burning with brimstone" (Revelation 19:20).

After proclaiming victory over the beast and the false prophet, the Lord will dwell with us, and we shall be His people. God Himself will be with us and will be our God! (Revelation 21:3–4). We shall "call His name Immanuel" ("God with us") (Isaiah 7:14). "God will wipe away every tear from their eyes; there shall be no more death, nor sorrow, nor crying. There shall be no more pain, for the former things have passed away" (Revelation 21:4). As deep as the pain of our world is now, that is how great the joy will be when Jesus Christ is with us again! Like Habakkuk of old, we shall exclaim, "Yet I will rejoice on the LORD, I will joy in the God of my salvation. The Lord God is my strength; He will make my feet like deer's feet, And He will make me walk on my high hills" (Habakkuk 3:18–19).

Christian believers, "Wait on the LORD; Be of good courage, And He shall strengthen your heart; Wait, I say on the LORD!" (Psalm 27:14).

IMMANUEL: GOD IS WITH US and there is great hope in things yet to come! Amen.

RIGHTEOUSNESS

"Jesus Christ achieved righteousness through living the perfect human life."* "For He made Him who knew no sin to be sin for us, that we might become the righteousness of God in Him" (2 Corinthians 5:21).

---
* Pastor Rick Booye, Trail Christian Fellowship (Trail, Oregon), Seminar, *Knowing Christ*, 9/24/16.

THE RIGHTEOUS WILL SEE GOD'S FACE

God is righteous. "Righteousness and justice are the foundation of His throne" (Psalm 97:2). "To be righteous [is to] be in the right, be justified, be just." *Vine's Complete Expository Dictionary of Old and New Testament Words*, 205. What does it mean to be *right*? *The New Strong's Exhaustive Concordance of the Bible* defines *right* as "that which is just and fair." There are abundant examples in the Bible of what is *right*. "The statutes of the LORD [God's Law] are right" (Psalm 19:8). Obeying those statutes is right (See e.g. Ephesians 6:1). "The word of the LORD is right" (Psalm 33:4). The way of the Lord is right (Psalm 107:7). Righteous thinking is right (Proverbs 12:5). Thinking like Jesus is right. Everything about the Lord is righteousness (Jeremiah 23:6).

Christian believers know right being, right thinking, and right action solely because of the Holy Spirit of God within us. Without the moral reference of God, the thoughts and actions from one's own mind are that of a person with a sinful nature (under "the law of sin" Romans 7:23) and are not right.

God can do no evil. All that He does is right. All that He is—is right. He is righteousness and perfection. Life in the Garden of Eden prior to the rebellion of Adam and Eve against God (as encouraged by Satan (the serpent)) reflected what God intended life to be on earth. All things were right. God called His works prior to the rebellion of man *good* (See Genesis 1:4–25) for He is good (Psalm 100:5). God's creation was goodness and righteous—all things bright and beautiful. Once He created His works of goodness and perfection, He'd established the highest standard (His moral reference) against which all things are to be measured in the universe.

But then in His infinite wisdom, God allowed darkness to exist. It is within this darkness that the ruler of the earth, Satan, exists. It is where the devil attempts to undermine, disrupt, usurp or destroy all that which is of God—that which is good. Satan's works are the

B. NEIL SHAW

opposite of God's: evil, dishonest, malicious, envious, hateful of God, unrighteous and unjust (See Roman 1:29–32).

Thus, without God, the Moral Designer, there would be no standards, no morals by which goodness, righteousness and justice are measured or determined. There would only be evil, for without the contrast of the light shining upon the dark, the earth would be as God described it in Genesis 1:2, "darkness was on the face of the deep."

God is just; He is justice. He implements His righteousness through justice. To be just is to be equitable—fair. In the law of man, there is a part of the law called the *law of equity*. That body of law was developed by the judiciary over the millennium for the purpose of right dealing and fairness in adjusting in an impartial manner the conflicting rights or claims between adverse parties. It is the natural right or justice of God. It is based on precepts of the conscience derived from the moral reference to God, His statutes, and His Word. It is man's innate sense of right-dealing and fair play instilled in him by God. In essence, it is application of the Lord's *Golden Rule*, "Therefore, whatever you want men to do to you, do also to them, for this is the Law and the Prophets" (Matthew 7:12; Luke 6:31). Fair and equitable dealing are the basic guidelines of equity courts and they are based on the Just Law of God.

"The LORD is righteous...His countenance beholds the upright" (Psalm 11:7). Who are the upright before God? They are His people called by Him. By His grace His people are brought into a right personal relationship with Him. This righteousness is unattainable by obedience to any law, or by any merit of man's own, or any other condition than that of *faith in Christ*. James Boice, *Foundations of the Christian Faith*, 424-425. "He made Him who knew no sin to be sin for us, that we might become the righteousness of God in Him" (2 Corinthians 5:21). It is by faith in Jesus Christ that we strive to become righteous like Him. He died so that we could become righteous.

Doing what is right in God's eyes feels right. In the days before I knew Jesus Christ, like the Israelites of old, I often did what was right in my own eyes (Judges 21:25). Unfortunately, so many in our culture of today still live by that standard: whatever is right in their own mind, so long as it doesn't harm others, is OK. They do this without any moral reference to God. However, even before I accepted Jesus into my life, there was an innate sense within me that caused me to hesitate if I was about to do something that violated God's laws. Being unaware that it was God's Holy Spirit trying to communicate with my spirit, I called that conflict within me a "guilty conscience" (See Romans 2:15). But in reality, it was God reaching out to me and through His Holy Spirit working on me to strive to become righteous like Him. It was God seeking to instill integrity of character in me—to do that which was righteous and just—like Him (John 14:26).

Now, after many years of growing by the spiritual milk of the Word of God (1 Corinthians 3:2) and walking deeper in the Holy river of water of life with the Lord, He has placed in me a burning desire to do as He does—to do what is right and just and true. I have trusted the Lord with all my heart and seek to lean less on my own understanding (*self*). I want to acknowledge Him in every way possible—and He has directed my path with many blessings (Proverbs 3:5–6). For that I am thankful.

O Lord, may we who have faith in you be righteous and just in everything we are and do in life. "He who practices righteousness is righteous, just as He is righteous" (1 John 3:7).

PETER: FROM WRETCHEDNESS
TO RIGHTEOUSNESS

As children of God, it should be our heart's desire to seek the righteousness of God and to be righteous in all ways (2 Corinthians 5:21). "The Lord is righteous in all His ways, Gracious in all His works" (Psalm 145:17). What are the righteous ways of God? Psalm 37 gives us just some examples of His righteous ways: He "upholds the righteous" (37:17); He provides all we need (37:18–19); He "gives" generously (37:21); He never forsakes us (37:25); He blesses His children (37:26); He "loves justice" (37:28); He protects us forever (37:28); He speaks "wisdom" (37:30); He speaks what is just (37:30); He exhorts us "to inherit the land" (37:34); He marks us "blameless" and "upright" (37:37); He gives us "peace" (37:37); He gives us salvation through His grace and mercy (37:39); He is our "strength in the time of trouble" (37:39); and He is our refuge "from the wicked" (37:40).

The apostle Peter is a fine example of a man who, being chosen of God, went from a life of wretchedness (a Pauline term—see Romans 7:24) to live a life of righteousness. His life gives us great hope that we too, as believers in Jesus Christ, can achieve a life of righteousness in Christ.

Matthew 4:18 first mentions Peter. It tells us that he was a fisherman from Bethsaida, a fishing village on the northeast coast of the Sea of Galilee. Professional fishermen are reputed to be hard-working, risk-taking, no-nonsense, salt-of-the-earth types. Peter was certainly that type of man. But along with the good, he had his negative traits. He was worldly, even a stumbling block to Jesus at times (Matthew 16:23). He was always trying to control things (Matthew 17:4). Sometimes he was dishonest (Mark 14:68, 71). He was not consistently dependable (Mark 14:37). He was initially prideful, over-confident, and cocky to the point that he even tried to rebuke the Lord! (Matthew 16:22). He was disrespectful at times (Mark 10:28). He was jealous and competitive (John 21:21). He was short-tempered and used profanity (Matthew 26:74). Is this the man who the Lord called "Cephus," the rock upon whom the Lord would build His church? (Matthew 16:18).

But Peter was a quick learner and as we trace his life with Jesus through the Bible, we find that the Holy Spirit in-dwelled Himself in Peter and ultimately he became a man in the way of the righteousness of God. He emulated all that he was taught by Jesus. He exemplified Galatians 2:20, "I have been crucified with Christ; it is no longer I who live, but Christ lives in me; and the life which I now live in the flesh I live by faith in the Son of God, who loved me and gave Himself for me."

He started out as a man of little faith (Matthew 14:31). He became a man with great insight when he said to the Lord, "You are the Christ, the Son of the living God" (Matthew 16:16). He ultimately became repentant of his sinful, earthly ways (Matthew 26:75).

As his spirit became aligned with God's Holy Spirit, he saw his own sinfulness and was humble (Luke 5:80). He was charged by the Lord to be a shepherd of the Lord's flock (John 21:15–17). He took charge as a leader of the righteous (Acts 1:15–22). He became a man of the Lord's Word (Acts 2:14–36). He became empowered by the Holy Spirit and performed miracles (Acts 4:8; 3:1–10). He was a man who dedicated his life through the exhortation of things right, to the glory of the Father (Acts 3:11–26).

He became a teacher of righteousness as evidenced by the letters he wrote to the believers,

> "For this is the will of God, that by doing good [being righteous] you may put to silence the ignorance of foolish men—as free, yet not using liberty as a cloak for vice, but as bondservants of God. Honor all people. Love the brotherhood. Fear God. Honor the king" (1 Peter 2:15–17). "Finally, all of you be of one mind, having compassion for one another; love as brothers, be tenderhearted, be courteous" (1 Peter 3:8).

B. NEIL SHAW

Reading all three of the epistles Peter wrote to his fellow Christian believers, one quickly sees Christ living in him (Galatians 2:20). You see a wise, gentle, righteous man, not a rough-on-the-edges salt-of-the-earth type of man.

Peter was truly a living example of a man who grew in Christ from wretchedness to righteousness.

SACRIFICE

"He takes away the first that He may establish the second. By that will we have been sanctified through the offering of the body of Jesus Christ once for all" (Hebrews 10:9–10). "But this Man, after He had offered one sacrifice for sins forever, sat down at the right hand of God" (Hebrews 10:12).

CUTTING COVENANT: THE LORD'S SUPREME SACRIFICE

"On the same day the LORD made a covenant with Abram, saying, 'To your descendants I have given this land, from the river of Egypt to the great river, the River Euphrates'" (Genesis 15:18). Thus the Lord made a solemn contract with Abram (later called *Abraham* by the Lord) by which He promised Abram and his descendants the land of Israel.

In order to be binding, every contract must be supported by a cost (the "consideration") to the person making the offer to enter into the contract (covenant). God entered into a unilateral (only one party making the promise) covenant with Abram pursuant to which He covenanted to give to him the land from the River of Egypt (the Nile) to the great river, the River Euphrates. This was known as the *Abrahamic Covenant*. In order to bind His covenant, the Lord instructed Abram,

> "Bring Me a three-year old heifer, a three-year old female goat, a three-year old ram, a turtledove, and a young pigeon. Then he [Abram] brought all these to Him and cut them in two, down the middle, and placed each piece opposite the other..." (Genesis 15:9–10). "Now when the sun was going down, a deep sleep fell upon Abram; and behold, horror and great darkness fell upon him...when the sun went down and it was dark, that behold, there appeared a smoking oven and a burning torch [revealing the presence of God] that passed between those pieces" (Genesis 15:12, 17).

In ancient times in order to bind a contract, the parties cut an animal in two, stood in "the midst of the carcass, and clasped each other's wrist to show they were deadly serious about keeping their end of the bargain." *Jon Courson's Application Commentary, Old Testament*, at Genesis 15:10. This is called "cutting covenant." In effect, by passing between the slaughtered animals' pieces, the oath taker was saying that if He didn't comply with his oath then what had been done to the sacrificial animals should be done to him.

God later saw it necessary to cut another covenant with His people—the *Mosaic Covenant* (also known as the *Ten Commandments*). God gave them His Law to shed moral light on their sinful ways—to give them His moral reference. The only consideration God expected in return from His people was obedience. But the people, by their sinful nature, disobeyed His Law. As it turned out no one but God's Son, Jesus Christ, a Man without sin, was able to fulfill all of God's commandments—and He did so.

Being a gracious God and slow to anger, the Lord cut yet another covenant with His children, a new and final covenant (the *New Covenant*) which He spoke through His prophet Jeremiah,

> "Behold, the days are coming, says the LORD, when I will make a new covenant with the house of Israel and with the house of Judah—not according to the covenant [the Law] that I made with their fathers in the day that I took them by the hand to lead them out of the land of Egypt, My covenant which they broke, though I was a husband to them, says the LORD. But this is the covenant that I will make with the house of Israel after those days, says the LORD: I will put My law in their minds, and write it on their hearts; I will be their God, and they will be My people...I will forgive their iniquity, and their sin I will remember no more" (Jeremiah 31:31–34).

In order to be binding, the New Covenant also had to be supported by consideration, that is, a cost to the Person making the promise (the "Promissor"). The writer of Hebrews wrote, "It is necessary that this One also have something to offer" (Hebrews 8:3). There had to be a

B. NEIL SHAW

cost to the Promissor—the Promissor being God the Father. God's consideration for His unilateral New Covenant was the sacrifice of His only Son on the cross.

Once again, the New Covenant of God was a unilateral covenant. God's covenants to mankind, being made by a loving Father, are always unilateral.

Under the Law, the high priest entered the Most Holy Place in the temple once a year, and never without the blood of sacrificed animals "which he offered for himself and for the people's sins committed in ignorance" (Hebrews 9:7).

> "And according to the law almost all things are purified with blood, and without [the] shedding of blood there is no remission [of sins]" (Hebrews 9:22). "For the life of the flesh is in the blood, and I have given it to you upon the altar to make atonement for your souls; for it is the blood that makes atonement for the soul" (Leviticus 17:11).

However, the sacrifices being offered to support the Old Covenant "cannot make him who performed the service perfect in regard to the conscience" (Hebrews 9:9). The sacrifices under the Law of Moses were not able to clear the consciences of the worshipers. Under the ceremonial sacrifices of the Law, there was no permanent remission of sin.

In order to assuage His wrath at the people for their sinful and disobedient ways and to bind His New Covenant, God Himself offered consideration for the New Covenant that He unilaterally made to His People. He sent His Son Jesus Christ to enter the Most Holy Place in the temple in heaven itself to appear for us in the Father's presence (Hebrews 9:11, 24). "With His own blood He entered the Most Holy Place once for all, having obtained eternal redemption" (Hebrews 9:12). "For by one offering He has perfected forever those who are being sanctified" —His elect (Hebrews 10:14).

Just as at the time of the Lord's Abrahamic Covenant, when Jesus breathed His last on the cross "there was darkness over the whole land until the ninth hour" (Mark 15:33). As with the Abrahamic Covenant where the animals were cut in two in a symbolic cutting of covenant, the veil of the temple separating the Most Holy Place "was torn in two from top to bottom" (Mark 15:38). "The thick veil that separated the holy place from the holy of holies was a barrier between people and God. Only the death of Christ could tear that veil...and open the way into the *heavenly* sanctuary where God dwells." Warren Wiersbe, *Be Confident*, 113–114. Just as Abram cut in two the heifer, the goat and the ram to provide an offering, with His blood Christ cut His covenant by cutting the veil separating us from God. Now through Christ, mankind can draw near to God. He has reconciled us with God the Father and has assuaged the wrath of God for man's sinful ways.

> "Therefore, brethren, having boldness to enter the Holiest by the blood of Jesus, by a new and living way which He consecrated for us, through the veil, that is, His flesh, and having a High Priest over the house of God, let us draw near with a true heart in full assurance of faith, having our hearts sprinkled from an evil conscience and our bodies washed with pure water. Let us hold fast the confession of our hope without wavering, for He who promised is faithful." (Hebrews 10:19–23).

Thank you Jesus for Your supreme sacrifice for us!

SALVATION

We all are sinners (Romans 3:10–12). Unless saved from our sinful nature, we shall ultimately die an eternal death separate from God. "For the wages of sin is death, but the gift of God is eternal life in Christ Jesus our Lord" (Romans 6:23). We all need salvation from our sinful nature. Salvation is the gift of God given by grace and received by personal faith in the Lord Jesus Christ, whose precious blood was shed on Calvary for the forgiveness of our sins so that we may be with Him forever.

BUT WHY?

Have you ever seen your memories? By that I mean physically looking at something from your past? Doing so gives great perspective about life. Recently, my wife and I had occasion to visit our home town. While there, we decided to visit our old neighborhood and see the house where we raised our children. It's been many years since we lived in that house. Seeing it again was a profound experience. We felt like we were the characters in the play *Our Town* by Thornton Wilder. We found ourselves peering into another era—into a slice of our youth. The house looked smaller, but beautiful. We could almost hear the sounds of our family in times gone by: the good times, the bad times, the laughing, crying, praying, sleeping, eating, playing—just plain living life.

But we also saw in those memories reminders about the brevity of life. The psalmist wrote, "Man is like a breath; His days are like a passing shadow" (Psalm 144:4). At some point, we all wake up one morning and discover that we are old—better said, "We are advanced in years." On that lovely spring day in the eastern United States we saw life fleeting before our eyes. Seeing our memories made it clear that every moment we are here on earth is precious and must be cherished.

BUT WHY? Why are we here? What could possibly be God's purpose in giving us such a small window called life on earth? After all He is the One who sent us here in the first place (See Psalm 139:13). Is it possible that He sent us here solely for the purpose of finding our way back to him? Why did He give us such a limited amount of time to fulfill His purpose for us? Is it possible for us to find our way to God by ourselves? If we don't seek God and if we reject that He even exists, when we die is that the end of what we call life? The idea that when we die we no longer exist, are gone forever, and that life is over would be very troublesome indeed if we didn't know Jesus Christ. Therefore, it has to be God's highest purpose for us while on this earth to know and believe in His Son Jesus Christ for He is the only

Way to our salvation and the Way back to the Father and eternal life with Him (John 14:6).

The Bible answers all of these questions and in so doing, gives us who have faith in Jesus Christ, great assurance that when we die it will not be the end of it all. In Genesis 3, Adam disobeyed God's command not to eat of the forbidden tree. His defiance of God was the first sin and as Adam's descendants we have all inherited the result of his defiance (Romans 5:12). Sin is part of our nature (Romans 3:9). The wages of that sin are death (Romans 6:23). Therefore because we are sinners and carry the genes of Adam, we must be saved from the death condemnation of sin. Romans 6:23 further states, "But the gift of God is eternal life in Christ Jesus our Lord." Our death-oriented path of life can be changed through God's grace to a path of eternal life. Not only life eternal, but a full life in the present, saved from sin.

Jesus Christ said, "I am the resurrection and the life. He who believes in Me, though he may die, shall live. And whoever lives and believes in Me shall never die" (John 11:25–26). It is only by His grace that we can be saved through faith in Him. "It is the gift of God" (Ephesians 2:8). The apostle Paul, quoting Deuteronomy 30:14 in part, wrote, "If you confess with your mouth the Lord Jesus and believe in your heart that God has raised Him from the dead, you will be saved. For with the heart one believes unto righteousness, and with the mouth confession is made unto salvation" (Romans 10:9–10).

But we have a role in the salvation gift graciously bestowed upon us by our Lord. Watchman Nee succinctly addresses this issue, "The sinner must exercise faith and a believing into the Lord Jesus. By so doing, he is united with Him in His death and resurrection and receives eternal life (John 17:3)—which is spiritual life—unto regeneration." Watchman Nee, *The Spiritual Man*, Vol. I, 64.

The apostle Peter, speaking before the Sanhedrin, said, "Nor is there salvation in any other [than Jesus Christ], for there is no other name under heaven given among men by which we must be saved" (Acts 4:12). Faith in Jesus Christ is the only way to be saved and that is our role in the regenerative process. Once saved, the Lord rescues us from Satan's dominion and enables us to fulfill God's purpose for us in life—finding our way back to Him. "He has delivered us from the power of darkness and conveyed us into the kingdom of the Son of His love, in whom we have redemption through His blood, the forgiveness of sins" (Colossians 1:13–14). Our salvation by the Lord is permanent, forever, for eternity—a life eternal with God (John 3:16).

The old John Newton hymn, *Amazing Grace*, summarizes it all,

> "Amazing grace how sweet the sound
> That saved a wretch like me
> I once was lost but now I'm found
> Was blind but now I see.
> Twas grace that taught my heart to fear
> And grace my fears relieved
> How precious did that grace appear
> The hour I first believed."

It is a fond feeling to have memories to look back on, to see, and to learn from. However, in that experience of seeing our memories, we quickly realize that our minutes, hours and days of life and living here on earth are precious and that God's gracious gift of salvation is the only lasting thing in our lives.

NOTHING IS IMPOSSIBLE WITH GOD

"He is not here," said the angel to the women at Christ's tomb. "For He is risen, as He said...He is risen from the dead" (Matthew 28:6–7). Christ overcame death and was resurrected back to life.

But some say, "That is impossible. Once a person dies, he's dead." That is Satan talking! In my view, one of the most important verses in the Bible is, "With God nothing will be impossible" (Luke 1:37). A variation of Luke's statement is Matthew's wherein he wrote, "With God all things are possible" (Matthew 19:26). Can anyone honestly say in view of all the miracles of creation that we can see, hear, touch, smell and taste, that resurrection is impossible? Is anything too hard for the Lord? "Ah, LORD God! Behold, You have made the heavens and the earth by Your great power and outstretched arm. There is nothing too hard for You" (Jeremiah 32:17).

At least once in the life of a human being, he or she ponders, "Where did all of this come from? Why am I here? What happens when I die?" Believers in the Lord know that the answer to these questions is that we are a creation of a Designer, a Master Creator—God, and that He has a plan for us. Only He, the Potter, knows why He shaped us, the clay. He is a wondrous God!

> "For by Him all things were created that are in heaven and that are on earth, visible and invisible, whether thrones or dominions or principalities or powers. All things were created through Him and for Him. And He is before all things, and in Him all things consist" (Colossians 1:16–17).

Even an atom, the basic material substance of which all things are made, with its various patterns of electrons, neutrons and protons, is held together by a force that no one has been able to explain. The earth rotates on a consistent axis in the middle of space and yet stays at the same distance from the sun since the day it was formed by God.

But no one can explain this phenomenon. Only the Designer knows the formula for His creations.

If you've ever had a medical procedure and in so doing became aware of the intricacies of the human body, you would conclude that the human body in and of itself is miraculous in design. It couldn't have just happened or evolved out of some other substance without a plan or design. If you've had a medical procedure and did research of the inter-workings of that part of your body affected by the procedure, you quickly realized that it is a miracle how the body functions with its miles of blood vessels, nerves, bones, joints, heart, lungs, liver, and other vital organs.

The life support system on earth is not just a coincidence: the air we breathe is perfect for human existence; the temperature range for life to survive is just right; the sky, the land, the water—they are all designed by God for life to exist. If God can create life, what is so hard to understand that He Himself came to be with us as a Person in the form of His Son, died on His cross, and rose again from the dead? The prophet Job said to the Lord, "I know that You can do everything, And that no purpose of Yours can be withheld from You" (Job 42:2).

God's purpose in all things is to do good for those who love him (Romans 8:28). The apostle Paul wrote about the goodness of God as reflected in the life and death of His Son [Christ Jesus],

> "Who, being in the form of God...made Himself of no reputation, taking the form of a bondservant, and coming in the likeness of men. And being found in appearance as a man, He humbled Himself and became obedient to the point of death, even the death of the cross" (Philippians 2:6–8).

Being the second Person of the Trinitarian God, Jesus Christ, came to earth for our salvation. He took on the sins of the world, overcame death by His resurrection, rose from death into life, and then ascended into heaven where he sits at the right hand of the Father

(Romans 8:34). Does it seem impossible? No, nothing is impossible with God!

Belief in the resurrection of Jesus Christ is essential for one's salvation from sin and eternal life with God. Paul, who at one time not only disbelieved in Christ but persecuted those who believed in Christ, wrote in his letter to the Corinthian believers, "For I delivered to you first of all that which I also received: that Christ died for our sins according to the Scriptures, and that He was buried, that He rose again the third day according to the Scriptures, and that He was seen by Cephas, then by the twelve. After that He was seen by over five hundred brethren at once" (1 Corinthians 15:3–6).

Without a belief in Christ's resurrection, Christianity is meaningless. Paul explained to the Corinthian believers why it was so important to believe that Christ rose from the dead. He wrote, "And if Christ is not risen, then our preaching is empty and your faith is also empty...And if Christ is not risen, your faith is futile; you are still in your sins!" (1 Corinthians 15:14, 17). See 1 Corinthians 15 wherein Paul wrote at length about the resurrection of Christ.

But why did Jesus have to die and be resurrected? Because "All have sinned and fall short of the glory of God [what God intended man to be], being justified [declared guiltless] freely by His grace through the redemption that is in Christ Jesus, whom God set forth as a propitiation [sacrifice of atonement] by His blood, through faith" (Romans 3:23–25). Without a belief in Christ's propitiation of the wrath of God (which wrath was due to man's rebellion against God— see Romans 1:18–32), a sinful man is destined for eternal punishment. By the grace of God, believers in the resurrected Christ are saved for eternal life with God.

As He promised, one day Jesus Christ will return to earth from heaven. What if He asks if you believe in His death and resurrection? What will be your answer? What if He tells you that you will be with Him for eternity if you believe in His death and resurrection? What will be your answer? If, as the Bible states that God created the earth, the heavens and all of creation, why is it so difficult to believe that He sent His Son to take the form of a man on earth to assure our salvation in eternity? Ask yourself, "Is there a one-tenth of one-percent (1/10 of 1%) possibility that the Holy Bible is the truth, the inerrant Word of God?" If you believe there is even the slightest possibility of the inerrancy of the Bible, how can you reject its truths about Christ and His resurrection from death to life? Rejection of Jesus Christ means an eternal life of condemnation after you die! Belief in Him means eternal life with God forever—in His kingdom of heaven. Is that the chance you want to take in rejecting Him?

Scripture asks, "Is anything too hard for the LORD?" (Genesis 18:14). Scripture answers, "With God all things are possible" (Matthew 19:26; Mark 10:27; Luke 1:37; Luke 18:27).

Believe God's Word. Believe in Him.

ON THE ROAD TO HEAVEN— WORKING OUT OUR SALVATION

The apostle Paul said to the Philippians, "Work out your own salvation with fear and trembling; for it is God who works in you both to will and to do for His good pleasure" (Philippians 2:12–13). This statement seems to imply that we must *do* something in order to be saved. But in his letter to the Ephesians, Paul also said, "For by grace you have been saved through faith, and that not of yourselves; it is the gift of God, not of works, lest anyone should boast" (Ephesians 2:8–9). We cannot earn our salvation from sin by following the Law of God. We cannot earn our way into heaven by being good—because we are not good (Romans 7:18). We are sinners and have been since Adam first sinned (See Genesis 3). Only by faith in Jesus Christ and by His grace bestowed upon us can we be justified (as if we never sinned) (Romans 3:20, 28).

Salvation is a process by which man is delivered from the power and penalty of sin. Salvation starts with the gracious gift of our Lord and Savior Jesus Christ. That gift from God is called *rebirth*, being born again, for Jesus said, "You must be born again" (John 3:7).

God created us in three parts: the flesh, the soul (the mind—will and emotions), and the spirit (1Thessalonians 5:23). The flesh is the earthly temple for the soul and the spirit. Spirit is the means by which we communicate with God. The desire of the flesh is *self*. The desire of spirit is God. The flesh and the spirit are opposing forces within us. They are competitors in a race for our life (Galatians 5:17). Our sinful nature (our "fleshly lusts") wars "against the soul" (1 Peter 2:11).

The apostle Paul struggled with this issue (See Romans 7:15, 17–20) and so do we. Although he recognized that as a believer in Christ his salvation was intact, he continued to do sinful acts from time to time. He'd do something that he didn't want to do, or he'd not do something that he wanted to do. We all have this conflict within us. For example, we find ourselves speaking a profanity when we accidentally hit our finger with a hammer while driving a nail into a board. When that happens, we ask, "Where did that (profanity) come from?" Paul answered that question. He opined that it comes from "sin that dwells in me" (Romans 7:20).

Prior to our spiritual rebirth, the flesh and our sin nature are dominant and our spirit dormant (Romans 7:1). From infancy, we seek physical or worldly things to satisfy our flesh. We're *selfish*. Often, the accumulation of worldly things separates us even further from God. Then God puts events and circumstances in our life that cause us to cry out to Him in confusion and desperation. One example of this is ill health. When we hear that we are ill, we cry out to Him, He hears our cry and He answers our prayers. Although we do not deserve it, His Holy Spirit imparts new life to our dormant spirit (John 3:6).

Once reborn, there's more work to be done in us since rebirth begins in a state of spiritual infancy. Salvation is a lifelong maturation process of becoming Christ-like. Though as baby Christians He may not have "revealed what we shall be" in Christ, we hope to ultimately "see Him as He is" and "be like Him" for "everyone who has this hope in Him purifies himself, just as He is pure," a lifelong process (1 John 3:2–3). Perhaps that is what Paul meant when he said to "work out your own salvation with fear and trembling" (Philippians 2:12). But does that mean we have to *do* something to be saved? Yes, we must have *faith* that the Lord will do a good work in us.

How does the Lord do His work in us? The flesh consists of our *sin nature* and *self*. As to sin, He's already done the work in us by dying on His cross, the supreme sacrifice (atonement) by which our sins, through His grace, are forgiven. He who was without sin took on the sin of the world—took it away from us who believe in Him, and saved us (1 John 3:5).

As to *self*, Jesus said, "If anyone desires to come after Me, let him deny himself, and take up his cross, and follow Me. For whoever desires to save his life will lose it, but whoever loses his life for My sake will find it" (Matthew 16:24–25). The Lord, through His grace, not only forgives us of our sins, but He also delivers our *self* from the power of sin—that is, if we are willing. It is a choice (free will) given to us to deny one's *self*, feel the pain and suffering (our cross) "for His sake," and follow Jesus to abundant life (Philippians 1:29). Our *self* then becomes less, He becomes more, and we become more like Him.

> "Therefore be imitators of God as dear children. And walk in love, as Christ has also loved us and given Himself for us, an offering and a sacrifice to God for a sweet smelling aroma" (Ephesians 5:1–2).

As we mature in our spiritual walk with Christ, it becomes second nature for us to resist falsehoods, to speak the truth, to obey His commandments, to speak wholesome talk, to seek to be kind and compassionate to one another, to forgive each other just as Christ forgave us, and in the process, find that our bitterness and anger in life are lessened, if not eliminated (See Ephesians 4:25–32). In our perseverance, goodness, righteousness and truth, the fruits of our light, will become more apparent and one day (at the "end"), God will have completed His gracious gift and worked out our salvation in us.

"He who has begun a good work in you will complete it until the day of Jesus Christ" (Philippians 1:6).

THE LORD'S SEVENFOLD PROMISES OF SALVATION

What is salvation? The dictionary definition of *salvation* is, "'Salvation' is used in the [New Testament]...(b) of the spiritual and eternal deliverance granted immediately by God to those who accept His conditions of repentance and faith in the Lord Jesus, in whom alone it is to be obtained...and upon confession of Him as Lord." *Vine's Complete Expository Dictionary of Old and New Testament Words*, 545.

Sin is a condition of separation from God as a result of man breaking His Law. We are all sinners, for Jesus said, "No one is good but One, that is God" (Mark 10:18). As Christians, the recognition that we are sinners and need salvation is an essential first step in the process of salvation. God gave us a choice: righteousness with Him, or sinfulness with the evil one. The process of choice more often happens in the negative. By rejection or disbelief in God, we are left with the spiritual ruler of the earth: Satan. Our "choice" of the latter causes us to be separated from God for eternity, because the penalty of sin is death and eternal judgment. But if we are saved and believe in a Savior, that is, delivered by Him from the power of sin, the Lord's gift to us is eternal life with Him (Romans 6:23). Eternal life with God is heaven. Eternal life with Satan is eternal condemnation in the "lake of fire burning with brimstone" (Revelation 19:20).

As sinners, how can we be saved? The Bible says that we must believe and confess by our mouth that Jesus is Lord and Savior since salvation only comes through faith in Jesus Christ (Romans 10:8–10). Jesus Christ died for our sins. His sacrifice enabled us to be forgiven, redeemed and saved from sin. Jesus said, "I am the way, the truth, and the life. No one comes to the Father except through Me" (John 14:6). The apostle Paul wrote to the Roman believers, "Whoever calls on the name of the LORD shall be saved" (Romans 10:13; Joel 2:32).

Having confessed that Jesus Christ is Lord and that He died for us and then rose from the dead, and having placed our faith in Him for everything, He tells us by His Word that "whoever believes in Him should not perish but have everlasting life" (John 3:16).

What does this mean—that we shall have everlasting or eternal life? By His Word, Jesus tells us what this means. He gives us His *sevenfold promises of salvation.*

In the Book of the Revelation of Jesus Christ, Jesus makes seven promises to those who overcome the temptations of the world and are victorious, who stay the course, who resist the desires of the flesh, and who remain true to Him, even unto death. Paul sums it up in describing those to whom Jesus Christ has given the sevenfold promises of salvation, "Finally, there is laid up for me the crown of righteousness, which the Lord, the righteous Judge, will give to me on that Day, and not to me only, but also to all who have loved His appearing" (2 Timothy 4:8). As believers in Christ, we can look forward with great excitement to a life that will be forever true, noble, right, pure, lovely, admirable, excellent and praiseworthy (Philippians 4:8), being forever reconciled to the Lord!

Revelation, the last book of the Bible, is preceded by the epistles of James, Peter, John and Jude, all of whom speak of false teachers and days of great persecution by the world of believers in Christ. In the first century, Christians were being persecuted for their faith in Jesus Christ. In addition, churches were being invaded and undermined by "false prophets" who taught false theologies, causing confusion and despair amongst the believers. Some of the believers were losing hope; but still, many overcame the attacks by the evil one.

In Revelation 1, the Lord appears to His apostle John, the one He loved, and tells him to write to the seven churches in Asia Minor. These seven churches were representative of all churches, both then and now. At a time when there was great persecution, the Lord tells John to write of the great hope of the things to come. In addition to exhortations for their apostasy, Jesus Christ commends many of the churches for their good works. But for those believers who overcame the temptations taught by the false teachers and the persecutions of the world, that is, those who stayed the course, He gave seven promises of what salvation and the eternal life with Him will be like.

In each letter to the seven churches, Jesus says, "He who has an ear, let him hear what the Spirit says to the churches" (Revelation 2:7). Therefore, read carefully His sevenfold promises of salvation addressed to the true believers in the seven churches and to all of us who believe in Him:

1. Letter to the Church in Ephesus, "To him who overcomes, I will give to eat from the tree of life, which is the midst of the Paradise of God" (Revelation 2:7).
2. Letter to the Church in Smyrna, "He who overcomes shall not be hurt by the second death" (Revelation 2:11).
3. Letter to the Church in Pergamum, "To him who overcomes I will give some of the hidden manna to eat. And I will give him a white stone, and on the stone a new name written which no one knows except him who receives it" (Revelation 2:17).
4. Letter to the Church in Thyatira, "And he who overcomes, and keeps My works until the end, to him I will give power over the nations...as I also have received from my Father; and I will give him the morning star" (Revelation 2:26–28).
5. Letter to the Church in Sardis, "He who overcomes shall be clothed in white garments and I will not blot out his name from the Book of Life; but I will confess his name before My Father and before His angels" (Revelation 3:5).
6. Letter to the Church in Philadelphia, "He who overcomes, I will make him a pillar in the temple of My God, and he shall go out no more. I will write on him the name of My God and the name of the city of My God, the New Jerusalem, which comes down out of heaven from My God. And I will write on him My new name" (Revelation 3:12).
7. Letter to the Church in Laodicea, "To him who overcomes, I will grant to sit with Me on My throne, as I also overcame and sat down with my Father on His throne" (Revelation 3:21).

Imagine, we who have been chosen by our blessed Lord to believe, we to whom He has given ears to hear and eyes to see Him, we who were lost and now are found, shall be richly rewarded when we leave this earth and go to His heaven! Earthly worries and concerns will be irrelevant. Pain and suffering will be a thing of the past. Crying? Only for joy! Finances? Not applicable! Anger and frustration? Gone! Fear? None!

He tells us unequivocally how it will be, "All who persevere shall derive from Christ, as the Tree of Life, perfection and confirmation in holiness and happiness, not in the earthly paradise, but in the heavenly." *Matthew Henry's Concise Commentary on the Whole Bible*, 1266. We shall have no need to fear God's eternal judgment for He assures us that we shall not be thrown into the Lake of Fire, that is, the second death. Hunger and famine shall be no more since we shall forever eat of the manna that comes from heaven for He said, "I am the bread of life...he who feeds on Me will live because of me" (John 6:48, 57). No longer will we experience rejection by blackball, but acceptance with a white stone from God with our new name written on it. We shall share with Him His coming reign over the world as prophesied in Psalm 2:8. We shall receive Christ as our new substance and life just as He rises as a morning star over the darkness of the world's persecution and is victorious over it. We shall be dressed in white as high priests serving our glorious Lord singing, "Holy, holy, holy, Lord God Almighty, Who was and is and is to come!" (Revelation 4:8; Isaiah 6:3).

Our pure relationship with Jesus Christ will be permanently guaranteed since our names will be forever recorded in His Book of Life and we shall for all time belong to His eternal kingdom. He will acknowledge our name before the Father and His angels assuring our heavenly citizenship. We shall be believers in His temple in a New Jerusalem where jasper, gold, sapphire, emeralds, diamonds, pearls, and other precious minerals will be as commonplace as the sand of the sea. We shall be recognized as worthy as the most noble hero of any nation. And last, but best of all, we who suffer with Christ in this earthly plain even to the point of death, will be with Him as He is exalted in glory and honor, forever and ever, sitting with Him on His wonderful throne.

What is salvation? It is the gift of God brought to man by His grace and received by personal faith in the Lord Jesus Christ, whose precious blood was shed on Calvary for the forgiveness of our sins so that we may be with Him forever. Praise be His holy name, forever and ever. Amen.

SIN

"Whatever is not from faith is sin" (Romans 14:23). "Sin is lawlessness" (1 John 3:4). "All unrighteousness is sin" (1 John 5:17). "To him who knows to do good and does not do it, to him it is sin" (James 4:17).

SIN: WE DO HAVE A CHOICE

There was a time in my life when I actually thought I was a good man. In my view, I didn't commit any crimes, I worked hard, I didn't smoke or drink, I cared for and loved my family, and I regarded myself as an honest person. "Who me?" I would have said in response to the question, "Are you a sinner?" "No," I would respond, "I'm not a sinner!" But that was a time when I didn't know Jesus Christ as my Savior. That's of course not to say that knowing Jesus renders one a sinner. But knowing Jesus, the Man who knew no sin, the Man of the Light, the Man of Life, causes one to see and hear how all, including me, are sinners—people in a dark world.

The Bible is full of stories of people who thought like me. One example is the young rich man described in Matthew 19:16–26. He approached Jesus and asked Him how he could achieve eternal life—what could he do for his salvation. In asking this question of Jesus, he called Jesus a "Good Teacher." Jesus addressed the rich man's reference to Him as "Good." He replied that no one is good except God. Jesus also told him that if he wanted "to enter into life" (Matthew 19:17) he should comply with God's commandments. But instead of accepting Jesus' teaching, the young man continued to question Him by asking which commandment he needed to obey (as if there were some commandments he wasn't required to obey!). Being the gracious Lord that He is, Jesus gently repeated to the young man the commandments of God dealing with murder, adultery, theft, dishonesty, and honor of his mother and father and exhorted him to love his neighbor (Matthew 19:18–19). The man responded to Jesus' exhortations by affirming that he'd kept all of these commandments. But he also asked Jesus whether there was anything lacking in him. Jesus knew the man's heart and replied, "If you want to be perfect, go, sell what you have and give to the poor, and you will have treasure in heaven; and come, follow Me" (Matthew 19:21).

Realizing that Jesus could see his sin, the young man withdrew with sadness. The commandment that the young man did not fulfill was the Tenth Commandment of God which states, "You shall not covet your neighbor's house" (Exodus 20:17). The rich young man treasured his worldly possessions more than God. He idolized what he owned. He coveted his possessions. Sin is a condition of estrangement from God as a result of breaking God's law. Because the young man broke God's commandment, he was a sinner in the Father's eyes.

No person, other than Jesus Christ, can keep all of the commandments of God. We are all sinners and have been since the fall of Adam and Eve in Genesis 3. As descendants, we carry their sinful burden. The apostle Paul reiterated the lessons of the Psalms when he wrote, "As it is written: 'There is none righteous, no, not one'" (Romans 3:10). In his wisdom, King Solomon came to the same conclusion, "For there is not a just man on earth who does good And does not sin" (Ecclesiastes 7:20). Paul even went so far as to refer to himself as the chief sinner (1 Timothy 1:15). If Paul was the chief sinner, what does that make us? Hopeless? "By no means!" (as Paul often wrote).

Watchman Nee wrote,

> "When God created man He gave him a perfect freedom...he had perfect freedom of choice. If he chose to obey God, he could; if he decided to rebel against God, he could do that too...The original purpose of God is that the human soul [mind] should receive and assimilate the truth and substance of God's spiritual life [the Holy Spirit]. He gave gifts to men in order that man might take God's knowledge and will as his own. If man's spirit and soul would maintain their created perfection, healthiness and liveliness, his body would then be able to continue forever without change. If he would exercise his will by taking and eating the fruit of life, God's own life undoubtedly would enter his spirit, permeate his soul, transform his inner man, and translate his body into incorruptibility. He then

would literally be in possession of 'eternal life.'" *The Spiritual Man*, Vol. I, 43–44.

The Lord wants us to obey Him and not do as Adam did. Even if in the past we have chosen not to obey Him, He still loves us as a Father and wants us to follow His guiding light (John 12:46–47).

The Lord not only gives us the gift of choice, but without condition gives us His grace to be free of our sinful ways. The gift of the Father's love and grace is what saves us from our fallen state. Paul wrote,

> "For the grace of God that brings salvation has appeared to all men, teaching us that, denying ungodliness and worldly lusts, we should live soberly, righteously, and godly in the present age, looking for the blessed hope and glorious appearing of our great God and Savior Jesus Christ, who gave Himself for us, that He might redeem us from every lawless deed and purify for Himself His own special people, zealous for good works" (Titus 2:11–14).

Life doesn't have to be hard to be good. But without Christ, it is so hard to be good, in fact it's impossible (Matthew 19:26). Unless we actively cooperate, God will not undertake anything for us. We can exercise our free will by choosing Jesus Christ as our Lord and Savior and be saved for eternity. It's that simple. For Jesus said, "I am the way, the truth, and the life. No one comes to the Father except through Me." (John 14:6).

Choose the Lord Jesus Christ and sin no more. It is our God-given choice.

TESTIMONY

The testimony of a Christian believer is a powerful gift given to him or her by the grace of Jesus Christ. The Holy Bible consists of thousands of pages of eyewitness testimony by God-inspired men and women (2 Timothy 3:16). The apostle John is just one of many whose God-breathed testimony about Jesus Christ is irrefutable. He wrote about that which he had seen, "That which was from the beginning, which we have heard, which we have seen with our eyes, which we have looked upon, and our hands have handled, concerning the Word of life" (1 John 1:1).

A DIRECT EXPERIENCE WITH GOD

I was 43 and in trouble. My work-a-holism was affecting my family and my marriage was falling apart. I was under tremendous pressure at work and I was having what many call a "mid-life crisis." With respect to my marriage, perhaps it would have been less painful to walk away and divorce, but something urged us on to try and work out our problems.

My wife and I were searching for answers. In an effort to find the truth, we tried various New Age programs such as Lifespring and EST but nothing provided answers. Nothing filled the emptiness in our souls.

Then, on a Tuesday evening, while attending another "life seminar" in the mountains of Vermont, I experienced a vision in my mind's eye of Jesus Christ being crucified on the cross. In my vision, I saw Christ on the cross surrounded by brilliant white light. Incredibly, it was as if I was at Golgotha watching Jesus being put to death. Tears filled my eyes and I cried uncontrollably. Not only did I feel great sadness for what I was witnessing (the death of a Man), but at the same time I experienced great love and joy realizing that He was sacrificing Himself for me. "But God demonstrates His own love toward us, in that while we were still sinners, Christ died for us" (Romans 5:8). Deep love filled my heart and the glory of God filled my soul!

That direct experience with God was a life changer! My life and that of my family haven't been the same since that eventful September evening in 1983.

At first, I didn't know what to make of this—seeing Christ crucified! But when my wife also experienced a special revelation of Jesus some six months later (she experienced His presence), the path He wanted us to follow became clear. He gave us a deep yearning to learn all we could about Him (2 Corinthians 5:1–4). The apostle Paul's words sum up our longing at the time for spiritual answers (answers about Jesus Christ),

"Yet indeed I also count all things loss for the excellence of the knowledge of Christ Jesus my Lord...that I may know Him and the power of His resurrection, and the fellowship of His sufferings, being conformed to His death, if, by any means, I may attain to the resurrection from the dead" (Philippians 3:8, 10–11). (See also Romans 8:22–23).

Since that time of special wonder, our lives with Christ have been filled with faith, hope and love, not to mention marital bliss.

Visions of God are wonderful "mountain-top experiences" if and when they happen. But once you have descended from the mountain-top back into the valley, life still has to be lived—not by visions or miracles, but by the written Word of God. The issue of why the Lord revealed Himself to us through visions is not the important question. What is important is that He adopted us and led us to His "pure river of water of life" (Revelation 22:1), a place to which He leads all of His children, that is, those who receive Him and believe in His Name (John 1:12–13). For that we shall be forever grateful!

Oh, and by the way, my wife and I just CELEBRATED 54 years of marriage! Thank you Lord, "You will show me the path of life [the kingdom of heaven]; In Your presence is fullness of joy; At Your right hand are pleasures forevermore" (Psalm 16:11).

Author's note: For further insight on the subject of visions of Jesus Christ, see the article by Sandy Feit in *In Touch*, January, 2010 (*www.intouch.org*) entitled, *Just a Dream? Visions of Jesus: A Not-So-Rare Phenomenon*.

TRIUMPH

"Now thanks be to God who always leads us in triumph in Christ, and through us diffuses the fragrance of His knowledge in every place" (2 Corinthians 2:14).

TRIUMPH: A STUDY OF PALM SUNDAY

The story of Jesus' triumphal entry into Jerusalem in fulfillment of the biblical prophecies of His death and resurrection are set forth in Matthew 21:1–11, Mark 11:1–11, Luke 19:28–44 and John 12:12–19. The prophecy of Jesus' triumphal entry into Jerusalem is written in Zechariah 9:9. Zechariah was a prophet who accompanied the Israelites back to Jerusalem from captivity in Babylon. He wrote this prophecy between 520 and 480 BC, more than 500 years before Christ. Jesus fulfilled Zechariah's prophecy, "Rejoice greatly, O Daughter of Zion! Shout, O Daughter of Jerusalem! Behold, your King is coming to you; He is just and having salvation, Lowly and riding on a donkey, a colt, the foal of a donkey" (Zechariah 9:9).

Jesus may have chosen the colt "since the donkey was a lowly animal of peace [as compared to a horse, an instrument of war] as well as a princely mount before the horse came into common use. The royal mount used by David and his sons was the mule." *NIV Study Bible*, 1805, note at Zechariah 9:9. King David ordered his advisors to "Take with you the servants of your lord, and have Solomon my son ride on my own mule and take him down to Gihon" where they were to anoint his son Solomon as king over Israel (1 Kings 1:33). Consistent with His Davidic lineage, Jesus chose His ancestor's means of transportation, an animal in the mule family, the smaller animal, a donkey—and an even smaller animal in the same family, a colt. This was also consistent with His humble character.

Zechariah 9:9 is not only significant because of its prophetic accuracy, but it is another example of seeing Jesus in the Old Testament (Covenant). The Old Testament is replete with references (prophecies) or appearances of Jesus. It is all about Him. "And beginning at Moses and all the Prophets, He expounded to them in all the Scriptures the things concerning Himself" (Luke 24:27).

Out of the four Gospels describing Jesus' triumphal entry into Jerusalem, only Matthew (21:2) refers to a donkey and a colt. This was in line with Matthew's objective in writing to the Jewish people about Jesus. He references Zechariah's prophecy by referring to both a donkey and her colt. The other three Gospels mention only the colt. Matthew shows how Jesus' actions fulfilled the prophet's words, thus giving another indication that Jesus was indeed the Messiah. When Jesus entered Jerusalem on a donkey's colt, He affirmed His Messianic royalty as well as His humility.

On His final journey to Jerusalem to face the Father's charge on His life as a Man, Jesus' triumphant entry down the Mount of Olives and then up to Mount Zion in the City of Jerusalem was carefully planned by Him. He instructed two of His disciples to go into the nearby village and untie the donkey and her colt and bring them to Him (Matthew 21:1–3). "All of this was done that it might be fulfilled which was spoken by the prophet" [in Zechariah 9:9] (Matthew 21:4).

Bethphage is a little village at the top of the Mount of Olives. It is the place from which the famous photo is often taken of the Temple Mount and the mosque which the Muslims have erected on it with its gold dome. The village of Bethany where Lazarus, Martha and Mary, Jesus' friends, lived, is just down from Bethphage on the eastern slope of the Mount of Olives on the road to Jericho. Although not stated in the Bible, it is possible that Jesus may have stayed with His friends in Bethany the night before He triumphantly rode into Jerusalem. Perhaps the owner of the donkey and her colt was a friend of Lazerus' or one of Jesus' disciples who resided in Bethphage.

Matthew 21 continues, "So the disciples went and did as Jesus commanded them. They brought the donkey and the colt, laid their clothes on them, and set Him on them" (Matthew 21:6–7). Notice that Jesus asked His disciples to bring both the donkey (mother) and the colt (child), perhaps to keep both animals calm. Those familiar with animals know that separating a mother and its offspring often causes the mother great consternation. When our neighbor, a sheep farmer, takes the little lambs away from their mothers, there is loud crying for hours from the mother sheep.

Jesus' triumphal entry into Jerusalem in one aspect resembled the parades of Roman generals who marched into Rome after victory on the battlefield. The people cheering on the Roman legionnaires were celebrating (or anticipating) military success over their enemies. In Jesus' case, the people expected Him to be their military leader who would overthrow the murderous reign of the Romans over Israel. Josephus wrote about the triumphal parades of the Roman generals,

> "And as soon as ever it was day, Vespasian and Titus came out crowned with laurel, and clothed in those ancient purple habits which were proper to their family...Then did he retire to that gate which was called the Gate of the Pomp...and when they had put on their triumphal garments...they sent the triumph forward, and marched through the theatres, that they might be the more easily seen by the multitude." *The Complete Works of Flavius Josephus*, Book VII, 594, translated by William Whiston, A.M.*

Whereas the triumphal entry of Roman generals on their war chariots was marked with pugnacious pomposity, the triumphal entry of the Lord Jesus into Jerusalem was marked with peaceful passivity and meekness as He rode in on a colt. Crowds of people lined the road as Jesus proceeded towards the city. Thinking that He would be their military leader to break the bonds of the Romans, they spread palm branches on the road in front of Him. The display of palm branches was a tradition of the Israelites to show honor to their military leaders. As He passed by, the multitude shouted in Hebrew (transliterated), "Awnaw Yahweh. Hosheaw naw" (Matthew 21: 8–9).

The word, "Hosanna," is derived from the Hebrew words "hosheaw naw" which mean "save us now!" These words were probably quoted purposely by His joyful believers from Psalm 118:25–26: "Save now, I pray, O LORD; O LORD, I pray, send now prosperity. Blessed is he who comes in the name of the LORD! We have blessed you from the house of the LORD."

---

* Taken from *The Complete Works of Josephus*,© Copyright 1981, translated by Wm. Whiston (Foreword by Wm. S. LaSor). Published by Kregel Publications, Grand Rapids, MI. Used by permission of the publisher. All rights reserved.

The branches placed on the road before Jesus were palm branches (hence the designation "Palm Sunday"). The symbolism of the palms is important here. Palm trees are referenced numerous times in the Bible. In 1 Kings 6:29 it is described how King Solomon "carved on the walls of the temple figures of cherubim, palm trees, and open flowers." They may have been intended to be symbolic reminders of the splendor of God's Garden of Eden in Genesis 2:8.

In Leviticus 23:37, the Lord commanded the Israelites to celebrate the Lord's Feast of Tabernacles (Succoth) and to live in booths for seven days as a reminder of the temporary shelters the Israelites lived in as they traveled through the desert on their way to the promised land (Leviticus 23:42). The booths were made of "branches of palm trees, the boughs of leafy trees and willows of the brook" (Leviticus 23:40).

The prophet Zechariah foretold how on the day of the Lord, God would defend Jerusalem against all the nations of the world and preserve a remnant of the children of Israel. He prophesied that "The people shall dwell in it; And no longer shall there be utter destruction, But Jerusalem shall be safely inhabited" (Zechariah 14:11). Then the Lord commanded "that everyone who is left of all the nations which came against Jerusalem shall go up from year to year to worship the King, the LORD of hosts, and to keep the feast of Tabernacles" (Zechariah 14:16). In that annual celebration, the nations of the world will celebrate the Lord for seven days in their temporary booths.

Many of the people encouraging the Lord in His triumphal entry had a selfish motivation in their exuberance. They were looking for a military leader to overthrow the bonds of oppression of the Romans. Remembering the use of palms by Simon Maccabeus in his victory over the Seleucids and his restoration of the temple from the abominable desolation of Antiochus Epiphanes, the people waved and spread palms on the road down the Mount of Olives as Jesus entered the Holy City. "On the 23rd day of the second month, in the year 171 [141 B.C.], there was a great celebration in the city because this terrible threat to the security of Israel had come to an end. Simon [Maccabeus] and his men entered the fort singing hymns of praise and thanksgiving, while carrying palm branches and playing harps, cymbals and lyres" (1 Maccabees 13:51).

But palm branches are enduring symbols, not of war and triumph, but of eternal peace, light and strength. Believers in Jesus Christ shall be waving them in joyful celebration before the throne of the Lord,

> "After these things [wrote the apostle John] I looked, and behold, a great multitude which no one could number, of all nations, tribes, peoples, and tongues, standing before the throne and before the Lamb, clothed with white robes, with palm branches in their hands, and crying out with a loud voice, saying, 'Salvation belongs to our God who sits on the throne, and to the Lamb!'" (Revelation 7:9–10).

TROUBLES

Jesus said, "In the world you will have tribulation; but be of good cheer, I have overcome the world" (John 16:33).

STORMS OF LIFE

Our mortal lives are but a test created for us by the Lord to determine the eternal path we shall choose. The Lord not only gave us the gift of life, but He also gave us free will, that is, the will to choose Him and enjoy eternal life, or the will to reject Him and suffer death and eternal darkness separated from God.

> "And Moses said to the people, 'Do not fear; for God has come to test you, and that His fear [respect] may be before you, so that you may not sin' (Exodus 20:20). And you shall remember that the LORD your God led you all the way these forty years in the wilderness, to humble you and test you, to know what was in your heart, whether you would keep His commandments or not. So He humbled you...that He might make you know that man shall not live by bread alone; but man lives by every word that proceeds from the mouth of the LORD" (Deuteronomy 8:2–3).

Within the overall test of life itself, our Lord also sends us occasional "mini-tests." These take the form of life's troubles. These tribulations are intended to enable us to see where we stand in our faith as the main test of life progresses to the time of determination of our eternal path.

In September, 2005, I learned that I had a very serious spinal illness called "cervical myelopathy." Five of my cervical vertebrae were each collapsing into the next one, the uncorrected result of which could have been paralysis. One vertebra was projecting three-fourths into the wall of my spinal cord! The physician told me that if I had a sudden jarring of some kind causing my spinal cord to break that I would probably spend the rest of my life in a wheelchair.

I lamented, "Why would the Lord allow this to happen to me?" Now that the operation is over, the answer has become apparent: the

Lord was showing me how my life has changed as compared to the days when I didn't know Him. As I've elected to walk deeper with Jesus Christ in His Living Waters, my ship of life with Him at the helm is running a stronger, steadier course as I traverse life's storms (tests).

I've recounted below in journal form that life storm as it played out and how it showed me that I've experienced a change for the better in my life due solely to His hand.

Wednesday, October 5, 6:00AM: Because of the complexity of the operation I faced, after much prayer, I was guided to seek out the most experienced physicians, that is, doctors who teach other surgeons to do spinal surgery at Barrow Neurosurgical Institute (BNI) in Phoenix, Arizona. Although I awoke today with a degree of uncertainty as to where the day would take me, my morning devotions have given me a peace as they always do. I read comforting words in Psalm 91, "Because he has set his love upon Me, therefore I will deliver him; I will set him on high, because he has known My name. He shall call upon Me, and I will answer him; I will be with him in trouble" (Psalm 91:14–15). As I face this *risky* operation tomorrow, I feel His arms around me and move forward without fear or trepidation.

Wednesday, October 5, 9:00AM: It was a short walk from the hotel to the sprawling St. Joseph's Hospital and Medical Center wherein the physicians of Barrow perform their surgeries. It is comforting to see the huge cross over the hospital in the distance. After examining me, Dr. Volker Sonntag, MD, an internationally known neurosurgeon, advised that not only did he have to remove four of my discs, but also one of my vertebrae (a "corpectomy") since that vertebra (C5) was embedded in the wall of my spinal cord. The risks of the operation included paralysis and a host of other concerns. He explained that it made sense to fix the problem while it was *not irreversible* (i.e. a severed cord) and while I was in relatively good condition. We'd been praying for more certainty to the issues I faced and here was the confirmation. The Lord answers all of our prayers.

"For the eyes of the LORD are on the righteous, and His ears are open to their prayers" (1 Peter 3:12; see also John 9:31).

Thursday, October 6, 5:00AM: After prayers, we headed to BNI for my surgery. As we walked to the hospital, the name of the Lord identified by the prophet in Isaiah 7:14 came to mind, "Immanuel," which means *God with us*. When we arrived at the hospital, they had me change into one of those notorious one sided gowns and I climbed onto a gurney in a room that is just adjacent to the operating rooms. The anesthesiologist introduced himself, explained what I could expect and then proceeded to hook up an IV in my left hand. My mind was filled with these words, "Trust in the LORD with all your heart, And lean not on your own understanding; In all your ways acknowledge Him, and He shall direct your paths" (Proverbs 3:5–6). When the doctor turned on the IV, that's about all I can remember until I woke after the operation.

Thursday, October 6, late afternoon: I heard the words, "Wake up Barry." The nurse checked my vital signs and asked me to move my arms while she held them in place; the same for my legs. Everything worked fine! My wife told me that as I was being wheeled out of the operating room, I spoke the word *hallelujah* which means Praise the Lord! The operation turned out to be more difficult because the vertebra to be removed was embedded deeply in my spinal cord. Dr. Sonntag had to dig it out without puncturing the cord and without severing any nerves. I was in there for four and one-half hours. Notwithstanding the degree of difficulty, I was blessed by the competence and wisdom of experienced physicians presented to me by my Lord and Savior Jesus Christ. Thank you Lord for the gracious gifts bestowed upon these learned physicians who served me through the storm.

Some time later: I'm home again! All went well. The Lord saw me through the storm. Now I start the long road of healing, the healing by His hands. I look back on the storm I just passed through and sense something different about this storm. It was probably one of the most severe storms I'd faced and yet, I'd had a peace about it that I'd not previously experienced. Throughout the process, I had a knowing that *all would be well, no matter the outcome.* The apostle Paul refers to this sense of well-being as the "armor of God." He wrote, "Therefore take up the whole armor of God, that you may be able to withstand in the evil day, and having done all, to stand" (Ephesians 6:13).

There's been a change in my life—a change for the better. I know that with the armor of God around me, I can face any storm that may come my way. For "God is faithful, who will not allow you be tempted beyond what you are able" (1 Corinthians 10:13). He gives me the strength and courage to face life's troubles with a peace that transcends all understanding.

TRUTH

Jesus Christ is Truth (John 14:6). Faith in Him enables us to enter into "the mystery of His will," which as His disciples, He has "made known to us" (Ephesians 1:9). Knowing the will of Christ is knowing the truth. Knowing and speaking truth glorifies God (Joshua 7:19).

TRUTH IS THE ONLY WAY

It is vitally important for our eternal well-being that we endeavor in all things to be truthful in everything we think, say and do. Jesus Christ told us, His disciples, to emulate Him in everything. He said that He is the Truth (John 14:6),

> "For this cause I was born, and for this cause I have come into the world, that I should bear witness to the truth. Everyone who is of the truth hears My voice" (John 18:37). "If you abide in My word, you are My disciples indeed. And you shall know the truth, and the truth shall make you free" (John 8:31–32).

Pontius Pilate cynically asked Jesus, "What is truth?" (John 18:38). In Hebrew, the word for truth is *emet* which means firmness, stability, fidelity, and a reliable basis of support. It is associated with behavior (Genesis 24:49), promises (2 Samuel 7:28), kindness and faithfulness (Genesis 47:29), justice (Nehemiah 9:13) and sincerity (Joshua 24:14). It also suggests that something is open, uncovered, revealed for what it is, that is, real and genuine, rather than imaginary or false. Bridges for Peace, *Israel Teaching Letter*, July, 2005.

The Bible, the manual of life, gives many illustrations of the principle taught by our Lord that we must be truthful in all things, for "Lying lips are an abomination to the LORD, But those who deal truthfully are His delight" (Proverbs 12:22).

The Old Testament is a picture of the principles taught by Jesus Christ in the New Testament. Speaking through Joshua, God cautioned the Israelites who were about to see the walls of Jericho fall to stay away from the things that are consecrated to the Lord— the "accursed things." Those secret things of God were "silver and gold articles...and vessels of bronze and iron." (Joshua 6:18–19). The accursed things were to go "into the treasury of the LORD." (Joshua 6:19). But one of the Israelites, Achan of the tribe of Judah, took some of the accursed things of God and hid them for himself. God was angry at all of the Israelites for Achan's offense (Joshua 7:1). After the fall of Jericho, Joshua sent 3000 men to defeat Ai, but the small Jewish army was routed (Joshua 7:4). Joshua cried out to the Lord for an explanation for this defeat. The Lord responded by telling him that Israel couldn't defeat its enemies because it had sinned by violating His covenant concerning the accursed things. The Lord said to Joshua, "Israel has sinned, and they have also transgressed My covenant which I commanded them. For they have even taken some of the accursed things, and have both stolen and deceived; and they have also put it among their own stuff" (Joshua 7:11). The Lord told Joshua to purge the sinner from their ranks (Joshua 7:12).

Achan knew that he had acted wrongly against the Lord, but he hid this truth from Joshua. Following the Lord's instructions, Joshua questioned the Israelites tribe by tribe, clan by clan, family by family, and man by man. With the Lord's guidance he determined that Achan was the man who'd committed the sin against the Lord by stealing the devoted things. When confronted by Joshua, Achan admitted that he'd stolen God's accursed things and hid them in his tent. For this sin all Israel stoned him to death (Joshua 7:25). Once the sins of covetousness and untruth were purged from their midst, the Israelites again attacked Ai. But this time they easily defeated the enemy.

What is the picture (truth) that is taught in the Old Testament story about Achan and being truthful? "The wrath of God is revealed from heaven against all ungodliness and unrighteousness of men, who suppress the truth in unrighteousness" (Romans 1:18). God cannot be fooled. Speaking untruth is not just a lie against men to whom it is uttered, but it is a sin against God (Acts 5:4). He is omniscient and knows what is true in each of our hearts (1 Samuel 16:7). Jesus Christ taught, "there is nothing covered that will not be revealed, nor hidden that will not be known" (Luke 12:2).

Another illustration of this biblical teaching that speaking untruth is a sin against God is in Chapter 5 of the Book of Acts dealing with the covetousness and mendacity of Ananias and Sapphira. Like

Achan, Ananias and Sapphira held back from the community of disciples some of the money they'd received from the sale of their property and then lied about it. Peter, an apostle whose spirit was aligned with the Holy Spirit and hence perceived the truth about the people before him, said, "You have not lied to men but to God." When Ananias heard this, he fell down and died (Acts 5:4–5).

Three hours later, Sapphira, Ananias' wife, lied to the disciples about keeping part of the money from the sale of their property. Again, Peter confronted her and told her that she was lying not just to him, but to the Holy Spirit. Hearing this "she fell down at his feet and breathed her last" (Acts 5:10).

Lying is a serious sin. It is not just untruth to men or women who are injured by its utterance or actions, *it is untruth spoken to God.* How foolish one is to think he or she can lie to God, our omniscient Father, and not be caught in that lie. The Holy Spirit works in us an amazing thing regarding our speaking of the truth. When I speak the truth, the retelling of the same truth at a later time flows naturally and consistently from me. It is consistent, because it is the truth. However, if I lie, the retelling will be inconsistent with the prior version of my statement (a lie) because I can't remember accurately what I previously said. The Bible is truth because it is always consistent.

As the Bible repeatedly states, the Lord wants us to live our lives following Him and His teachings. He wants us to be Christ-like. He wants us to speak the truth to each other and to love no false oath. Speaking through His prophet, the Lord said,

> "Speak each man the truth to his neighbor; Give judgment in your gates for truth, justice, and peace; Let none of you think evil in your heart against your neighbor; And do not love a false oath. For all these are things that I hate" (Zechariah 8:16–17).

"By your words you will be justified, and by your words you will be condemned" (Matthew 12:37). "Walk as children of light (for the fruit of the Spirit is in all goodness, righteousness and truth), finding out what is acceptable to the Lord" (Ephesians 5:8–10).

Oh, Lord, "Remove from me the way of lying, And grant me Your law graciously. I have chosen the way of truth" (Psalm 119:29–30).

Truth is the only Way.

THE TRUTHS OF OUR LORD SET US FREE

Jesus said to those who believed in Him, "If you abide in My word, you are My disciples indeed. And you shall know the truth, and the truth shall set you free" (John 8:31–32).

This is the time of year [July 4th] when we remember the great sacrifices of our forefathers who valued freedom from tyranny above their own lives. Who were these great men of faith? What were their beliefs? What truths did they know when they wrote the Declaration on that day in July, 1776? They wrote,

> "We hold these truths to be self-evident, that all men are created equal, that they are endowed by their Creator with certain unalienable Rights, that among these are Life, Liberty and the pursuit of Happiness."

What was the Spiritual basis for their willingness to sacrifice all they had?

Thomas Jefferson, our third president, was the author of the Declaration of Independence assisted by John Adams, our second president, and by Benjamin Franklin, our first foreign ambassador. These men lived their lives unafraid of the "reproach of men" (Isaiah 51:7). They were all successful, affluent citizens of the then British colonies who threw off the yoke of a tyrannical monarch in order to be free. "Now the Lord is the Spirit; and where the Spirit of the Lord is, there is liberty" (2 Corinthians 3:17). They were willing to give up everything for freedom.

There is controversy about the religious beliefs of Thomas Jefferson. Respected historian David Barton wrote a book about the criticisms of Jefferson entitled *The Jefferson Lies*. In his book, author Barton discussed at length the false truths that have been told about Jefferson. Jefferson was raised in and baptized in the Anglican Church. His views on orthodox Christian doctrine were controversial as he didn't agree with the Divinity of Christ but viewed Christ's teachings as the most majestic in morality the world has seen. In a letter to one of his contemporaries he referred to himself as a real Christian.

Of the three on the Declaration Committee, John Adams was the strongest believer in the Lord. He was more consistent than Jefferson or Franklin in his religious practices. He wrote in 1756 of the gifts of God as expressions of God's love, the greatest of which in his view was the gift of an inquiring mind. Adams virtually looked to God in everything he did. That has been my prayer for each of the recent presidents of the United States—that like King Solomon and President Adams, each strives for wisdom from God in guiding our country.

Although Benjamin Franklin was a Deist as were many in his time, at the Constitutional Convention of 1787 he called for prayer, for a day to be set aside to fast in the Commonwealth of Pennsylvania, and for recognition in their prayers to their dependence on a Supreme Being.

Many of the founding fathers of our great nation were in awe of the teachings of our Lord in His Word. The Lord gave them great courage and inspired them to stand for what they believed to be the truths of all time. They were guided by the Word of God which tells us, "Stand fast therefore in the liberty by which Christ has made us free, and do not be entangled again with a yoke of bondage" (Galatians 5:1). They had a higher belief in truths that were self-evident. Among those was a belief that a tyrannical king may have been placed in a position of power by God solely for the purpose of providing a reason for them to declare to the world that all men "are endowed by their Creator with certain unalienable Rights, that among these are Life, Liberty and the pursuit of Happiness." God led them to place their names, their lives, their fortunes, and their honor as living sacrifices for freedom in their land. They signed their names to these truths and wrote, "And for the support of this Declaration, with a firm reliance on the protection of divine Providence, we mutually pledge to each other our Lives, our Fortunes and our sacred honor."

The truths shown to our forefathers by our Lord set them free. Thank you, Lord for your Holy Truths. Indeed, they have truly set us free!

WISDOM

"Oh, the depth of the riches both of the wisdom and knowledge of God! How unsearchable are His judgments and His ways past finding out!" (Romans 11:33).*

---

* The apostle Paul's outpouring of his love for God - a doxology

WISDOM IS HEAVENLY KNOWLEDGE

Wisdom is heavenly knowledge. It is acquiring an understanding of what is true. It is discernment of what is right or wrong. It is enduring through all the ages.

Without God, there is no wisdom. "For the Lord gives wisdom; From His mouth come knowledge and understanding" (Proverbs 2:6). The apostle James wrote, "If any of you lacks wisdom, let him ask of God, who gives to all liberally and without reproach, and it will be given to him" (James 1:5). It is the Word of God that tells us that in order to have wisdom about anything, we must pray to Him, consult His Word, and seek His guidance for righteous knowledge and understanding (Proverbs 2:1–5). Consistent with this Biblical wisdom, Jesus taught, "Ask, and it will be given to you; seek, and you will find; knock, and it will be opened to you. For everyone who asks receives, and he who seeks finds, and to him who knocks, it will be opened" (Matthew 7:7–8).

There are numerous illustrations of this principle in the Scriptures. Solomon, the wisest of the kings of Israel, had a loving reverence for the Lord and a keen willingness to submit to His Lordship and the commands of His Word. He concluded, "The fear [reverence] of the LORD is the beginning of wisdom, And the knowledge of the Holy One is understanding" (Proverbs 9:10).

One night Solomon dreamed about the Lord. In his dream the Lord asked him what He could give him, perhaps to assist him in ruling over God's children, the Israelites. Responding to the Lord in his dream, Solomon humbled himself before the Lord admitting that he was an inexperienced "little child" who was uncertain how to govern his people. He asked the Lord to give him "an understanding heart to judge" God's people so that he might "discern between good and evil" (1 Kings 3:5–9). The Lord was pleased with Solomon's request for wisdom in governing Israel. He was especially pleased that Solomon hadn't asked for selfish things such as a "long life...riches" or for the destruction of his enemies (1 Kings 3:11). The Lord granted

Solomon what he prayed for, namely, "understanding to discern justice" and "a wise and understanding heart" (1 Kings 3:11–12). The Lord was so pleased with Solomon that He even gave him the things he hadn't asked for consisting of "both riches and honor, so that there shall not be anyone like you among the kings all your days" (1 Kings 3:13). Solomon became "wiser than all men" (1 Kings 4:31).

Solomon's wisdom was founded on his unconditional trust in the Lord. With heavenly knowledge and Godly wisdom, Solomon wrote the greatest Proverb,

> "Trust in the LORD with all your heart, And lean not on your own understanding; In all your ways acknowledge Him, and He shall direct your paths" (Proverbs 3:5–6).

Solomon's wise Proverb has worked for me many times in my life. When faced with troubles and challenges in life, I have prayed Solomon's Proverb and it has worked to get me through those situations with peaceful clarity.

Jehoshaphat was another good and wise king of Israel who loved the Lord and sought God's wisdom in all things. Jehoshaphat faced a menacing army of Moabites and Ammonites whose aim was to destroy Israel. Looking to God for an answer to the overwhelming odds against him, Jehoshaphat proclaimed a nationwide fast. He exhorted the people to pray to the Lord for guidance and protection against the terrible danger they faced (2 Chronicles 20:2–12). While in prayer, the Spirit of the Lord came upon Jahaziel, one of the Levite priests serving in the Temple. The Lord spoke words of encouragement and reassurance to King Jehoshaphat and the Israelites through Jahaziel. He said through the words of His prophet, "Listen, all of you of Judah and you inhabitants of Jerusalem, and you, King Jehoshaphat...Do not be afraid or dismayed because of this great multitude, for the battle is not yours, but God's...Tomorrow go down against them...for the LORD is with you" (2 Chronicles 20:15–17). The next morning, as the enemies of Israel marched upon them, the Lord set ambushes against the aggressors. When the Israelites reached the place where the battle was to be joined, they found only dead bodies—not one of their enemies had escaped. "The fear of God was on all the kingdoms of those countries when they heard that the LORD had fought against the enemies of Israel. Then the realm of Jehoshaphat was quiet, for his God gave him rest all around" (2 Chronicles 20:29–30).

The apostle Paul wrote often of the infinite knowledge and wisdom of God. You can hear the exuberance in his doxology describing the extent and depth of God's boundless wisdom,

> "Oh, the depth of the riches both of the wisdom and knowledge of God! How unsearchable are His judgments, and His ways past finding out! 'For who has known the mind of the Lord? Or who has become his counselor? Or who has first given to Him, And it shall be repaid to him?' For of him and through him and to him are all things, to whom be glory forever! Amen" (Romans 11:33–36).

From his prayer, you can see and hear the apostle's joyful heart as he wrote his letter to the Roman believers. His words reflect a person who truly felt the presence of the Lord!

So, dear saints, seek the Lord's heavenly knowledge in all situations in life. If we trust in Him and lean not on our own understanding, He will impart to us His great wisdom, our paths will be straight, and we shall have great joy forever!

WITNESS

Jesus said, "But you shall receive power when the Holy Spirit has come upon you; and you shall be witnesses to Me in Jerusalem, and in all Judea and Samaria, and to the end of the earth" (Acts 1:8).

A LIFE-CHANGING VISION

In this post-modern era, supernatural events are viewed with skepticism by the secular culture. They say, "If I can't see it, hear it, smell it, touch it or taste it, or if science can't prove it, then it isn't so." But the secularists' rejection of the spiritual dimension does not mean it doesn't exist. Accepting the material and rejecting the spiritual part of life defies common sense.

There I was, living a worldly life, raising my family, earning a living—accumulating material things. But something was missing. In my desire for material things, I'd become a workaholic. After years of going through the world's motions, I felt empty. No matter how many *things* I'd accumulated—a house, car, fine clothes—none filled the yearning in my heart for something greater in my life. One day I woke up to find the very foundations of my family shaken. My marriage was falling apart. Divorce was threatening its ugly head. I was always working and my children were growing up without me. But, not knowing any better, I dove even deeper into my work. Keeping busy took my mind off the pit in my stomach.

My soul groaned, but I didn't know for what. My spirit was low. Deep fear, insecurity and sadness permeated my existence. I was in a downward spiral sinking into an endless pit. I felt so alone. Who or what could relieve me of my pain?

I questioned everything in my life. At age forty-three I couldn't still my mind from questions such as, "Why I am here? What is the purpose of all this? Where am I going—am I going to die soon? (Although the way I was feeling in that mid-life crisis, at times I felt like perhaps it would be best if it would end soon—put me out of my misery)! With respect to my family, what had I done wrong? What is right and what is wrong in life (and how did I know what was right versus wrong)?" Bear in mind, I was asking these questions as a Jewish man who didn't know Jesus Christ.

It was these purpose of life questions for which I was seeking answers. Looking back to that time, the words of King David rang true for me. He wrote, "[Lord] Turn Yourself to me, and have mercy on me, For I am desolate and afflicted. The troubles of my heart have enlarged; Bring me out of my distresses!" (Psalm 25:16–17).

The Lord was working on me. He had other things in store for me, but he needed me to cry out to Him. The words of the psalmist succinctly point out what the Lord had in store for me at that desperate time in my life. He wrote, "The righteous cry out, and the LORD hears, And delivers them out of all their troubles. The LORD is near to those who have a broken heart, And saves such as have a contrite spirit" (Psalm 34:17–18).

In my quest to fill the emptiness in my spirit, I "happened" to attend a seminar, *Dynamics of Life*, billed as "an introspective self-examination into life's issues." The setting for the seminar (retreat) was magnificent. It took place in Shelbourne, Vermont in a one-hundred room mansion on the shores of Lake Champlain. The mansion was classic. Its year of construction was on a cornerstone: 1899. It had been the summer home of a very wealthy New York magnate.

There were twenty-five of us in the group. We were told that our assignment for the next seven days was to come off the freeway where we'd been racing through life at an abnormally fast pace, to eat well, not smoke, not drink coffee (no aspirin for the headache that resulted from cutting out coffee), to get lots of rest and exercise, keep clean, and slow down to life's natural pace. The group instructor pointed to a gull gliding naturally on the updrafts over the lake at a gentle speed. He told us to aim for that pace of life in the upcoming days. The objectives in the seminar were to "raise your level of awareness" and "seek truth for yourselves," whatever that might be.

It was Tuesday evening, the third day of the seminar. The group was doing dyads (two persons facing each other)—we were sitting on the floor of the library of the mansion in rows of two. We were instructed to ask the person facing us, "Who are you?" In asking that question, I suddenly became aware that I was actually asking myself, "Who am I?" (At the time, I hadn't a clue that this was a bottom line life issue for me—I was unsure of who I really was and where my place in the world was supposed to be)! Focusing deeper into that question, my eyes began to grow heavy. Within moments, I felt drained, as if I had no energy. I could no longer sit upright and I fell back on a pillow that, for some reason, had been placed in back of me.

Thinking back about that sudden loss of energy reminds me of those incidents in the Bible where people having visions lost all their physical energy. For example, "So he [the angel Gabriel] came near where I stood, and when he came I was afraid and fell on my face; but he said to me, 'Understand, son of man, that the vision refers to the time of the end.' Now, as he was speaking with me, I was in a deep sleep with my face to the ground" (Daniel 8:17–18).

Daniel also described his experience while having another Godly vision and wrote,

> "Therefore I was left alone when I saw this great vision, and no strength remained in me; for my vigor was turned to frailty in me, and I retained no strength" (Daniel 10:8).

In Acts 9:3–4, Luke described the apostle Paul's Damascus Road experience with the Lord, "As he journeyed he came near Damascus, and suddenly a light shone around him from heaven. Then he fell to the ground, and heard a voice saying to him, 'Saul, Saul, why are you persecuting Me?'"

As I lay there energy-less, I began to see a brilliant white light in my mind's eye (my eyes were closed). The light was oval in shape and it sizzled on the edges as if it was energized by a powerful force in the universe. Then I saw a person in the middle of the oval—a man in a loin cloth hanging on a cross. There was no question in my mind who He was: Jesus Christ on the cross.

As certain as you see the words on this page, in my mind's eye it was as if I was at Golgotha in real time seeing Christ being crucified. I felt and went through all of the cathartic emotions one can experience if he or she was witnessing the crucifixion of the Creator of the Universe. I began crying from the depths of my soul. I felt deep sadness for what I was witnessing—a Man dying on a cross. At the same time, I felt indescribable joy for I somehow knew that I was witnessing the greatest act that could be performed for another on earth, namely, the sacrifice of His life for the salvation of mankind (including me) from the sins of the world. I was overwhelmed by what I was seeing. "But," I asked myself, "why me?" After all, I was just a Jewish man who didn't even know Christ! How could this be happening?

After what seemed like hours, I came back from my vision and returned to a consciousness of the dimly lit library and the other participants in the seminar. My direct experience probably lasted for a few minutes, however, my overwhelmed emotional state endured for quite some time. I was physically and emotionally spent, and yet I felt a peace that I'd not ever experienced in my life. Everything in my life seemed unimportant except for what I'd just experienced. In the days that followed, everything I saw, heard, or touched had a different meaning to me. It is difficult to this day to put this experience into words, for the words are inadequate.

After the seminar concluded, I flew home. I remember that plane ride. I knew in my heart that even if the plane went down and I was killed, all would be well with my soul. For almost a year, I found myself occasionally looking into the sky and tears would come into my eyes. My universe couldn't believe I was so mellow. I'd gone from an "A plus" type of personality to perhaps a "C minus" type. My business partners didn't believe the change that had occurred in me. All who knew me could see that I'd been through some life-changing experience.

Life soon settled down for me in this valley of shifting shadows on earth. However, as I live my life looking up from the valley, I shall never forget that overwhelming mountaintop experience with my Savior. As time has gone by, I have come to understand that the vision I saw that evening in September, 1983 was the Lord Jesus Christ who in His wonderful grace came to me and showed me that He died for me (and for everyone) so that I could be saved from my sinful ways. "The secret of the LORD is with those who fear Him, And He will

B. NEIL SHAW

show them His covenant" (Psalm 25:14). In those precious moments in 1983 I experienced the greatest love, peace, joy, and encouragement that only Jesus Christ offers to humanity.

Paul described it perfectly, "The peace of God, which surpasses all understanding, will guard your hearts and minds through Christ Jesus" (Philippians 4:7). That direct experience with the Lord was the start of a beautiful journey for me and my family, a journey into a life that, through His grace, I now know as a disciple of Jesus Christ. For that I am forever grateful.

Thank you Jesus! To You be the glory.

WORKS

"Thus also faith by itself, if it does not
have works, is dead" (James 2:17).

WORKING MY WAY INTO HEAVEN?
IT DOES NOT WORK!

When I was growing up as a young Jewish boy, my father instilled in me the love of God. I also came to believe that if I was good, obeyed the Ten Commandments (the "Law"), and did good things, I would return to God in heaven when I died. I believed that *goodness* was not doing the bad things God's Commandments forbid such as lying, coveting, murder, stealing etc. Being *good* also meant being polite, helping others, being kind, and obeying the law.

With these beliefs in mind, I mistakenly set out in life to achieve *goodness* through my own efforts. I truly believed that hard work at whatever I did would be rewarded by God, materially and spiritually. Because our family was not very religious, I wasn't very familiar with the Bible. I wasn't aware that the Bible says that in God's eyes, "They have all turned aside, They have together become corrupt; There is none who does good, No, not one" (Psalm 14:3). (See also Romans 3:9–18).

Later in life, at age 40 (the typical midlife crisis age), troubles hit me from all directions—my family life, my work and my universe in general. My *works* beliefs weren't working. I felt as though I'd accomplished nothing in my life and that all of my *works* had ill-served me. I'd been living with a mindset fixed on automatic and didn't realize that I'd spent most of my life driven by a personal addiction, work-a-holism. The world I lived in my everyday life was collapsing around me. I felt like I was spiraling down to the bottom of my existence and there was no way out. I was in a spiritual state of darkness and was looking for a way out.

Both my wife and I were searching for answers for a way out of the marital abyss we found ourselves in. That search led us to Jesus Christ

In 1983, in a vision, Jesus plucked me out of a crowd and changed my life (see the prior essay, *A Life-Changing Vision*, for a more detailed account of visions which led us on a path to Christ). But the conflict between my new-found faith and my innate belief that I had to work my way into heaven still gnawed at my soul. That vision of Jesus Christ opened my eyes and ears, but I needed answers to the questions the vision of Christ had raised in me. Being the omniscient God that He is, the Lord knew I was searching for answers. So He led me to His Word, the Bible. In his letter to the Roman believers, the apostle Paul wrote, "And do not be conformed to this world, but be transformed by the renewing of your mind [through the Word of God], that you may prove what is that good and acceptable and perfect will of God" (Romans 12:2). He further wrote, "Faith comes by hearing, and hearing by the word of God" (Romans 10:17). A hunger for His truths grew in me as the years went by. Morning devotions and the daily study of His Word soon became routine. The Bible provided the answers.

Over the years, walking with the Lord has deepened my faith and changed my view of doing good works. God has shown me the proper order of things: faith first, then study and knowledge of the Bible, and then works as the fruit of the Holy Spirit at work within me. Watchman Nee in *The Spiritual Man* (Vol. I, 110-111) discussed the issue of faith in the Lord as compared to works of the flesh (the Law), "God's children in Galatia had descended into the error of doing good by the flesh. They had begun in the Holy Spirit; they did not continue therein to be made perfect. They wanted instead to be perfected through their righteousness, even the righteousness according to law."

Paul asked the believers in Galatia, "Are you so foolish? Having begun in the Spirit, are you now being made perfect by the flesh?" (Galatians 3:3). "For if I build again those things which I destroyed, I make myself a transgressor. For I through the law died to the law that I might live to God" (Galatians 2:18–19). Watchman Nee explained that Paul (in his letter to the Galatians) "was pointing at those who, having been saved and having received the Holy Spirit, still insisted on gaining righteousness [being right with God] according to law (vv.16, 17, 21) through their own flesh." Brother Nee continued, "Now if by doing righteously we try to 'build up again those things'

B. NEIL SHAW

which we have destroyed, then Paul concludes 'we prove ourselves a transgressor.' The Apostle is hence telling us that inasmuch as sinners cannot be saved through their efforts, so we who have been regenerated likewise cannot be perfected through any righteous acts of our own flesh." *supra* at 111.

Paul also wrote in Galatians 2:15–16 about his discussion with Peter about works. He wrote,

> "We who are Jews by nature, and not sinners of the Gentiles, knowing that a man is not justified [forgiven of sin] by the works of the law but by faith in Jesus Christ, even we have believed in Christ Jesus, the works of the law; for by the works of the law no flesh shall be justified." (See also Romans 3:28).

So what are we to *do*? Are we not to *do* anything good? Shouldn't we strive to do righteous things in life? Should we not do good works at all? The apostle James wrote,

> "What does it profit, my brethren, if someone says he has faith but does not have works? Can faith save him? If a brother or a sister is naked and destitute of daily food, and one of you says to them, 'Depart in peace, be warmed and filled,' but you do not give them the things which are needed for the body, what does it profit? Thus also faith by itself, if it does not have works, is dead" (James 2:14–17). James concluded, "For as the body without the spirit is dead, so faith without works is dead also" (James 2:26).

We are instructed by the Word of the Lord to seek righteousness through faith in Jesus Christ and all things will naturally follow. The desire to serve the Lord by doing good things will be the natural fruit of our faith. This is the answer to the questions, "What are we to do?" "Are we not to do anything?": we cannot earn or work our way into heaven, but by faith we are to seek His kingdom first, and all of His blessings including the opportunity to do good for others which are the fruits of righteousness, will by His grace be given to us (Matthew 6:33).

WORSHIP

The Lord is a "jealous God" (Exodus 20:5). He commanded His people, "You shall have no other Gods before Me" (Exodus 20:3) —The First Commandment. He, and only He, is to be worshiped.

WORSHIP THE LORD

The Lord commanded the children of Israel to worship only Him. He spoke these commandments (First and Second) to Moses on Mt. Sinai,

> "You shall have no other gods before Me. You shall not make for yourself a carved image—any likeness of anything that is in heaven above, or that is in the earth beneath, or that is in the water under the earth; you shall not bow down to them nor serve them. For I, the LORD your God, am a jealous God" (Exodus 20:3–5).

By His own words, El Shaddai, God Almighty, is a jealous God. He told His prophet, "I am the LORD, that is My name; And My glory I will not give to another, Nor My praise to carved images" (Isaiah 42:8). He wants our worship of Him to be sincere, focused, reverent, and exclusive. He condemns those whose worship is irreverent.

Many in Israel in ancient times were insincere in their worship of the Lord. They were practicing man-made religious rituals in the temple, but were not truly worshiping God. The religious leaders were honoring the Lord with their lips, but not their hearts (Isaiah 29:13). The hearts of the people were hardened and though they could see with their eyes, they could not see God; though they could hear with their ears, they could not hear God (Isaiah 6:10). Their worship of God was taught by rules of men, not God's (Isaiah 29:13). As a result, the angered Lord lashed out at rebellious Israel. He told them that their sacrifices to Him were meaningless, the incense they burned in His temple was detestable, and their appointed feasts were filled with iniquity and insincerity (Isaiah 1:13–14). They worshiped carved images just as their predecessors had done in the land of Canaan (Isaiah 42:8). They lived without moral reference to God. In His wrath against them, the Lord allowed the Assyrians and then the Babylonians to attack the children of Israel.

In this post-modern era, a depraved culture lives more and more without moral reference to God (just as the ancient Israelites did), and many look to idols for spiritual fulfillment. They reject God. Instead, they devote their God-given lives to idols: money, power, sex, materialism, and yes, even sports. They suppress their innate desire for something greater than themselves. The apostle Paul wrote about this in his letter to the Romans,

> "Professing to be wise, they became fools, and changed the glory of the incorruptible God into an image made like corruptible man—and birds and four-footed animals and creeping things [carved images]. Therefore God also gave them up to uncleanness, in the lusts of their hearts, to dishonor their bodies among themselves, who exchanged the truth of God for the lie, and worshiped and served the creature rather than the Creator, who is blessed forever. Amen" (Romans 1:22–25).

But whether you are a believer or not, the human spirit yearns to know God, the Supreme Being, for He is The Greater as compared to the lesser, the spirit in man. The psalmist wrote, "As the deer pants for the water brooks, So pants my soul for You, O God" (Psalm 42:1). Creation groans for God (Romans 8:22). But the ever-increasing busyness and time-constrained life of modern culture suppresses that groaning rendering it numb—unconscious. But what is this "human spirit" that needs to know and worship God?

By God's design, we humans are spirit, soul and body. "When God first created man, He formed him of dust from the ground, and then breathed 'the breath of life' into his nostrils. As soon as the breath of life, *which became man's spirit*, came into contact with man's body, the soul was produced." Watchman Nee, *The Spiritual Man*, Vol. I, 23 (my emphasis added).

Every communication of and with God occurs through the Holy Spirit with and into the human spirit. The human spirit is "usually referred to in Scripture as the heart." Pastor Ray Stedman, *infra*. "But God has revealed them to us through His Spirit. For the Spirit searches all things, yes, the deep things of God. For what man knows the things of a man except the spirit of the man which is in him?" (1 Corinthians 2:10–11). The significance of the human spirit is that it is the means by which we not only know God, but it is the means by which we worship Him through the Holy Spirit within us..

When we first came to Christ and were re-born in Him, His Holy Spirit entered into us (1 Corinthians 3:16) and with great joy our human spirit was totally aligned for the first time with His Spirit. We became believers in Christ and this was confirmed by the Holy Spirit, "The Spirit Himself bears witness with our spirit that we are children of God" (Romans 8:16).

I remember that important day in my life (rebirth or regeneration) and how wonderful life seemed. Everything in life was working together for good—like a well-oiled machine at its peak performance. The apostle Paul's writing to the Roman believers rang true for me, perhaps for the first time in my life. He wrote, "And we know that all things work together for good to those who love God, to those who are the called according to His purpose" (Romans 8:28). That regeneration marked the complete reconciliation of God's Holy Spirit now within me with my human spirit. How congruous I felt! What a state of being!

But regeneration is not the only time in life we can achieve such a high state of well-being. The Lord desires that we worship Him and only Him (See the First and Second Commandments cited above). In worshiping the Lord, He desires that we be aware of His presence and that we have a knowing within that our spirit is completely aligned with His Holy Spirit. When we are able to focus our entire attention, free of distraction, on the praise words being sung to the Lord, it is the utmost of worship that we can give to the Lord—and that is what He wants from all of us. When that state of being occurs, a glorious sensation manifests itself within us, a sense of joy, peace, contentment and love within our soul. When that happens to me, I smile for there is nothing in this life that is better than worshiping the Lord and sensing His presence.

The late Pastor Ray Stedman wrote in a sermon, *Why Worship*, about the meaning of true worship of God,

> "...Jesus said: '**God is a Spirit; and they who worship him must worship him in spirit and truth.**'" (John 4:24 KJV). With these words, Jesus indicated the fundamental elements of true worship...Our human spirit is designed to communicate and interrelate with the Spirit of God. This is what Jesus means when he says we must worship God 'in spirit.' He is referring to our human spirit which is usually referred to in Scripture as the heart.

> "We talk about doing this with our whole heart. By this we mean our spirit is fully engaged—we are functioning at the fundamental level of our humanity. We are said to be involved *wholeheartedly*. Therefore, to worship 'in spirit' means that our worship must be genuine and heart-felt. We must mean it and feel it deeply. We must be fully committed to what we are doing as an expression of what we actually feel."

Pastor Stedman described the *truth* part of worship as meaning the God we worship must be the true God, Jesus Christ, and no other.

Worship of the Lord is an act of reverence and should be done *wholeheartedly* with all of one's mind, body, soul and spirit focused on Him. In doing so, a believer will sense the glory the prophet experienced when he "saw the Lord sitting on a throne, high and lifted up, and the train of His robe filled the temple" (Isaiah 6:1). With joy, we shall feel the peace of our human spirit aligned with the Holy Spirit of God within us. We shall feel His presence. The Psalmist surely felt this as he prayed, "I will bless the LORD at all times; His praise shall continually be in my mouth. My soul shall make its boast in the LORD; The humble shall hear of it and be glad. Oh, magnify the LORD with me, And let us exalt His name together" (Psalm 34:1–3).

As the last verse in The Book of Psalms reads, "Let everything that has breath praise the LORD. Praise the LORD!" (Psalm 150:6), so we say it here, the end of this work! Praise the Lord!

"Blessed be the LORD forevermore!
Amen and Amen" (Psalm 89:52).

The End

APPENDIX 1

ATTRIBUTION OF SOURCES
OF QUOTED MATERIAL

The following authors and/or publishers have been quoted by the author in this book:

HOLY BIBLE QUOTATIONS: Scripture taken from the *Holy Bible, New King James Version* ®. Copyright © 1982 by Thomas Nelson. Used by permission. All rights reserved.

OTHER QUOTATION SOURCES:

Berry, W. Grinton, *Foxe's Book of Martyrs,* Baker Books, a division of Baker Book House Company, Grand Rapids, MI 49516. Copyright © 2001. All rights reserved. Fair use per publisher.

Boice, James Montgomery, *Foundations of Christian Faith, a Comprehensive & Readable Theology,* Revised Edition. Copyright © 1986 by InterVarsity Christian Fellowship of the United States of America. All rights reserved. Fair use per publisher.

Booye, Rick, Senior Pastor of Trail Christian Fellowship, Eagle Point, Oregon. Sermon regarding Heaven. Copyright ©. All rights reserved. Used by permission.

Chambers, Oswald, *My Utmost for His Highest.* Quotation taken from *My Utmost for His Highest* by Oswald Chambers. Copyright © 1935 by Dodd Mead & Co., renewed copyright © 1963 by Oswald Chambers Publications Assn., Ltd., and is used by permission of Discovery House, Grand Rapids, MI 49501. All rights reserved.

Comer, John Mark, and Griffin, Gerald, song (hymn): *Empty Me.* Copyright © 2003 50 Miles (ASCAP) Gene Way Designee (ASCAP) Thirsty Moon River Publ. Inc. (ASCAP) (Adm. at CapitolCMGPublishing.com). All rights reserved. Used by permission.

Courson, Jon, *Jon Courson's Application Commentary - Old Testament Volume 1.* Copyright © 2005 by Nelson Reference & Electronic, a division of Thomas Nelson Publishers. All rights reserved. Fair use per publisher.

Courson, Jon, *Jon Courson's Application Commentary - New Testament.* Copyright © 2003 by Thomas Nelson, Inc. All rights reserved. Fair use per publisher.

Fenelon, Francois, *The Seeking Heart.* SeedSowers Christian Books. Copyright © 1992, SeedSowers.com. All rights reserved. Used by permission.

Frost, Robert, poet. Poem: The Road Not Taken. Public domain.

Gaebelein, Frank E., editor, *The Expositor's Bible Commentary Volume 9*, a *Commentary on the Book of John* by Merrill C. Tenney. Copyright © 1981 by the Zondervan Corporation. All rights reserved. Fair use per publisher.

Henry, Matthew, *Matthew Henry's Concise Commentary on the Whole Bible.* Copyright © 1997 by Thomas Nelson, Inc. All rights reserved. Public domain per publisher.

A' Kempis, Thomas, *The Imitation of Christ,* translated by William C. Creasey. Quotations from *The Imitation of Christ* by Thomas A' Kempis translated by William C. Creasey are used by the permission of Mercer University Press, Macon, GA 31207. Copyright ©. All rights reserved.

Laubach, Frank C., a prayer ("An Inspiration") from *The Game with Minutes* published by Dr. Robert S. Laubach, his son, in the book *Letters by a Modern Mystic* by Frank C. Laubach . *Letters by a Modern Mystic* was published by Dr. Robert Laubach with Purposeful Design Publications, Colorado Springs, CO 80962- 5130. Copyright ©. All rights reserved. Used by permission.

Lawrence, Brother, *The Practice of the Presence of God.* Copyright © 1982 by Whitaker House. All rights reserved. Used by permission.

Lewis, C. S., *Mere Christianity.* Copyright © C. S. Lewis Pte, Ltd. 1942, 1943, 1944, 1952. Copyright © renewed 1980, C. S. Lewis Pte. Ltd. All rights reserved. Harper, San Francisco 2001 Edition. Used by permission.

Link, Julie A., *Our Daily Bread* ®, Copyright © 2001 by Our
    Daily Bread Ministries, Grand Rapids, MI. All rights
    reserved. Reprinted by permission.

McGee, Dr. J. Vernon, *Thru the Bible with J. Vernon McGee*.
    Quotations taken from *Thru the Bible with J. Vernon
    McGee, Volume IV: Matthew-Romans*. Copyright
    © 1994 by J. Vernon McGee. All rights reserved.
    Used by permission of Thomas Nelson, Inc., www.
    thomasnelson.com. Other quotations from *Thru the
    Bible with J. Vernon McGee*, Volumes I, II, and V are
    fair use per the publisher.

Nee, Watchman, *The Spiritual Man*. Copyright © 1968.
    Reprinted as a combined edition, 1977. Christian
    Fellowship Publishers, Inc., Richmond, VA. 23235.
    All rights reserved. Used by permission.

The NIV Study Bible, New International Version. Copyright
    © 1985 by The Zondervan Corporation. All rights
    reserved. Fair use per publisher.

Perowne, J. J. Stewart, *Commentary on the Psalms*. Quotations
    taken from *Commentary on the Psalms,* Copyright ©
    1989 by J. J. Stewart Perowne. Published by Kregel
    Publications, Grand Rapids, MI. All rights reserved.
    Used by permission.

Stanley, Dr. Charles F., *The Glorious Journey*. Copyright ©
    1996 by Charles F. Stanley. Quotations taken from *The
    Glorious Journey* by Dr. Charles F. Stanley published
    by Thomas Nelson, Inc., Nashville, TN. All rights
    reserved. Fair use per publisher.

Stedman, Dr. Ray, *Adventuring Through the Bible*. Quotations taken from *Adventuring Through the Bible*, Copyright © 1997 by Elaine Stedman. Used by permission of Discovery House Publishers, Box 3566, Grand Rapids, MI 49501. All rights reserved.

Stedman, Dr. Ray, sermon entitled, *Why Worship*. Copyright ©. Used by permission of Elaine Stedman Higuera. All rights reserved.

Thomas, W. H. Griffith, *Commentary on Romans*. Quotations taken from "Commentary on Romans," Copyright © 1974 by W.H. Griffith Thomas. Published by Kregel Publications, Grand Rapids, MI. All rights reserved. Used by permission of the publisher.

Tyndale House Publishers, *Life Application Bible, New King James Version*. Notes and Bible helps copyright © 1988, 1989, 1990, 1991, 1996, 2004 by Tyndale House Publishers, Inc. New Testament Notes and Bible Helps copyright © 1986 owned by assignment by Tyndale House Publishers, Inc. Harmony of the Gospels copyright ©1986 by James C. Galvin. Maps in text copyright © 1986, 1988 by Tyndale House Publishers, Inc. All rights reserved. Used by permission of Tyndale House Publishers, Inc..

Vine, W. E., *Vine's Complete Expository Dictionary of Old and New Testament Words*. Copyright © 1984, 1996, Thomas Nelson, Inc., Nashville, TN. All rights reserved. Fair use per publisher.

Whiston, William, *The Complete Works of Flavius Josephus*. Quotations taken from *The Complete Works of Flavius Josephus*, Copyright © 1960, 1978, 1981 by Kregel

ABOUT THE AUTHOR

B. Neil Shaw is a retired attorney whose mission in life is to share the Word of God with others and to do this with pen in hand. This work is an assemblage of essays written by the author over a period of ten years for a Christian magazine, The Christian Journal. Mr. Shaw is a husband, father, grandfather, and great grandfather and enjoys writing his manuscripts in the majestic mountains of Southern Oregon. When he writes, he does so in the company of the Holy Spirit (for inspiration) and his two companions, Sophie, a Bernese Mountain dog, and Quincy, his Goldendoodle (for a reminder that unconditional love is what it's all about)